:008

)8

2009

TOUR DE FRANCE

Tour de France

RICHARD COBB

DUCKWORTH

First published in 1976 by
Gerald Duckworth & Co. Ltd.
The Old Piano Factory
43 Gloucester Crescent, London NW1.

ISBN 0 7156 0720 0

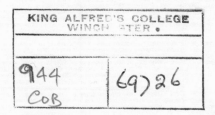
Acknowledgments are due to the editors of the following journals for
permission to reprint: the *Guardian* for 2, 3 and 5; the *Listener* for 21
and 25; the *New Statesman* for 4, 6 and 9; the *Spectator* for 19; the
Times Literary Supplement for 1, 7, 8, 11, 12, 13, 14, 15, 16, 17, 18,
20, 22, 23, 24, 26, 27, 28, 29 and 30.

Made and printed in Great Britain by
The Garden City Press Limited
Letchworth, Hertfordshire SG6 1JS

Contents

à mes amis
de la rue des Quatre Vents
Arthur et Madeleine Birembaut

Preface

Most of the articles and reviews contained in the present volume were previously published in the *Times Literary Supplement*, the *Listener*, the *Guardian*, the *Spectator* and the *New Statesman*. Between 1949 and 1959 I had written a number of books and articles in French, and the opportunity once more to write in English came quite unexpectedly through the post, in the shape of a book, an abridged version of Restif's *Les Nuits de Paris*, sent to me some time in 1959 by John Willett, whom I had known in Normandy, and who had then but recently become Assistant Editor of the *Times Literary Supplement*, a paper I had never read before.

It was the beginning of a long and, at least for me, extremely fruitful relationship. Arthur Crook, the Editor, his successor John Gross, and John Willett henceforth plied me with a varied diet of provocations, enticements, serious commitments and *amuse-gueules*, ranging from *pissotières*, French sport, French fortune-telling and the good Marie Bénard, to the trying Mary Wollstonecraft, the domestic architecture of eighteenth-century Paris, French slang, and regiments of Maigrets. Some of the earlier reviews were printed in *A Second Identity* (OUP 1969), to which this volume is a successor.

My various and successive tempters and temptresses have included, besides the above, John Sturrock, assistant editor of the *TLS*; Claire Tomalin of the *New Statesman*, William Webb of the *Guardian* and Derwent May of the *Listener*. They would, at one moment, shake in my face the red flag of Quantification, the black flag of *Boul-Mich* nihilism, the yellow lion of Flemish nationalism; at another, the faceless, symbol-less banner of sociology, the quirks of popular language; now charming me with gentle things, now moving me with the economy of eighteenth-century poverty, now tempting me with academic gossip and Common-Room reminiscence, playing on my taste for the macabre, enchanting me with negro pages, secret doors, and the paraphernalia of seduction and *enlèvement*.

These are the hands that have fed me, and while, of course, I take full responsibility for what I have written, I am entirely obliged to them for the fact that they have always seemed to know me better than I know myself, and so for the unexpected range of subjects and personalities. I am someone who needs to know for whom he is writing; indeed, I would rather write for him or her than for the paper, though there was an undoubted suitability in evoking Robespierre for the *New Statesman* and the pseudo-revolution of May 1968 for the *Spectator*. The relationship between reviewer and literary editor should be a personal one. I tend to carry personalities further still, often finding it difficult not to identify this or that historical personage with people I have known. Robespierres, as anyone knows, are still with us, self-righteousness being a hardy plant, especially under glass : Marxism, the chapel, academe. I managed to heap on the head of the murdered van Severen all the loathing that I have always felt both for every type of Fascism, whether of the Right or of the Left, and for Flemish nationalism.

Now that the Tour de France itself takes in England as part of its route, there is perhaps no need to account for the presence, in a volume of essays devoted mostly to French history and language, to the Belgian Simenon, and to Paris, of Captain Swing—as English as you make them —Maurice Bowra, or the incomparable Lord Hervey. Even "Hodge", at least if he lived in East Kent, would have some vague awareness, perhaps through smugglers or fishermen, of what had happened a month before in Paris, in July 1830. The Warden of Wadham belonged to the whole of Europe, indeed to the whole civilised world. And the family of Lord Hervey gave the name of *Bristol* to at least one hotel in almost every European capital, as well as adding to the French vocabulary an alternative name for a visiting card (*en rentrant j'ai trouvé le bristol qu'il m'avait laissé en mon absence*). May the Tour de France take in more and more of England, and may the time soon come when Churchill's marvellously inspired suggestion of a double nationality— Franco-English—be revived and realised, though it is hard to see why the French should want to put themselves in harness with such a broken-down old carthorse.

Although I have been described, in a letter to the *Times Literary Supplement,* as only an "occasional tourist" in Paris (and one who could enjoy the luxury of observing the city and its inhabitants from *outside*, though not presumably *sous les ponts*) I was in fact fortunate enough to acquire a base in the city in which I was able to write, and from which I could set out, on repeated *tours de France*, for exactly twenty years. It was the rue de Tournon that enabled me to get a new start, on writing, on research and on living. The preamble, "Danton 71, 48", was written specially for his volume, since it was from this telephone number, and this fifth-floor address, that my real *tour de France* began.

Wolvercote 1975   R.C.C.

Preamble
Danton 71, 48

"Bonjour, Monsieur Kopp." "Bonjour, Monsieur Cobb." And so it was, the late beginning of a day that offered little promise, as I put my key, *chambre No. 25*, right at the top of the steep house, 105 rue Monsieur-le-Prince, on its hook, at the entry to the Bar-Restaurant on the ground floor. By that time M. Kopp, a totally bald Alsatian with little piggy eyes, would be already standing behind the bar in blue overalls, serving a *vin blanc sec* to one of the regulars, an elderly *appariteur* from the Sorbonne, who in the course of the day would move over *chez Thomas, vins charbons,* on the other side of the street, below the level of the long, hopeless façade of the Lycée Saint-Louis, the grimmest of Paris schools. By then it was generally close to midday, and Madame Kopp would have chalked up the menu for lunch. This had started conventionally with *pot-au-feu* or *biftèque-frites*, but a little before selling up the Kopps made at least a token gesture to the prevailing mode by proposing a *couscous* that was above all peppery and that might ensnare, once only, the occasional passing Swede or Englishman. They would not try again. Christian and I knew better.

"Bonjour, Monsieur Kopp." "Bonjour, Monsieur Cobb." This time, M. Kopp had come up to the fourth floor, to bring me a registered letter : he displayed a natural and quite commendable curiosity about my mail, and the letters bearing the head of the King of Denmark that reached Christian every six weeks or so, for such letters would offer the prospect of the payment of back rent. It was normal for Monsieur Kopp to be familiar with Copenhagen and its function as a royal capital, but as a result of my mother's much-awaited letters and parcels (containing clothing), his knowledge of English geography extended down to the level of that other royal city, Tunbridge Wells. On the rare and privileged occasion when a letter arrived, he would display an almost deferential affability and a somewhat sickening jollity, even to the extent of offering us a drink at the bar.

But this time the affability, already creased in welcoming wrinkles on his podgy face, was wiped off in a second, as if by the stroke of some invisible towel. The door of my room would only half open against the end of the bed, so that the first and quite unexpected object that caught my landlord's attention was the head, as bald as his own, of a little man, tucked up to the chin, but with his made-up wide bow-tie—the sort of *noeud papillon*, in diagonals, that one would associate with Jules Berry, in one of his more sinister, meaner parts, such as in *Le Jour se lève*—sticking out coyly over the red counterpane. The head was where mine should have been, and it was only by leaning over at a right angle that M. Kopp could take in mine as well, over on the wall side. His piggy eyes starting out of his head, M. Kopp launched into a long, severe tirade about police regulations, introducing unregistered strangers into licensed hotels, one never knew what might happen, there were the other *locataires* to be considered, and so on and so forth. Faced with such unfamiliar vehemence, and believing that he was about to expel me, *je me suis fait tout petit*, explaining that I knew about such regulations but that this had been an exceptional case. But I could see that in fact Kopp, who in many ways was quite an indulgent and even patient land-lord, especially on the subject of the alcoholic habits of Christian and myself, did not really have the Prefecture in mind, but that he was deeply disappointed in such a revelation of what he took to be my secret habits. To discover me in bed with a man, at eleven o'clock in the morning, was beyond the limits of his normally blasé Alsatian tolerance. Realising this, I hastened to pull back the bedclothes, two old blankets reinforced with my overcoat and Army leather jerkin, to reveal my small bow-tied companion fully-clothed, even to waistcoat, trousers, suspenders and (holed) socks. He had put his coat and yellow shoes on the end of the bed. Later, when the little man had gone, after thanking me profusely and cadging a Métro ticket off me, I went down below and explained to Kopp that I had met him *chez Thomas*, that he was an antique dealer (though clearly much out of custom, and down in the *Puces* category—for the *Puces* had not yet become fashionable with visiting American academics), that he had been very drunk and had been weeping on my bony and rather unwelcoming shoulder, at a repetitive evocation, shuddering between sobs and hiccoughs, of an empty, unin-viting room somewhere in the depths of the wretched XIIme, and that, as the last Métro had long since departed, I had taken pity on him, deciding that he would never make it back on foot to the horrors of Daumesnil, and had, *en chevalier errant,* offered him half of my bed, an offer accepted with an alacrity that, even in the state I had been in, I had found slightly alarming. But I need not have worried, for *le petit antiquaire* (if that is what he was, which I doubt) had gone right off to sleep, like a child, though during the night he had kept on kicking me convulsively with his hot and sticky socked feet. I think M. Kopp was partially reassured; and I allowed him the luxury of a further homily delivered on the subject of unknown guests : there were a lot of strange people around, antique dealers with bow-ties were ready suspects, I must moderate my natural hospitality, *les Anglais étaient des naïfs*. Kopp took something of a fatherly interest in his *deux lascars*.

As I climbed up to the fourth floor, after taking the last Métro from the Ternes, where I had been having my weekly supper with a family, the smell of cheap calvados (*Le Père Magloire*) was wafted down towards me, becoming stronger at each storey. On the landing of the third floor, there was a *signe avant-coureur* of disaster : Christian's rimless spectacles were lying on a stair, one of the glasses broken. At the top, blocking the entrance to his "room" (it was a sort of cubby-hole with an internal window facing on to the stairs, and a huge bed like a sarcophagus on a red stone pedestal taking up all the space, so that there was not even room for a chair, and when Christian was actually in the room it looked as if he were Lying in State; but this time, and it was not the first, he had not made it) lay his enormous and inert body, as he breathed heavily, emitting sickly waves of calvados at each breath. I went down the street to *chez Thomas*, and got the *bougnat* himself to come up and help me lift the Great Dane on to his tomb-bed. The Copenhagen Mail had clearly come in (he had been meeting the *Etoile du Nord* each day for the previous week) at last; and with it cold ham, pickles, cheese, dried fish, in fact enough to keep both of us going for a week. And, *embarras de richesses,* there had also come a letter from Christian's uncle in Wisconsin, enclosing a ten dollar bill, some of which, as it turned out, had survived the calvados, and was later to be the means by which I was rescued from a café in les Halles, where I had been left in pawn, while Christian went off to change five dollars with my friend Maurice, rue d'Obligado. At least there did not appear to be any rationing in Denmark.

Those who are condemned to live (or choose to live) in very small, table-less, and, in the case of my Danish Communist friend (characteristically he belonged to the *wrong* one of the two rival Danish Communist parties), windowless, rooms, are likely to put off returning to them for as long as possible (this, no doubt, is how I recognised in the bow-tied antique dealer a fellow traveller in the night). In our own case, this generally meant staying in Thomas' tiny, semi-concealed bar till two or three in the morning. There were three steps down from the level of the pavement, and, on entry, one was liable to see M. Thomas' cheery round face and torso emerging from a trap-door in the floor, on the way up from the cellar. Although behind the bar there was the usual notice : *La Maison ne fait pas de crédit*, this is just what the Thomas did, and Christian and I were chalked up *sur l'ardoise*, as well as the peak-capped *appariteurs* from the Sorbonne, and a female couple in their fifties, one of whom wore a pair of off-white stockings that were always falling down round her ankles, revealing the blue geography of a complicated network of varicose veins; so that there was no danger

of going thirsty, even when the Copenhagen Mail had *not* come in. As
the evening progressed, so would a repertoire, unchangeable and inexorable in the rigidity of succession: "Quelle est Belle Ma Normandie"
(this, my favourite, would generally come round midnight), "Les Blés
d'Or" (later), "Le Temps des Cérises" (later still), something about
eating ham with M. le Curé (towards the early hours), and "Il ne faut
pas rouler par-dessous la table" to cap the evening before going to bed,
often accompanied by a sudden, gentle slide in that general direction
(Christian tended to go down slowly and majestically, like a huge building, hit slow-motion by dynamite). *Chez Thomas* supplied all our needs
for sociability; it was our family, a fact emphasised by the presence,
often well into the night, of the daughter of the house, a pretty little
dark-haired girl of eight, who seemed to find Christian and myself
hilariously funny; it was our home, our refuge—and we were allowed
into the tiny kitchen at the back, dug apparently into rock and with
what appeared to be a medieval vaulted ceiling—and our eating place,
for Madame Thomas, a woman of generous girth and disposition,
offered a plentiful round of *saucisson d'Auvergne*, brought, like the
young red wine, from their own village.

Nor did the function of *chez Thomas* end there. For one of the
regular customers was an Italian girl whose marriage had gone on the
rocks and who took it out of Thomas' red wine. I can no longer remember her name but she and Christian took an instant fancy to one
another, and soon we were a trio, with myself in the role of honorary
brother. Anyhow I no longer had to enlist the help of M. Thomas to
carry the massive Scandinavian upstairs, though on one occasion, after
Christian had come back from the Gare du Nord with the visible
evidence that the Northern Star was not only shining, but was in, I
discovered on reaching Kopp's that they had *both* collapsed, Christian
on the first landing, the girl on the fourth. This time I called in Madame
Thomas as well as her husband.

Under this sort of regime, though our eating improved, and was no
longer confined to the contents of the Copenhagen Mail, regular work
and, above all, writing, are almost impossible. Christian's Danish nineteenth-century radical poet, a Scandinavian *quarante-huitard* (and the
Centenary was approaching), who had himself been in Paris and who
was the ostensible reason for my friend's presence there, had to remain
increasingly unchronicled. I think Christian only managed a couple
of visits to the Archives de la Police, which, it is true, were situated on
the sixth floor, at the very top of the Police Judiciaire. He did manage
to obtain a Press card, as unpaid reporter of *Land og Volk,* but his
reports on the French political scene at the beginning of the period of
the Cold War were both intermittent and, I suspect, doctrinally unsound.
The *hébertistes*, although they received my solicitous company for a few

hours each afternoon—provided I did not call in *chez Thomas* at midday—completely failed to occupy my evenings, nights, or mornings.

Then came a treble change. Christian and the Italian girl got married at the *mairie du VIme*, M. Thomas and I acting as bridegroom's witnesses, Madame Thomas as the bride's. We had the wedding lunch in the Thomas' kitchen; the *appariteurs* were there, the lady with the white stockings fell under the table after singing "Les Blés d'Or". The Thomas found the couple a room and tiny kitchen further down the street. Shortly after, I too was able to depart from *chez Kopp*, though every now and then, when passing by the top end of the rue Monsieur-le-Prince, I would look in on the glaucous-eyed Alsatian, who noted with visible astonishment—for he was an observant man, as people in his trade have to be—my improved physical appearance and even evidence of a regular routine. "Bonjour, Monsieur Cobb." "Bonjour, Monsieur Kopp." I was not sad to have left my box-like room—it was the best thing that happened to me since my demobilisation—but I was quite sad when, one day, I saw a sign up over the Hôtel-Restaurant marked on the glass door *chez Kopp* : *Changement de Propriétaire*. And there have been a great many of those since.

At much the same time, for reasons I never fully understood—I think it had something to do with the increased charges of a *patente*—the Thomas sold up their business, M. Thomas becoming a taxi-driver. He remained independent, however, owning his own car and observing his own hours. They continued to live in the street; and occasionally I would be greeted by the stocky Auvergnat, as he waited, wearing his perpetual cap, at the rank by the Métro station. The *vins-charbons* had a brief metamorphosis as a *crêperie bretonne*, before its final degradation as a fashionable bar selling whisky, with high stools and concealed lights, and with the most unfunny name in neon lights, *Au Trou du Cul*. It was the sort of place patronised by young technocrats from La Résidence Ris-Orangis or la Défense, who came there with their wives and colleagues, on Friday and Saturday nights, blocking the pavements with their insolent cars, and waking up the whole neighbourhood with their row when they started up their vehicles at two or three in the morning. The rue Monsieur-le-Prince had started moving into the Fifth Republic even before France itself, and the process has been going on, at an increasing momentum, ever since. The female couple moved down the road to the Bar Condé on the corner of the rue de Condé. But there was no singing there. I do not know what became of the *appariteurs* and the two or three *retraités* who had formed part of the regular clientèle *chez Thomas*.

I found my new room almost by accident, soon after it had been vacated by an American girl. It was still quite small, and was of peculiar shape, the wall on the right curving in at a slight bulge, so that it was not

quite rectangular. I had been given the choice of this or a larger room
next to it, further towards the centre of the flat, and had opted for the
smaller room, partly because I liked to work in a confined space, partly
because it enjoyed greater privacy, being at the end of a long, narrow
corridor, and separated only by the kitchen next door from the back
entrance. It was on the fifth floor of an *hôtel particulier—Cour et Jardin*,
the latter approached by a double staircase leading from the courtyard
to the principal groundfloor apartment—built in the 1770s, by a Parisian
architect, for his own use and for letting out. Later I discovered that the
house was classified *monument historique*, though I lived in it for a
number of years before acquiring this information.

The house was next to the fine eighteenth-century barracks of the
garde républicaine serving the Palais du Luxembourg; and I was sometimes woken up by the rolling of drums and by snatches of some fast
marching tune. The room had a very high ceiling, and a French window
down to the level of the parquet floor protected by a low railing. It faced
north, towards the Seine, and on to a cobbled, resonant and, in the
summer, wonderfully quiet and cool courtyard, surrounded with pots
and climbing plants. The only sun that I ever got was from the bright
reflections, at sunset on summer evenings, from the windows of the flat
directly opposite. I had a sizeable table, facing the window; and at my
back stood an old-fashioned marble fireplace (of the sort that one felt
might at any moment emit a Magritte-like locomotive, with steam
coming out of its stack) surmounted by a tall gilded mirror fitted into
the wall, which gave the impression of depth, adding what seemed like
an anteroom. A small bed, over which hung three bookshelves, and a
narrow wardrobe which I could reach with my feet when in bed,
occupied all the left side of the room, so that I could open the door
inwards from my bed. To the right there was a condemned door in a
recess, leading to a larger room, occupied for much of my time by a
medical student and his current girl or girls—at one stage there were
two of them, who generally alternated, but who, on one noisy occasion,
arrived in succession.

Sitting up in bed, I could see into the room on the other side of the
courtyard, which was the bedroom of one of the children of a barrister.
And I could also observe the barrister's wife or the maid, busy in the
kitchen next to it. In the spring I could see the house martins, caught by
the early morning sun, as they wheeled round the roof, as if hesitating
to fly right through my open window. Late at night, from the deep
well of the sonorous courtyard, I could hear, in my half-sleep, the muffled
request, in male or female voice, and sometimes, impatiently, in both :
Cordon, s'il vous plaît, as from a distant cavern, and there would follow
the far-away clang of the enormous dark green *porte-cochère*, that was
decorated on the outside with the heads of emblematic lions, their

tongues hanging out, holding in their jaws two large brass rings. At various times in the night, one could just pick up the insistent peep-peep of the police alarm standing on the corner by the PTT, just off the rue de Vaugirard—a reassuring sound, because it made one appreciate the strength and size of the *porte-cochère* and the silent fortress of the closed house.

The weekday morning sounds were equally predictable, and, therefore, likewise reassuring: at 5, the furtive, but purposeful, and vaguely obscene scraping in the bins, by, or so I assumed, a *chiffonnier* or a tramp in search of scraps of food, cheese rinds, or rags; at 5.30, the wheezing of a car that would never start in one go, the property of someone living at the very top, in one of the maids' bedrooms; at 6.30, the clatter of the dustbins, and the confused shouts of the dustmen; at 7.30, the bugles from the barracks. Sunday would be marked by a still silence, as though all movement in the city had stopped, save for the cries of the house martins and the insistent cooing of pigeons, followed, at 8, by the metallic boom of the bells of Saint-Sulpice, and if the wind were from the north those, more majestic, of Notre-Dame. There was a particular quality about the Sunday stillness. And, all through the night and the very early morning, one could hear the slow, rather hesitant clock striking out the hours, as if uncertain of the exact count, from the façade of the Luxembourg. In the 1950s, any time between midnight and 3 a.m., but never *before* midnight or *after* 3, one could pick out the dull thud of explosions, sometimes so close as to allow for the sound of tinkling glass, and sometimes far away, little more than a slight beat. And, according to the volume of sound, one would try to estimate the probable location of the latest *plastiquage*, for the OAS were nothing if not regular with their bombs.

At 7.45 in the morning, with the utmost regularity (Sunday excepted), the Bouvier brothers, Philippe and Alain, would start quarrelling, in the red-tiled kitchen next door, their voices rising in a competitive crescendo, right in my back as I lay in bed, like two parakeets, as they prepared, in a clatter of pans, what passed for their breakfast: *je t'ai dit mille et mille fois, Alain, de ne pas mettre la soucoupe par terre—Philippe, j'en ai assez, tu es sale, tu es dégueulasse—Alain, tu as laissé le gaz allumé* (this shouted up the corridor)—*Philippe, tu as oublié de vider les ordures, c'était ton tour—Non, c'était le tien*—they went at it hammer and tongs, the morning seeming to bring out in each the maximum of acrimony, as they screamed at one another, in total indifference to their listening audience (myself, fully exposed to their high-pitched denunciations, the medical student and his girl still able to pick out each word, through the thickness of two walls, so totally wrapped up were they in their daily dialogue of mutual accusation) before going off separately, Philippe, on his Vespa, to his chemical laboratory, Alain, on foot, to the Faculty of Medicine. After they had gone, still arguing all the way down the corridor, the front door of the flat angrily slammed behind them, the flat would fall silent, save for the occasional *coup de balai* from the next room, when, rarely, one of the medical student's girls was taken with the domestic urge. If they ever made love in the morning, they were certainly very quiet about it. But sometimes there would be stifled laughter, and I would wonder if they were laughing at the latest Philippe versus Alain dialogue. When we met in the corridor or on the stair-case the student and I used to exchange our impressions of the two brothers, whom he was in the habit of describing as *complètement cinglés, quoi. Mabouls.*

If one of his girls was, now and then, shocked into action by the general disorder, this was a preoccupation that appeared to be totally remote to the bachelor brothers. For with their bachelorhood—and, when I went there, in 1948, Philippe must have been about twenty-four, Alain possibly eighteen or nineteen—went a magnificent *laisser-aller,* an amiable disorder. Judging from my nearby observation of the kitchen, they never washed a plate or a glass; there were, however, several complete *services de table*, through which they were apparently working, at the rate of a whole set a month, which would then be piled up dirty and perilously on any flat surface remaining, or on the tiled kitchen floor, so that to get out of the back door I had to wend my way through a series of Leaning Towers of Pisa consisting of plates and bowls, most of them of very handsome design. There were the remains of a motorcycle in the hall, and Alain was in the habit of mending his bicycle in what had, judging from the disposition of the furniture, been the drawing-room before the war. Philippe slept on a camp bed in what had been his father's study, which he had converted into a home laboratory, and from which, on Sundays, emerged sudden explosions, followed by screams of dispute from the far end of the flat. The dining-room table had been converted for ping-pong, a game that seemed to have been favoured by the brothers as a further occasion for highpitched acrimony. And, apart from the mounting towers of plates, the kitchen was generally cluttered with orange boxes of over-ripe fruit and rotting vegetables that Philippe went out to buy, once or twice a week, very early in the morning, from les Halles. Some, I think, also came from bins, for, according to the red-haired Breton *concierge*, the furtive 5 a.m. shuffling sound had been produced on at least one occasion by Philippe, as he examined, with his laboratory patience and prehensile dexterity, the remains rejected by the other *locataires*. She attributed such behaviour both to the bizarrerie of the two young men—*voyez-vous, M. Cobb, ils sont un peu sauvages*—and to the experiences that they had shared during the years of the Occupation. Certainly, from my point of view, they were ideal landlords, leaving me to my own devices, and receiving with amused amazement my request to borrow a step-ladder, propped up against the jumble in the corridor, so that I could whitewash the ceiling of my room, which was scattering plaster confetti on to the bed. They were equally tolerant of my regular efforts to polish the parquet floor of my room.

In the morning, at 7.30, Philippe, in virtue of *le droit d'aînesse* always slightly ahead of the more lackadaisical Alain, could be heard coming with his characteristic slow, uneven footsteps down the long corridor which, running from the ex-dining/ping-pong room to the kitchen and passing by my door, was crammed with boxes and parcels packed up in 1940 and never since undone, and containing, from a gingerly conducted survey that I had made during the brothers' vacation one summer, dresses, women's underwear, hats, sheets, and linen. He still had a bad limp which, like the parcels and boxes, dated back to the *Exode* of 1940, when at fourteen, with his mother and Alain, then aged nine, he had been machine-gunned in the shins by German planes on the road west, somewhere near le Mans. Alain had escaped unhurt; their mother had been killed, and Philippe had had to go to the mortuary at le Mans to identify her body. He had somehow eventually hobbled back to Paris, against the prevailing stream of refugees, holding his brother's hand. During the Occupation, the two boys had grown up untended in the unheated flat, Philippe coping as best he could, though Marie, the family's former maid, was able to keep an occasional eye on the mother-less household from the flat opposite, where she was in service to the barrister. I think Philippe's slow, timid gravity and perpetual sadness—his very pale blue eyes seldom lit up to any sign of merriment—must have dated from these terrible childhood experiences. Alain, on the other hand, had been preserved from them, his brother having somehow succeeded in concealing from him at the time the sight of their mother's body and the immediate and devastating fact of her death in the long corn, beside the summer road that in normal years would have lead to holidays at the seaside. In most ways, Philippe had had to take on the double role of elder brother and of guardian, their father apparently having completely opted out, living from 1940 in his native Geneva—he belonged to an old HSP family of the rue des Granges—and only rarely coming to Paris. Something of Philippe's resentment at the responsibilities thus thrust upon him could be detected in the fact that he had opted for French nationality—that of his dead mother, a Teissier du Cros, again an old Protestant family, from the Gard—and that he constantly referred to *les Helvètes* with the sort of derision that so many French people generally reserve for *les bons Belges*. Indeed, the nearest he ever got to being light-hearted was when he was imitating *l'accent gènevois* and making rude references to *le jet d'eau, vous savez, Monsieur, c'est le plus haut du monde*. Possibly for similar, though unstated, reasons, the brothers had become Catholic converts. Though they had cousins in Paris, they rarely saw them, and appeared to have cut themselves off from all human contacts save that of Marie.

Whether from choice, indifference, or meanness—and Philippe certainly was never prepared to throw anything away, even bringing home half-dead flowers that he had picked up in the street, or that he had bought at a cut price from the genial Algerian who had a flower stall on the corner of the rue de Seine and the rue des Quatre-Vents—the brothers lived in great discomfort, amidst the wreckage of the family furniture, camping in what, before 1940, must have been a comfortable and well-appointed flat. They slept without sheets and pyjamas, using old cushions from the salon as pillows and their overcoats as dressing-gowns. The central heating was turned on for only about a month, in January, and the water-heater for the bathroom every Sunday. When I acquired an oil-heater, *chez le Roumain* (I think in fact he was merely a gipsy), the *marchand de couleurs* in the rue des Quatre-Vents, Philippe was at pains to point out the heavy expenses in fuel which I would incur, and when I bought pillows and sheets from the BHV, they were both clearly disappointed that the legend of English toughness, drilled into them by their Protestant relatives, was not being borne out. Daninos, with his totally unconvincing *le Major Thompson*, was their *maître* in matters English; and I did not seem to fit the model.

Strangely, the telephone had survived from the pre-War period, or possibly Philippe had been unwilling to go to the expense of having it removed. Neither of the brothers ever use it; indeed, as far as I could make out, there was no one to whom they could have telephoned. Philippe had pinned up beside it a piece of paper divided into two columns, headed *M. Gaudeix* and *M. Cobb*, so that the medical student and I could mark down our daily calls. It was an easy number to remember, as it spelled out three Revolutions: DANton 71, 48.

The telephone arrangement was typical of everything else. It was as if we had entered into private treaties with the brothers, and, as long as these were observed—though they were unstated—they did not interfere. When, for instance, one of them met a partially clothed girl coming out of the lavatory, which was right at the end of the corridor, with a tiny window opening on to the back staircase, he would lean up against the wall, often provoking a minor cascade of parcels and boxes and battered suitcases, so as to let her pass, saying politely *Passez, Mademoiselle*. Yet they were not unobservant, nor devoid of malice, commenting, every now and then, with amused cynicism, on the latest state of play of my neighbour's love life. Otherwise, they were not interested, provided, however, that the girls came and went by the back door and the less prestigious, though still very handsome, back staircase, perhaps an unconscious twentieth-century transposition of the eighteenth-century theme of *Cour et Jardin*. As far as we were all concerned, however, we were all confined to the side of the *Cour*. Sometimes, through the French windows of the Klébers' *salon d'apparat*, approached by double steps, the stopping place once for approaching coaches and cabriolets, I could just make out a fountain covered in moss, an ivy-covered wall, and a small bit of grass, with a stone sphinx in the middle; but, for all I was concerned, it might have been painted on. In twenty years, I never set foot in *le jardin secret*.

Now I had a base from which, every now and then, to start off on the next stage in my *tour de France*, and to which to return, with enjoyment and reassurance, as to a place that I could domesticate, with a row of red and pink geraniums on the window ledge that I could see from down below and that somehow proclaimed the fact of my residence—and not just a temporary residence either, but a long-term proposition; and with pictures and plates on what little wall space remained available, a vase made by a potter from Les Bornes, near Bourges, on the mantelpiece, the flowers in it doubled by the tall mirror, a small shelf to the right of my table bought from *la maison du raffia (objets du Madagascar)* in the rue Danton. In the stillness of the day-time courtyard—as still as a night in Langres—with the children at school, the brothers at work, I could type without interruption, till lunch at four, dinner at nine.

And, from 1949, when I wrote my first article, till the early 60s, my works in French would steadily accumulate on the Greek black and red bedcover : articles for provincial reviews, a small book from *les Albums du Crocodile*, published from the profits of patent medicines (Rhône-Poulenc), another published in Toulouse, a steady mobilisation of Revolutionary Armies, the ever-present *problème des subsistances*, the pages concerning the years heavy in disaster and hopelessness : Years II, III, and IV, lying so lightly on my bed. At the end of each day that I did not visit the Archives, I would witness, with great satisfaction, the mounting pile of typed pages with footnotes trailing at the end of them like peacocks' tails.

I had occasional visitors; and, at one time, I had to make room, among the clutter of papers on the bed, for a dark freckled girl, the daughter of a doctor who practised somewhere near Enghien, and whose family came from the pretty town of Noyers in the Yonne, who came to me twice a week for English lessons. And it was here, too, at my table, that I received once a week Russian lessons from Madame Melgounoff, the widow of a SR. When I went out, I would stop at the *loge* for a chat with the red-haired Breton *concierge*, who kept me informed of the activities of all the *locataires*. *Ah, Monsieur Cobb, toujours le mot pour rire*. She thought I was a wag; and she found the stories about the Bouvier brothers a source of endless entertainment. They were both rather frightened of her, mainly, I suppose, because they were terrified of being engaged in conversation by *anyone* outside the immediate circle of the flat. The *concierge* did not need to inform me about the habits of the *propriétaire*, Mlle de Montigny, an aristocratic lady from Mayenne, whose family had owned the whole house for a good many years; for I could time myself from her nocturnal wanderings: till midnight the *Relais de l'Odéon*, after midnight, till 2 or 3 in the morning, the *tabac* at the top of the rue de Tournon, where she would sit for hours, watching the bridge-players. We would exchange brief greetings, like travellers on secret missions who knew each other's business, but do not wish to seem too enquiring. It was, however, from her that I acquired much of my knowledge of the Bouvier family background. There are two things above all that make one feel one *belongs* in a community or quarter: familiarity with the *concierge* and acceptance by the *propriétaire*, for both represent *la longue durée*, time past, the assurance of a future succession of months and years, just as the silence of a Paris Sunday admits one, *de plein pied*, to the intimacy of a city, on the day on which its inhabitants, dissolving into family units, allow themselves a respite, to breath, to dawdle, to look around, to sniff the air and look out for the buds in the Luxembourg—"later than last year". There was even reassurance in the morning concert of *piailleries* of the Bouvier brothers from the kitchen, an exchange governed as much by the *Trois Règles* as a play by Racine, and that, I felt, did not exclude affection and mutual dependence. After all, the tune and the invective had hardly changed at all for over fifteen years; and there seemed no reason to think it ever would, so closely bound up were Philippe and Alain in the closed, private world of their shared eccentricities, shared discomforts, and shared distrust of the outside (thought I suspect Alain did in fact have friends among his fellow medical students, and that he hesitated to bring them home on account of his brother). I was so completely happy, in my quiet fortress, in the stillness and cool resonance of the courtyard, the *porte-cochère* shutting out almost all sound of traffic and dispute as effectively as if we had been surrounded by a moat, or walking on one of my usual itineraries to this or that archive, that I would talk to myself out loud, mostly in French, for I had few occasions to use English, save when writing to my mother.

Yet, despite the moat, despite so many precautions, we were, all three of us, being threatened from close quarters; and the end came in a completely unexpected manner. The spartan habits of the brothers had been observed for some time from across the street, which, at the top end of the rue de Tournon, fans out as it climbs towards the Senate, increasing the gulf between the odds and the evens, and thus rendering, one would have thought, No. 12 even more impenetrable to the gaze of the curious. Directly opposite us, in adjoining bedrooms, at the top of a hotel, there lived two sisters, the one good-natured, jolly and perhaps rather foolish—later she married a publican from Guildford, and settled in the Army Belt—the other younger, a bit sharp, not without calculation and, with a widowed mother whose mind tended to wander, certainly avid for security. I do not know at what stage Monique had begun to take an interest in Philippe's daily routine. I suspect that she must have used binoculars or a telescope, for from what her sister was later to tell me it was clear that, before even meeting him, she had been aware of the exact disposition of the furniture, parts of cycles, laboratory equipment, and sundry junk in the brothers' two adjoining bedrooms, the four long windows of which faced east directly across the street. The prospect, one would have thought, would not have been particularly tempting to anyone outside the second-hand furniture trade, though it might have intrigued a Simenon, as a literary problem setting out a series of clues requiring an answer. To the casual observer, it would merely have spelt out indifference and neglect; to a female observer, no doubt, the clear evidence of the absence of femininity. And to her, indeed, the sheer enormity of the disorder might even have acted as a sort of difficult challenge. The curious thing was that Monique's window had in fact *une vue plongeante* on to *Alain*'s room, so that, in logic, it would have been the prime object of her solicitous scrutiny. Yet—and this is no doubt where both Simenon and his *alter ego*, Maigret, would have gone wrong—it was the room slightly on a tangent, the one on to which she could only command a *regard de biais*, so that at least a quarter of the room, including the camp bed, would, like the other side of the moon, ever remain shut off from view, that seemed almost from the start to have commanded most of her attention. All of this must of course be pure guess-work, though it was to be apparent that from a very early stage Monique had, as it were, *jeté son dévolu sur Philippe*, or had at least made him the prime object of her daily window-watching. In a conventional sense, he might have been described as better-looking than Alain, who did not possess his rather gloomy distinction and his washed-out blue eyes; and the limp may have aroused further interest in his watcher. Or Monique, a provincial girl (I think from the Charentes; it seems likely, for the dead father had been in the French Merchant Navy, and like so many of those who had made their career plying between Bordeaux and Pointe-Noire, he had eventually succumbed to the massive abuse of *pastis*) and with attitudes that were decidedly petit-bourgeois, may merely have decided that the elder brother was the more viable proposition. But it would be indecent to pursue the matter further. The fact is that she set her sights, literally, on Philippe, though, for some weeks, or possibly two months, he was sublimely unaware of this.

Monique at this time was out of work, or was in between two jobs.

This probably accounted for the beginning of her window-watching, for it would have been inadvisable for a girl on her own—and she was attractive—to have gone and sat in the Luxembourg. Furthermore, she would have been alone most of the day, for her sister was on full-time hospital work. This was important, for there was no great love between the two girls, and had her sister been present in the day, she would soon have become aware of her preoccupation with *en face*, and would have been likely to have pressed her as to its purpose. As it was, she could assume her watch unobserved and unsuspected. The initial stages were simple enough, for there was no difficulty about establishing Philippe's weekday time-table, punctual as he was to a degree of fanaticism : open the *porte-cochère* on to the street at 8.10 sharp, lift his Vespa over the bottom of the little door released by an electric catch—then off to the right, *pétardant*, past the Police alarm box and the PTT, turning left up the rue de Médicis, skirting the Luxembourg, at which stage he would be lost to her radar screen as he bowled along in the direction of his laboratory in the *banlieue-sud*. Then back, on the dot of 5.50, coming in low under her window. Child's play.

Her next move was to establish the pattern of *Alain*'s daily (and nightly) movements, and this entailed greater difficulties, for he was not such a man of habit, often stayed late in bed, and his working hours varied according as to whether he was going to the Faculty or was on hospital duty. For if, as at some stage she had decided, she were to speak to Philippe—*aborder* is more eloquent, with its naval connotations—it would have to be in Alain's absence. And the fact that the young doctor was sometimes on night shifts, like her own sister, once ascertained, could be usefully mobilised for her campaign.

I suppose that Monique next made a series of discreet enquiries in the local shops. If she went to the *tabac*, she would have come away *bredouille*, for, like a number of the old-established inhabitants of the street, the brothers never used it : the *patronne* had collaborated "horizontally" with *ces MM. de la Luftwaffe*, established in the Luxembourg, during the Occupation. I doubt in fact if *any* of the shops would have been very helpful, as the brothers hardly ever bought anything, and when they bought food, it was directly from les Halles, which were cheaper. And they certainly never went to cafés or restaurants. The sheer paucity of information may even have stimulated her interest in two people who, while living in a quarter, hardly seemed to belong to it. She would have had too much sense, on the other hand, to have made a direct approach to the *concierge*, and she could not at this stage have known about Marie and her former connections with the family. If she had had an ally in the PTT on the corner—a post office that once won the *Figaro* prize for the rudest *bureau de poste* in the whole of Paris—she would merely have discovered that the brothers received hardly any mail at all, save a monthly letter from Geneva, and a monthly *avis* from the *Comptes-Chèques-Postaux* of the rue des Favorites. In fact, I simply do not know what her next move would have been.

The one after—or the one *two* after—won my admiration for its ingenuity and cunning. One morning I received the visit of the elder sister. She introduced herself, saying that she lived opposite, worked as a nurse, was engaged to an Englishman in *le Surrey*, and what was it like living in England? Was *le Surrey* fun? Where could she take a crash-course in English? Would I translate a letter she had just had from *son Anglais*? And I started with this. There was no doubt about the English publican's interest, and I could see why. She was a buxom, pleasant girl, with an inviting frontage, pretty, bold brown eyes, and a very warm smile. She would look well behind a bar (where no doubt she still is). I liked her, and we talked away most of the morning. She wanted to know what I did, who lived in the flat, who owned it, and I told her. She let out that she had heard about my existence from her younger sister, but that she had come of her own accord, thinking I might be able to help. I said I would be delighted, and indeed saw her several more times, took her out for drinks, met her decidedly odd mother and eventually the publican, a moustached tweedy fellow without a word of French but as open and jolly as she was. I do not think she had, on this occasion, been the conscious instrument of her sister's curiosity; and as in appearance I am unmistakably English (*Monsieur Cobb, vous portez votre passeport sur la figure*) Monique would have had no difficulty in discovering that there was an Englishman living in No. 12, though she could not have known on what floor.

I suppose from then on it must have been plain sailing. My own guess is that she must indeed have *abordé* Philippe one evening, as he was lifting the Vespa over the little door. It is of course just possible, for no man can ever judge another man in matters of this kind, that it was Philippe who had taken the initiative, and had actually spoken to the pretty dark girl whom he had seen on a number of occasions in the street. My first, and shattering, intimation of change was a ring on the front-door one evening, quite late, 9.30 or so, when, a rare thing indeed, Philippe had gone out—Alain was on a night shift at Broussais—and there was this dark girl standing there. *Philippe est là?* she asked, and I said that he wasn't. *Il m'a dit de l'attendre*, so after some hesitation I showed her into what had once been the *salon*. I had no idea who she was, and did not connect her with my *anglomane* visitor of a few days before. But there was no doubt about the proprietarial tone of her enquiry.

After that, things moved fast. Philippe and Monique got married, Alain took up a locum in Tahiti, spent a year there, then came back briefly to clear up, returning to Papeete to set up in permanent practice.

Later he married a Tahitian. That was the end of the *piailleries* from
the kitchen. It was also the end of the disorder. The first danger signs
came when Monique, who was *rangeuse*, and given to little yellow
receptacles purchased from the basement of the BHV, set to work on
the corridor. The numerous relics of the late Madame Bouvier disappeared in a day. Then it was the turn of the hall : the motor-cycle was
all at once gone, to be replaced by arrangements in shells, and hanging
lamps. The lavatory came next, the ping-pong table was reconverted,
the kitchen was cleared. The medical student was the first to go; and I
knew I was only living on borrowed time. There was no row, no scene.
I was even told that I could keep the room to work in in the day. But
what was the point of that? It would only make things seem sadder. I
did not actually *leave*. I took things away bit by bit, but never *everything*, feeling that after twenty-one years the room and I had still some
right to one another. I daresay my books are still there. Philippe is, or was
quite recently. But all alone. Monique and the children went elsewhere,
after a divorce. The *concierge*—not the red-haired Bretonne, who went
west (I mean literally)—told one of the shopkeepers that M. Philippe
had taken to talking to himself and seemed more remote than ever. I
notice, each time I go past, that the four tall windows facing on to the
street constantly have their white wooden shutters closed, as though
Philippe had now gone a stage further and shut out the light of day.
But it was good while it lasted, and I had a good run for my money.

History by numbers*

That very entertaining and sharp Parisian, Jacques Prévert, has a poem
that goes :

Louis I
Louis II
Louis III
Louis IV
Louis V
Louis VI
Louis VII
Louis VIII
Louis IX
Louis X (dit le Hutin)
Louis XI
Louis XII
Louis XIII
Louis XIV
Louis XV
Louis XVI
Louis XVIII

> et plus personne plus rien...
> Qu'est-ce que c'est que ces gens-là
> qui ne sont pas foutus de compter jusqu'à vingt?

Was this then the cause of the disappearance of the ancient Bourbon
dynasty? That they were unable to come to terms with that latest of historical fads: Quantification? It could be so. Yet, it should be added, in
their favour, that they were already clearly on the right track, for do we
not have, both in old and modern French currency: *un demi-louis*, which
suggests that they could at least divide, a negative process perhaps and
one more difficult than that of multiplication?

One of the favourite sayings—and indeed he meant it almost as a
revealed truth—of my old Master, Georges Lefebvre, was: "Pour
faire de l'Histoire, il faut savoir compter." And it must be admitted
that he practised what he preached. There are some 300 pages of tables
as an annex to his immense thesis on *Les Paysans du Nord*, all of them
drawn up without any mechanical assistance whatsoever.

* *Times Literary Supplement*, 1971.

Georges Lefebvre, although often given to rather schematic analyses on the subject of class structures and of group conflicts within a given pre-industrial society—he claimed to be a Marxist historian—was well aware of the limits of the uses to which numbers could be put. He rightly relied on statistical evidence when it was a matter of assessing variable degrees of wealth, on the basis of fiscal returns, or of studying the *mercuriales* of grain prices. And he made due allowance for quantification in such propitious fields as population studies, morbidity rates, fertility, and so on. But he was far too wise a man, far too experienced, too much aware of the unaccountability of human behaviour and of the accident factor, both in individual and collective conduct, ever to think of quantifying the human act. When he referred to "ces lundis révolutionnaires", Dangerous Mondays, especially in respect of rural riot, he was not attempting to set down any sort of General Law on popular tumult. He was merely aware, on the basis of evidence taken from a very wide area and over a period of several decades, that Monday following Sunday, villages often took collective action on a Monday that they had decided on the previous day. This is not a Model; it is based on the simple fact that Monday comes after Sunday (and went on doing so even under the revolutionary calendar, although neither day officially existed any more).

He was a historian both too respectful of the complexity of his material and too experienced in the conduct of individuals ever to make too great a demand on his own preference for various forms of neo-positivism. He would no doubt have liked men to respond predictably to predictable pressures; but he also knew that, in most cases, they simply would not oblige. And, in 1945, he severely took to task a group of Soviet historians who sought to identify eighteenth-century French agrarian structures with those of nineteenth-century Russia, accusing them of confusing history with propaganda. In short, Lefebvre was an honest historian, as well as a wise one; he also wrote with great clarity, if with a certain dryness. He was, however, a very old man when he died, eleven years ago, and he would now be considered, especially by some of the younger members of the *Annales* school, as old-fashioned. For did he not write history in terms that could at once be understood by the layman?

Much more recently, a group of American historians—and quantifiers, in the nature of things, tend to be gregarious, preaching the Group Project, reigning over Group Institutes, and employing a hierarchy of subordinates even more extensive and much more deferential than the teeming below-stairs population of an affluent mid-Victorian home; their machinery is expensive, the expense has to be justified, and one way of doing this is by the sheer size of the armies of white-coated assistants employed in their clinical Historical Laboratories—more recently, a group of American historians have been subjecting 500 *Cahiers de Doléances* to a programme of computerisation on the basis of fifteen selected questions. I cannot guess what wonders will emerge from this vast and expensive *enquête*, but those that have been revealed so far appear to me to have been rather self-evident.

Of course, what is wrong is not so much the mechanistic process, but the arbitrary selection of the questions. History will always give you the answers which you wish to obtain, if you manhandle the subject sufficiently severely. If you put to the Three Estates, "Are you in favour of the retention of Privilege?" it is not entirely surprising that the hoped-for answer from the Second Estate comes out as 98 per cent in favour.

And the other fourteen questions selected are equally crude and equally inviting of simple, predictable answers. Yet our quantifying school will not be put off by such objections, for is not this Total History, the equation of History with the Social Sciences?

I am reminded of the sort of questionnaire that is sometimes submitted to those seeking residents' visas to the United States: "Would you, or would you not, assassinate the President of the United States?" There can only be one of two answers. A friend of mine who, when the question was put to him by an immigration official, replied, quite reasonably I feel, "I would like a couple of days to think that one over", was given a very bad mark indeed. He had sinned against the Laws of Quantification; his card, inserted in the machine, might break the machine; he had in fact behaved like a human being, that is, both frivolously and unpredictably.

Nor is this all. There is at present being undertaken an even more expensive and massive venture: the computerisation of 516 urban riots, turbulences, disturbances, *fracas*, *prises-de-barbe*, semi-riots, *revolvérisations*, lynchings, stabbings, slaughters, massacres, protests, collective threats, abusive slogans, provocative songs, in France, for the whole period 1815–1914. The end-product will no doubt reveal some highly interesting pattern: that, for instance, market riots occur on market days, in or near the market, that marriage riots take place after weddings, that funeral riots take place either outside the church or near the cemetery or along the course of a funeral procession, that Saturday riots take place on Saturday evenings, between 10 and 12 o'clock in the winter and between 11 and 1 o'clock in the summer, that is after the wineshops and *bals* have closed, that Sunday riots take place after Mass, that rent riots take place on rent days and that they are commoner in April and July than they are in January and October, that port riots take place in or near ports, that recruitment riots converge on railway stations or on barracks, that prison riots take place inside or opposite the prison, or both, that religious riots, especially in towns or *bourgs* in which there exist two or more antagonistic religious communities, favour Sundays, Catholic feast days, or St Bartholomew's Day, or the Passover. Perhaps we thought we knew already; but now we *really* know; we have a Model.

Riot has been tamed, dehumanised and scientificated. Of course, we do not know at what expense; for it would be unwise to inquire too closely into which category "riot"—not a very disciplined word in itself—has, *a priori,* been forced. Is this one a market riot, or is it not a funeral riot? Do we have here a hunger riot or a rent riot? Is this one a collective lynching—and so a riot—or is it not merely a private murder? *Make it fit.*

The French, too, have suffered from this terrible urge for discipline. Efforts have been made to measure, to quantify, the decline of faith, in, let us say, eighteenth- or nineteenth-century conditions. One would have thought that, of all human feelings, faith would prove the most recalcitrant to measurement; for is it not the most intimate of human feelings, the most unsoundable of individual commitments? One would have thought so—I would have thought so. But the task has not always daunted French inquiries into popular emotions and mentalities. One such has proposed, as a standard of measurement of the decline of faith, in the city of Marseille, between 1700 and 1789, the size and number of church candles used at funerals, baptisms and weddings. They were in fact getting smaller and less numerous progressively throughout the century. This historian concludes triumphantly that he has penetrated the innermost secrets of the Marseillais soul and that he has come away with quantitative proof of a decline in faith. It does not seem to have occurred to him that the same figures might be taken to witness for the exact opposite, might in fact indicate a revolt against ostentation and a manifestation of moral Jansenism.

The insistence on Quantification does not, alas, apply only to methods of historical research, where it can inflict no lasting harm, other than to produce a lot of history that is both bad and boring. It is also increasingly applied to the assessment of personal and academic merits, in the case of candidatures for graduate places at American universities or, more generally, for junior posts in similar institutions. Anyone who has ever been a history tutor or lecturer in an English university will know what I have in mind. There will be a long white envelope, with one's address written with an electric typewriter; inside will be a form, in some garish colour—green or yellow—no doubt to encourage any hint of mental instability. There will follow a series of questions covering the whole range of the candidate's personality, with, alongside, small rectangular boxes inviting the appropriate tick. For example, on "reliable". Is he

totally reliable
generally reliable
frequently reliable
reliable
occasionally reliable

rarely reliable
unreliable?

Sometimes—this seems to be the case especially in California, where Quantification, like madness, seems to have gone farther than anywhere else—the adverbs may even be replaced by numerical grades, thus: "assess the candidate's emotional stability, on a scale from 1 to 5". Intelligence, capacity for leadership, imagination, civic sense, etc. are put up for similar assessment. My own way of dealing with this type of dehumanising inquisition is to fill in the whole range of the rectangles. If this does not do much good to the candidate, at least, so I feel, it will blow up the machine, when the card, like a pianola score, is fed into the computer.

One can detect a similar concern for the laying down of a standard, all-coverage definition that will exclude all possibility of individual deviation from the norm and that will ban all forms of eccentricity—perhaps the greatest crime in the eyes of the solemn white-coated Quantifiers—in those dreadfully candid, archly self-conscious self-analyses that American graduates so often submit, in a pathetic and fumbling effort to convince us of their fundamental seriousness, of their ponderous worthiness, to Oxford Colleges or to other institutions of higher learning, when they are applying for graduate places. These rather sickening essays in self-deprecation, although they are not actually quantified, are also clearly based on a standard model, which then produces a series of "case histories", of mini-autobiographies that might have written themselves, that clearly owe much to the American obsession with Teutonic forms of amateur psychology and psychological jargon, and that are so totally repetitive as to be completely uninformative and equally dehumanised, denying as they do any spark of individuality or even of vitality :

In my freshman year, I was still primarily ego-orientated, working mainly on my own, but competing eagerly in individual sport in a selfish effort to win, while taking no part in group activities, and reading only the sports pages of the *New York Times*. I was also having some difficulty in adjusting myself mentally to my Mother's re-marriage. In my sophomore year, I joined the Asoka Table [or some similar earnest institution founded by solemn do-gooders], becoming aware both of my place in American society and of my responsibilities, as a person unduly privileged in socio-economic terms, toward the Third World. In my Freshman year, I participated in a group project for the rehabilitation of spastic Puerto Rican children and spent three weeks in the Peace Corps in San Tomé. In my Senior year, I edited *Crimson*, was president of debates, helped to burn down the Skeffington-Lodge Library and participated in a sit-down opposite the Pentagon. I now felt myself a fully integrated personality. I wish to come to Britain to study the socio-characterial motivations of the feminine membership of the IRA-Provisionals. I feel that in this way I can complete the process of my group-integration in contemporary sociological cross-fertilisation currents.

Apart from imposing upon the unfortunate reader dehumanising jargon and a linguistic orthodoxy wrapped in Teutono-American obscurity—and this is the price to be paid for Quantification in terms of literary loss— there is little historical value in establishing, beyond a shadow of a doubt, that, let us say, Robespierre represented $1/12$ of the Committee of Public Safety, $1/24$ of the Revolutionary Government and $1/660$ of the National Convention, that Paris represented $1/83$ of the French Republic or that the Bastille was stormed by, among others, $33\frac{1}{3}$ watchmakers. I do not care to learn that members of the upper bourgeoisie of Elbeuf possessed from 6 to 20 servants, that members of the middle bourgeoisie of Elbeuf possessed from 2 to 6 servants, and that members of the lower bourgeoisie of Elbeuf possessed from 0 to 2 servants. I do not know what sort of a non-person a 0 servant can be; and I even find it distasteful thus to equate the number of servants to the visible signs of wealth and status, along with knives and forks and silver teapots, pairs of sheets and household linen, even if this may in fact be a useful measurement for the assessment of relative wealth. Perhaps I am being sentimental, but it disturbs me to see poor country girls who have sweated it out below stairs, or frozen in the attic, the object of the lust of the Master and his sons, being further humiliated, long after their death, by thus being forced into graphs in the galley-ships of American doctoral candidates. These girls, after all, however poor, possessed their own identity, had faces, sometimes pretty ones, though generally pock-marked, often a generous and open disposition, a great deal of naivety, a proneness to revere and obey their fathers and to love and slave for their brothers, even if their intellectual baggage was as limited as their wardrobe. I am incensed to see them thus reduced to the status of the poor playing-card-gardeners of the terrible Queen of Hearts, as, hastily and in fear—they may have only been low playing cards, but even they could feel fear— they set about the task of painting white roses red. Contemporaries were more merciful; even if they branded convicts with the letters "G" or "V" or "VV" on their shoulders, they did at least allow them names, nick-names, assumed names, a brief summary of their personal appearance, a *portrait parlé*; "marchant d'un pas leste", "se tenant bien droit", "le regard hardi", "ayant l'air d'une bête sortant de la forêt". These at least are no anonymous brigands.

How too is one to quantify morality? Should we establish, as with wine or alcohol, a percentage range of badness? Are we agreed that Bernadette was 94 per cent Good? That Charlotte Corday was 83 per cent Pure? That Charles Churchill was 89 per cent Wicked? Where do we place Don Giovanni with, if we are to believe Leporello (*never* believe servants, especially gentlemen's gentlemen, on the subject of numbers) "ma in Espagna, mille tre"? It does seem rather a lot. But it is an exact figure. Or should we simply quantify morality according to the ancient formula so much favoured by College deans: "Once is all right, twice is a habit"?

Life is becoming already dehumanised enough without our further hastening that process of brutalisation by taking all vitality out of our history and by substituting for names and faces, either mathematical formulae, symbols such as those used most frequently by such French historical quantifiers as Vovelle, Sentou, Baehrel and Daumard, or George Rudé's rather lifeless and unimaginative regimentation of trades, occupational categories, and crowd composition. For though we may count, in a given riot, eighty-three hairdressers and thirty-two watercarriers, the eighty-three hairdressers represent eighty-three individual beings, and the thirty-two Aveyronnais have only this in common, that they carry water and that they all come from a single area of the Aveyron, all speaking a dialect that distinguishes them totally from the Parisians. Of course they do indeed thus represent an identifiable cultural and occupational group but, within that group, if we seek further, we are likely to discover the whole range of human emotions and individual temperaments.

This is not, of course, to dismiss out of hand the very valuable work carried out by George Rudé on the analysis of the composition of crowds and of primitive forms of popular protest. He has taken popular history a big step forward. But we must go further still. One wonders, for instance, what the Rudé approach would make of the situation in Central Belfast. It would be of some help, both by locating the two religious communities in their various, often contiguous, strongholds, as well as by "counting heads" within those areas; it might even be a useful aid to establishing a pattern of riot that clearly responds to seasonal pressures, to the calendar of Friday night. But it would not tell us what we really want to know, and no doubt what the Army wants to know: what sort of people enlist in the active ranks of the Provisionals? What are their personal motivations? What are the sources of their commitment to militancy?

Nineteen eighty-four is sufficiently near to us already, its Charles Fortes-like menus and architecture already encaging us in airport, motel and new university. Do we have to regard the process as irreversible and to lose our faith in history as above all a human and a cultural discipline? The loss would be incalculable if we did. For history is one of the last barriers preserving our society from a total loss of both individual and national identity. The greatest danger, in this respect, comes from within the discipline itself. Both the social scientists and the anthropologists can no doubt get along very well without us, and it is unlikely that we will ever get much profit from *their* company. But insistence on Quantification within the profession often indicates a sense of defeatism, a loss of faith in the merits of history as a study of people. If history is only to survive by dressing itself up as something that it can never be, then indeed we might as well scrap it.

Of course, there is a case—and a very good one—for Quantification too, even within the historical fold. Applied to dearth and famine, to terrorism, to the exploration of social structures, to criminality, to church attendance, to literacy, to wills and marriage contracts, to mortality rates, to currents of migration, it can be of immense assistance even to the more old-fashioned historian. And why strain ourselves in endless additions and multiplications, if a machine can do the job for us? The trouble is that Quantification will never give us the *whole* answer, can never take us the *whole* way. At some stage, the individual historian, working alone, will have once more to take over. The study of elections is a useful reminder that, even with the most up-to-date instruments to hand, history is still liable to bite the scientific, rubber-gloved hand that is attempting to discipline it. Personally I find such accidents most reassuring.

And I do not at all share the defeatism of some in my profession. For the endless fascination of history, its justification as a discipline, as a field of inquiry, as a form of culture, is the exploration of the wealth and variety of human motivations, the myriad variations of individual lives which will, I hope, always defy the monolithism of parties and doctrines, the blind disciplines of collective fanaticisms, the orthodoxies of fashion, by emphasising the apartness and the integrity of the individual. I think, indeed, despite the dark mechanised forces of the Social Sciences, the Armies of the Night, that there is still a future for historical studies, if only because individuals are still immensely important: M. Hulot has not been effectively disposed of as yet; and as long as we have him with us, there is still hope. Perhaps this too is an act of faith, a plea for human dignity? It may be so; but I think it is a more rewarding faith than a blind belief in the Collectivisation of Man.

2

Hervey

Readers of this attractive book* should not be deterred by its garish dust-cover. For the contents are almost as elegant as were the appearance and prose style of its subject.

The author opens with the celebrated phrase of Lady Mary Wortley Montagu : "This world consists of men, women and Herveys' (Horace Walpole was to put it more explicitly; that there were three sexes : men, women and Herveys). Whatever we are to make of the theme of "Miss Fanny", of Pulteney's "pretty, little, *Master Miss*", or of Pope's justly famous "This Bug with gilded wings, This painted Child of Dirt that stinks and stings" (the author, rather crossly, points out that Hervey took a bath every day); whatever the ambivalence of the sexual life of a man who had eight children, several mistresses, and two passionate and apparently active love affairs with men (Stephen Fox and Francesco Algarotti), there was indeed only one Hervey : a fact for which all who enjoy English prose must be everlastingly grateful. In a century in which malice was undoubtedly the most creative stimulus to literary production, no one can come up to Hervey's standards of chiselled unkindness. He has an economy of phrase and a perfection of cruelty unequalled even by Chesterfield's "Characters" or, later, by Junius. Only Pope can write with a sting as permanently venomous.

Hervey must always have a place both in English prose and history, as the author of the *Memoirs of the Reign of George II* (which, as Robert Halsband observes, might better be entitled the *Memoirs of the Reign of Queen Caroline*, the Queen regarding Hervey almost as her son—her own son, poor woman, was the appalling Prince of Wales—and supplying him with many of his most telling *bons mots* and with the principal character in his brilliant chronicle of Court life). He minutely observed and lovingly described details of the family squabbles between the second Hanoverian, his Queen, and "Monster" (and this he really was), their hated and hateful son. With the christening scene, the tiresome business of the Princess of Wales's pew in the Royal Chapel, the unforgettable pages on the last illness of the Queen, with Monster scarcely able to contain his impatience to see his mother dead, the betrothal of the hunch-

* Robert Halsband, *Lord Hervey, Eighteenth-Century Courtier*, Oxford 1973.
2—TDF * *

backed Prince of Orange, items of small talk between Hervey and the Queen—the Memoirs might stand, almost on their own, as a masterpiece in the literature of hate, lacquered nastiness and, at times, of an immoderation splendid in its clipped excess. Hervey must have been the source of many historical vocations—and of many commitments to a period that could produce such a devoted observer of human weaknesses, meannesses, pettinesses, and follies. Only *Les Liaisons dangereuses* can, on constant rereading, offer such unequivocal pleasure at the spectacle of utter wickedness combined with exultant malevolence.

Hervey was not only the greatest wit of his age. He was also, on occasions when his own career was not concerned, wise as well as observant. His assessment of the likely behaviour of the King, after the death of Queen Caroline, in a conversation with Walpole, is strikingly penetrating and was indeed to serve our greatest First Minister and most devastatingly sensible politician in good stead. His cynicism is as engaging as that of his patron and benefactor, Sir Robert, another staunch enemy of enthusiasm and cant. As a politician, Hervey may have been something of a lightweight, though he seems to have defended Walpole's policies, both eloquently and sensibly, in both Houses. As a courtier he made one grave mistake : he displayed a stubborn unwillingness to relinquish office. And his resultant bitterness towards the King is quite out of keeping with his previously expressed sentiments regarding a monarch glimpsed in the intimacy of his meanness and his lewdness. George II did not qualify for the expression of feelings so strong, though, thanks to Hervey, the historian must be grateful for the carefully recorded intemperance of his language.

Hervey's sexual life is an irrelevance. The author does his best to throw some light in these dark places, just as he endeavours to be fair on the patient Lady Hervey, on the vicious Lady Bristol, and to speculate on the reason why Hervey treated his wife so shabbily in his will. What matters is that we have the Memoirs, mutilated though they are by the action of his grandson.

The author is rightly fascinated by his subject. He writes with pleasing restraint, occasional preciosity, and constant modesty. For much of the time he only has to allow Hervey, or one of his enemies, to do the talking. He is rightly in sympathy with this painted Lord, as any person of taste cannot fail to be. The result is a wholly admirable book about a man who brought English prose to a kind of perfection never since equalled and who everlastingly reminds us of the rich joys attendant on observant malice.

3

Enid Starkie

Why write a book about an Oxford don?* And who is going to read a book about an Oxford don? Possibly, other Oxford dons, and certainly, Oxonians in provincial universites who would like to be Oxford dons. I have only once read a biography of an academic, that of Sir Lewis Namier by his widow, and there is little that I retain from that remarkable book save that in the General Conspiracy by Persons Unknown against Sir Lewis, the ticket collectors at Manchester London Road Station had been enrolled as Agents and that, on a visit to Israel, the historian had nearly Walked on the Waters.

Miss Richardson does not make such claims for Enid Starkie (who, she says, walked with the slightly rolling gait of the sailor; in one experience I had returning home with Miss Starkie, the roll had nothing to do with sea legs) but one gathers that she, too, thought herself to have been the victim of a conspiracy, on this occasion by persons known, presumably the General Board or whatever governs Oxford University, the aim of which was to prevent her from obtaining the Chair of French. Her biographer, perhaps not entirely intentionally, does at least convince us that, on the subject of this particular professorship, Oxford had for once been on the side of sense.

One might go on to ask : why write a biography of Enid Starkie? She has been well served by the sensitive and charmingly evocative obituary in *The Times*, by an impressionistic article in the *Cornhill Magazine*, as well as in the memories and affections of the vast number of people who, at one time or another, had the good fortune to have met her. A book seems rather a heavy tombstone to lay over that little lady. It is hard to think what Enid would have made of such a tribute; she craved recognition, but she would not have liked it to have been in any way solemn; and any biography, even a frivolous one, is a pretty solemn undertaking. As the author admits, Enid could have done it much better herself. Indeed, she did it, over and over again, especially in the small hours of the morning in widely varying versions.

Certainly her biography will not contribute either to scholarship or to our understanding of France. For Enid Starkie was an indifferent

*Joanna Richardson, *Enid Starkie,* London 1973.

scholar, with little sensitivity towards French prose, an inability to make
aesthetic judgments and a strong penchant for personal trivia. The
Oxford myth would have it that she deliberately spoke French with a
Dublin accent; I can certainly vouch for the fact that she spoke French
with a Dublin accent, and this was because she could not speak French
with a French accent. Nor do I think she had any acute understanding
of the French. Like many people, she liked being in France, appreciated
French food and drink, and, more than most people, she showed an
exceptional avidity for recognition by French officialdom. In her eagerness for publicity, she displayed the brash skills of an academic lion-
hunter, lining up for her collection Gide and Cocteau, organising their
Honorary Degrees, and exploiting their visits to Oxford as colourful
stunts for self-advertisement.

I doubt whether in fact she ever contemplated marrying a Parisian
working man or taking up some humble occupation in France; I believe
these were fantasies, and I don't think that she was ever quite as poor
during her student days in Paris in the twenties as she was subsequently
to make out. She may indeed have felt very close then to starving Serbs
and tubercular White Russians, but there was always the boat home,
as well as a small scholarship from her College. I have never quite fallen
for the Down-and-Out-in-Paris bit as far as Anglo-Saxons are concerned.
It smacks of self-dramatisation. Anyhow, she did not marry her waiter or
whatever he was.

She had the makings of a good historian; her book on Rimbaud in
Abyssinia is a historian's study and she had the historian's eagerness for
detail. I recall the promptitude with which she pumped a Marseille
friend of mine, whose brother was a surgeon, on the subject of the
Hôpital de la Conception. Yet it is odd to write of a poet such as
Rimbaud as an historian might write about a statesman or an adventurer,
or about a novelist like Flaubert as a craftsman, polishing his tools, when
in fact he was a creator.

Biographers tend to fall into the heredity trap. Georges Lefebvre was
cold and reserved because he came from Lille; the fact is he was cold
and reserved. Albert Mathiez was brutal and violent because he was a
peasant from the Jura; the fact is he was brutal and violent. Miss
Richardson attributes Enid's pugnacity to her Anglo-Irish ancestry. But
the two things that she retained from an impoverishedly genteel background in or on the fringes of the Castle Set were her intense snobbery, a
truly Anglo-Irish class snobbery, and an almost Balzacien meanness.
Hence her concern too for the rites of High Table. Hence too a wide-eyed
provincialism that stayed with her all her life and that made Oxford
seem in her eyes an oasis of sophistication, gossip and good talk.

Her biography is a reminder of just how parochial Oxford, as well
as Enid and Miss Richardson (who, at one stage, uses the horrible

phrase : "Enid had an Oxford mind") can sometimes be. She was quite right to stick to Oxford while constantly complaining about the place, how she felt out of place in a College (yet she actually *enjoyed* college meetings, which is about the worst thing I have ever heard about anybody), how she could not get on with English people (and they, in their silliness, were remarkably indulgent to displays of her Irish Act, and did not even mind her regular genuflexions of Anglophobia for French consumption). Her cultivated eccentricity was readily tolerated by many (but not by all), because she was part of the Oxford scene. Where else would she have got away with it?

In spite of her grievance over the Chair, her own career was very much the product of the University's democratic and decentralised structure. In Redbrick, she would have been ruled by a Department, subjected to Professors, whereas, in Oxford, her own Professor could only complain, sadly and quietly, about the antics of *cette clownesse* (but he, poor man, could not see the humour of it all, he was a Frenchman). If she was so anxious to have more time to write, why then did she devote so much time and energy to University stunts, to getting herself into Atticus, and why, when she actually did write, did she write so badly?

Perhaps, as Miss Richardson says, there was a fundamental contradiction between the public figure and the private woman, often desperately lonely and devoured by self-pity. Certainly, I never found her lurid or flamboyant, rather extremely understanding and discreet. I was well placed in respect of her, having been to the same school as her father and brother.

I saw more of her in Paris than in Oxford, especially during the period when she stayed at the Hôtel Racine (at a reduced rate, she told me with pride). Apart from the school ties, we had in common an almost professional pride in reminiscences on the subject of sponging, an activity for which the French have the politer and more exact phrase of *la pique-assietterie*. If in that Order I were a *Chevalier,* she was at least a *Grand Officier*. In France, she worked the Catholic ticket, I, the Protestant and Communist ones. I think there is no doubt that she got the better value. But she was the better placed, as an attractive young woman with blue eyes. There was something childlike about her eagerness to obtain something for nothing, and there is a splendid passage in one of her letters about how much there was to eat at an official banquet in Moscow.

The book is a modest, slightly inflated assessment of the career of a warm and life-enhancing personality. The author wisely lets Enid do most of the talking and not all of it is easy-going; for Enid had terrible bouts of self-pity and, apparently, a very unhappy emotional life. It is not easy to write excitingly about a university teacher and the experiences of a Chairman of Examiners would have been hard even for Boswell to have assimilated.

The only lasting monument to Enid will, however, remain in the affectionate memories of her cherished by the many and highly diverse friends that she enriched by her warmth and her inexhaustible fount of fantasy, irreverence, and captivating directness. She was, as Miss Richardson says, like a child who collects shells; and *her* shells were her many, many friends, and the hundreds of cards that they sent her at Christmas. No wonder she wrote so well about her own childhood. It was what she was closest to all her life.

4

Maurice Bowra*

It was New Year's Day 1971, or possibly 2nd January. Anyhow, having that morning read the New Year's Honours List, I called in at midday at Wadham lodge. "Is the Warden in?" I asked the very old porter. "Do you mean the real Warden or the Warden?" he replied. I took a chance on this and said: "The Warden." "Oh yes, HE's in, do you know where to go, Sir?" I went through to the tiny quad, and looked in through the curtains of the L-shaped flat on the ground floor of the left-side corner. It was rather like a tank; and, through the mesh, I could just make out the rather squat figure, sitting reading in a chair in the drawing-room. I had always thought that he had something of the look of a very old and wise hippo (at other moments, he resembled a Chinese mandarin, or an emblematic Chinese porcelain figure representing Age and Sagacity, and with just a hint, too, of ruthlessness; it is strange how often people resemble their birthplaces) and now he looked so more than ever. Although he was a small man, spied through the curtains, he looked much too big for his tank. I rang the bell, and he let me in, first of all doing me the honours of his new lodgings: "Rather like living in a roll-top desk," he commented, of the study, which indeed had a low, vaulted wooden roof in small slats. The drawing-room was decorated with Chinese silk screens and prints, and there was a profusion of porcelain vases and a bright mass of winter flowers.

The Warden seemed so patently pleased with his new lodgings that I caught his almost boyish enthusiasm about what might also have been described as a show-case, displaying a very rare, very valuable object. I told him that I had come to bring him greetings for the New Year and to congratulate him on his C.H. "Nothing at all, dear boy. Only a matter of *waiting*, you know. *You*'ll get it, too, you'll see, if you wait long enough. Just a matter of time." I felt my doubts about this. There were after all plenty of septuagenarians whom I knew who were *not* Companions of Honour. He repeated, two or three times more, in short, gurgling barks: "Just a matter of *waiting*." And then we left the subject, as exploded. But he seemed genuinely glad to see me; and we talked of two topics that nearly always came up when we met and that I had

*Hugh Lloyd-Jones (Editor), *Maurice Bowra: a celebration*, London 1974.

come to recognise as Theme Tunes that would enable the Full Orchestra gradually to come into play. After that, one played it by ear, as the volume of tone increased.

Perhaps it was my own good fortune to have known Maurice Bowra as an old man, in his middle sixties when I first returned to Oxford, after an absence of nearly twenty-five years. Many people would tell me that I had missed him at his best, that he was now in decline and had lost his touch. I could not vouch for this, but I think in fact I was lucky, for I generally like old people—they have so much to tell one—and I find that they respond. Certainly, for the ten years that I knew the Warden, dining in Wadham never lost its fascination. One went into Hall, where sherry would be served at High Table, with a feeling of expectation and excitement, as well as a sort of *trac*, just as one enters a theatre to attend a play of which one has heard much praise. And, with the sharp, assertive kick of the Warden's mallet—*les trois coups*—much better designed to introduce an Entertainment than an invocation to the Deity in the form of a Latin grace, the play had indeed begun, though one felt sure that the Warden, who was an Eating Man, and who, we learn from one of the most delightful pieces in the present collection—that by Hugh Lloyd-Jones—had had as a child in China "a cook who bore the title of 'Great Eating Professor'" (perhaps the only sort of Professor the Warden could tolerate), would have rendered thanks somewhere or other for the good food to come. One was immediately plunged into some breakneck, bubbling monologue, as though the Warden had taken up exactly where he had left off, at one's last visit to the Jacobean Masque, a term or two previously. And it would go on, in a series of short sharp jerks, rising and falling, a sudden crescendo, followed by the low gurgling of an Icelandic geyser. But it was neither a One Act Play, nor a One Actor's Play: all would be put in, and it was up to each, in the course of the evening, to discover his role. That was part of the fun. From my very first attendance, I was made aware of what was expected of me: first of all, to talk of a school friend of mine who shortly after leaving school had murdered his mother, in the thirties. How he *loved* that story! (and he loved it even more because, at the first telling, he spotted the visible and extreme embarrassment of one of the Fellows, who was from the same school as myself and the murderer), and how, seeing how he loved it, I loved telling it! He would have me over it, again and again, gurgling and panting approval and delight, and interspersing my detailed narrative with pithy comments: "a bit clumsy that", "not much sense of aim", "probably never held a racket in his life", "not much of a fives player, I should say" (these interjections punctuating my account of the boy pursuing his mother round the house, hacking at her with an axe), "Ho ho, broke down, in O'Connell Street, too, rich, rich" (the boy having run out of petrol in the centre of town, with his mother's body in the back of the Austin Seven), "a bit of a prig, typical, typical, they generally are" (this when my narrative reached the stage when the boy, attempting to dispose of the body, by pushing it, with the car, over a cliff, into the sea, found his path blocked by a couple of lovers in another car, who went on and on making love)—"disgusting", commented my friend, "*animals*". He never seemed to tire of the matricide, and would display me, with a sort of circus pride, to newcomers: "Come on, Cobb, let's have the Mother's Story, you left a bit out last time ..." Well, it *was* a good one, at least in the telling.

The other subject was of less general interest to the company at large, though of great interest to the two of us. It concerned an academic who, at one time, had been my head, and who had grievously sinned against the Warden's personal code, by placing, as he saw it, his country before a friend. This man he described as "The Card", a description that was Edwardianly apt, *au physique comme au moral*. Indeed, after the Warden's first evocation of the Card, I would always picture the man as wearing a boater and blazer, with white ducks and tennis shoes. On my first visit to Wadham, I recall above all a sudden rapid burst of talk emitting from the Warden, that sounded like a deafening, rattling, reverberating game of skittles, or an American Bowling Alley with the serried ranks of the Professors of both ancient Universities as pins: down they went, one after another, each under a direct, cracking hit: "a noodle", "a grammarian", "a compiler", and so on. It was done with wonderful skill, brio and fruity enjoyment. Luckily I had not reached that dangerous eminence in those days.

All the evocations included in *A Celebration* give at least some indication of the Warden's wonderful powers as a conversationalist, an entertainer, and a life-enhancing person, to have known whom was both unforgettable and enriching. He believed above all in friendship, and took much trouble with it. I was every now and then the fortunate recipient of an article, an off-print, a book, or a novel, which I would find in Balliol lodge, with a brief note: "Dear Cobb, you will like this", "this will amuse you", "this man is a *consummate* liar". No one who met him is ever likely to forget him. Yet it is extremely difficult to communicate in a book the bubbling vigour of the man, the extraordinary modulations of his utterly unpredictable voice, his love of conversation, his ability to draw others out. He was not himself at his best in print, and he is too elusive, darting too swiftly, to be pinned down in the print of others. One or two of the recollections are not without vulgarity. One is as unwilling to spy on the Warden without his trousers as one would be to see one's mother in her bath; and I do not really care to know the shape of the Warden's navel, though Noel Annan's description of him swimming, like an Admiral standing on the bridge of his sinking battleship, is brilliant. I certainly could have done without the poetry. There is another, childlike swimming scene in Anthony Quinton's piece. *Mercurius*, a retired divine from the Turl, is witty, wise, and generous. Anthony Powell describes a curiously unrelated set of circumstances, in which characters bump into one another, over the years, rather as in one of the Widmerpool novels (Bowra, incidentally, had a unique collection of Widmerpools, to which he was constantly adding). I cannot comment on his scholarship. But I am surprised that so many of the contributors should have detected in the Warden a deep note of sadness and dissatisfaction; and some even make him appear rather unpleasant. Perhaps I did not know him long enough. But I think it is the true measure of his constant kindness that the most moving account of him should have been written by Leslie Mitchell, a Wadham undergraduate. It is stated here, too, that he did not set very much store by graduates and graduate work—he was, after all, one of those wonderful, gilded luxuries of the twenties, and if Oxford cannot afford luxuries, it would be a dull place indeed—yet, in the last three years of his life, he earned the deep affection and gratitude of an African graduate, an Angolan, studying comparative law, in whom he took a constant and intelligent interest, and who, from whatever eminence he now occupies in his own country, will recall the Warden as one who, in his three years in Oxford, helped him on his way, with friendship, advice, and encouragement, endeavouring to bring him out, talking to him in French, and personally intervening to obtain for him a room in the central part of the College. This, apart from the flow of words which poured forth from him like volcanic lava, rumbling and roaring, suddenly subsiding, as suddenly re-emerging from a newly-opened tunnel, was what was unique about him: an ability to take trouble, not just once, with a few kind words, but again and again, what might be described as *la bonté avisée*. And this is how, in a matter of years, he made of Wadham one of the most distinguished Colleges in the University. He *cared*: about people, about liberty, about the quality of life, about beauty, about style.

5

Besterman's Voltaire

The appearance of a full-scale biography of Voltaire by Theodore Besterman is an event.* For no one would appear to be better equipped than the editor of *Correspondance* and the founder and director of the Institut et Musée Voltaire in Geneva. The author, who sleeps in Voltaires' bed and lives in Voltaire's house, is certainly not the last to recognise his own competence in the matter; 720 footnotes prefixed with the abbreviation *Best.*, and almost as many cross-references to articles published by the author, help to bring that point home. He refers frequently to the prime importance of the *Correspondance* as a source. "This was the first Voltaire letter to see print," he comments, "20,000 more were to follow" (guess the name of the editor); and, throughout the book, he speaks from the rostrum, as the only fully qualified *maître-ès-Voltaire*: "I venture to say", "I have been able to show, and this is even more interesting", "this new play ... was generally regarded, though not by me, as Voltaire's best tragedy", "the beginnings of this love affair were completely unknown until a few years ago, when I had the good fortune to lay my hands on ..." (and there has been an awful lot of laying on of hands since); then there is the agonising admission: "I am not often in the unhappy dilemma of agreeing with Voltaire's enemies, but this time I am."

Voltaire Studies had to wait for the Coming of the Only True Interpreter of the Word (having got one of the houses, he is also the Only Authorised Guide). Those who ventured out before the Master get short shrift, especially if they are French. We hear of "the ignorance or incapacity of the authors (like Luchet and Duvernet)". Lounsbury, later "the ineffable Lounsbury", is the author of "one of the most insensitive and intemperate books ever published by a scholar". Some "ignorant paradox-mongers ... have alleged Voltaire to be impotent". Peter Gay, the only historian to be cited, has a "taste for paradox". George Saintsbury's "every word on Voltaire is an impertinence".

Worse, certain manuscripts "are now in the possession of a dealer called Kraus, who has not allowed me to check them—so rare an attitude that it deserves to be recorded" (poor Kraus does not even get a Mr, or,

*Theodore Besterman, *Voltaire*, London 1969.

as the author would write, a mr). Others, mostly historians, who have had
interesting things to say about Voltaire—David Bien, Betty Behrens,
R. R. Palmer, Norman Hampson, Jean Sarrailh, Marcelin Desfourneaux,
Jean Ehrard—are not mentioned.

It is a pity, for the author might have profited from them. As a contribution to the history of the eighteenth century, *Voltaire* is inadequate,
trite, pedantic, and often inane. The author insists on inflicting on his
readers footnotes defining, not always accurately, such difficult words as
conseiller, parlement, abbé, président, ancien régime, dauphin and *lettre
de cachet*. Louis-le-Grand is described as "this Jesuit Eton", Louis XV's
France as "a totalitarian society".

"Many historians"—who *are* they?—"seem to have difficulty in
appreciating the fact that a *philosophe* of the Enlightenment is by no
means the same kind of animal as a philosopher in modern times". Later,
there is a reference to "the commonest and greatest of misapprehensions
[which] is to suppose that the Enlightenment was a coherent body of
doctrine or even a consistent mode of thought". He himself defines the
Enlightenment as the Belief in Progress. Elsewhere, he appears to equate
the *parlement* with democracy; Voltaire's intense hostility to these bodies
is never explained, the treatment of the Calas affair is totally inadequate,
in the light of recent research, and it is of little help to have Charles XII
and Frederick II constantly placed in the unlikely company of Hitler,
Mussolini, and Stalin.

Undergraduates will have to do their homework again, for Mr Besterman tells us that "most of the peasants of France still lived in a state of
feudal servitude". The abolition of the *parlements*—the most important
French political decision of the century—is shrouded in the cryptic
phrase: "Voltaire . . . followed the *changes* with the closest attention."
To understand the dispute between Voltaire and Rousseau over Geneva,
the reader will have to turn back to R. R. Palmer.

Mr Besterman appears to think that he has done his job as a historian
when he has established the date of a letter or a play or has been able to
prove that Voltaire's niece was his mistress, or has given creaking
"abstracts"—his own expression—of the plots of his plays (I recommend
these for comic reading): what he admires most about Voltaire, one
suspects, is the sheer *number* of letters that he wrote. Many of them he
throws, *in extenso*, but, of course, in translation, at the reader, without
any attempts to analyse their content.

This is poor history and poor criticism. Even as a biography, the title
is misleading, for the book is as much about Besterman as about Voltaire.
We have Besterman on Anti-Semitism, Besterman on the English and
French National Character (*we*, for he is one of *us*, come out the better).
Besterman on Shakespeare, Besterman on Bishops, on Progress, on the
Atomic Bomb, Besterman on Man's Future, Besterman on Spiritualism,

Besterman on God, on Karma, on Happiness, Besterman on Persons I Have Talked to (Cocteau and Bertrand Russell are in this gallery).

There are references to mini-skirts, quotations from Kipling, Rebecca West, F. H. Bradley, Wilde, Leslie Stephen ("this great father of greater daughters"), Shaw, Herbert Spencer and Giraudoux. *On est cultivé ou on ne l'est pas.* Voltaire often has to wait in the wings while the Master takes off into his Great Thoughts.

The style is appropriate to the solemnity of the Message and to the indigence of historical construction. "The cathedral of Chartres is more than a pile of stones, but the Sacré Coeur is not necessarily a finer struc-ture than the Temple of Karnak." (It is surprising that Toynbee is not included among the author's referees.) "We are living on borrowed time, we have mortgaged the future of the race." "Yet again deep called unto deep." There is a glimpse of "the flash of Racine's brilliant scalpel", another of "the Cartesian light that penetrates into every corner". Voltaire, who might have described the operation more concisely, is depicted : "Still, having set his shoulder to the wheel, [he] continued his efforts to get to the top of the mountain of royal favour . . ." There is an echo too of Hans Killer : "I do not hesitate to repeat that it is perfectly possible to disapprove constructional philosophy altogether."

In the rostrum, the Master speaks in Germanic tones; but he can also unbend on the subject of "the goings-on of Stratford", a phrase from Voltaire is translated as "my heart and my prick", a certain bishop is "bloody-minded" about Aberfan. He is vulgar as well as ponderous. Every quotation in French is translated, literally, in the footnotes, and the author's personal contribution to the language of Voltaire is to refer repeatedly to a place called "Strassburg".

The underlying, perhaps unconscious, theme of this meandering, ill-constructed book is *France Unfair to Besterman.* It is difficult to see what the French have done to him; perhaps they have not given him enough honorary degrees, perhaps he cannot forgive them for being what he is not—French—the same nationality as Voltaire. (They do not *deserve* Voltaire.)

He has "laid hands on" most of the letters of their greatest prose-writer, he is proceeding to edit his correspondence in English, and, while enjoying this savagely defended monopoly, he never fails to point to the dereliction of French scholarship in this respect (if he really had the interest of Voltaire at heart, he might at least have made the slight effort required to edit him in French, an effort that has been made, with self-effacement and devotion, by an Englishman, for Rousseau). He has one of Voltaire's houses, his bed, his clothes, his quills, his ink-well, his pictures, his busts, his garden (the walls of which, he claims, were rather clumsily rebuilt by the Genevan authorities, in 1967), most of his books. What more can he want? Voltaire, *all* of Voltaire, for his very own, for his personal enjoyment. But Voltaire is not the private property of Theodore Besterman; he belongs to all of us, even including his much-abused countrymen. No one would gather from the present ponderous monument that the endless charm of Voltaire is his language, in its clarity and its brilliantly achieved concision.

6

The poor of eighteenth-century France

Though Dr Hufton's subject is consistently a sad and desperate one, offering little hope of mitigation, and indeed hinting that the situation could only worsen (as, following the Revolution, it did) this is not in fact a sad book.* On the contrary, there are many elements of consolation, and the general themes that emerge most insistently from a study illuminated throughout by compassion, restraint, humour and acute insight are the ever-ready resilience of the very poor, their ability to adjust to situations that change with the seasons, the months and even the hours, their pathetic moderation of expectation and, finally, the febrility of popular leisure, with so much to cram into so short a space of time, so that leisure, like work, appears as a desperate race against the clock.

In the sheer strength of will to survive the French *indigents* are far from fatalistic, displaying an incessant ingenuity of invention, and a refusal to admit the likelihood that, if the present is bad, the immediate future can only be worse. Such determined, if limited optimism would be the despair of present-day economists, as it seems to have been of contemporary *Physiocrates*. So much of what Dr Hufton describes constitutes an Indian scene, but the human subjects of her book (probably rather more than a third of the total population, eight or nine million women, children and men, in that order) far from displaying an oriental passivity as to the role assigned to them in a brief and brutal life, are revealed as fighting back, step by step, against impending catastrophe, or even as doggedly progressing forward, often in crab-like fashion, either on a single leg, or supported on bare and partly toeless feet, or permanently bent as a result of hernias or a flogging. The overriding impression given by what might have been expected to be a relentless chronicle of deprivation is one of extreme vitality. Only the very small children, abandoned on the steps of churches or hospitals, or sent out to *nourrices,* or underfed, take their leave of life, in filth and rags, almost without a sound.

To take the first point, the poor of eighteenth-century France are so often revealed as masters—and, more rarely, mistresses—of the economic tightrope. It is a matter of using every hour of the day and, indeed, a

* Olwen Hufton, *The Poor of Eighteenth-Century France 1750–1789*, London 1974.

good deal of the night in successive forms of employment. Here, for instance, are harvesters who manage to cram in as many as three grain harvests, moving upwards to the slow rhythm of the growth of the stalks, between late July and September, and perhaps even, at the end, contriving to get in on the *vendanges* or on the olive crop. Or here is a man who eats away from home, from May to October, either as a building labourer in the cities, or as an itinerant pedlar-cum-beggar-cum-*amuseur public*-cum-handyman. There are those, mainly from the Rouergue, who go to Spain, taking menial jobs for the winter, and those who spend anything from three to nine years there before returning with their savings.

In the sheer variety of the poor man's itinerary, as in the carefully calculated balance of interlocking activities and skills, one is reminded physically of the many small compartments fitting into the trays of a *colporteur* and forming a box supported by a pair of straps around his neck : here, pins and needles, here candles and "fine strong laces", here matches, *livres bleus* and coloured prints, patent medicines, herbs and potions, a popular Pandora's box of many colours and as many ills, carried half way across France on a single neck. It is hardly surprising that the masculine poor should have acquired a topographical knowledge of the kingdom equalled only by the *hardi compagnon* on his *Tour de France,* and totally different from that of the eighteenth-century traveller in search of the picturesque. The *colporteur* would have no eyes for waterfalls and cascades; windmills would merely be landmarks to guide him on an itinerary transmitted to him by word of mouth, Gothic cathedrals would indicate locations suitable to various forms of dramatic begging, whether inside or outside, mountains would tax him on the upward climb, and even the sky would be more likely to be scrutinised as a potential threat than admired as an object of wonder by a man who could ill afford the discomforts and dangers of sodden clothes.

We, of course, can read of these fantastic seasonal migrations with comfortable excitement, seeing them as the gradual unfolding of a hitherto secret network of *étapes*, of stopping-places, of inns, ferries, stables, in which we can perceive the yellow of the broom and gorse in bloom on some Breton *lande,* the pink and red of the fruit trees on the great begging *route des abbayes* between Jumièges, le Bec and Rouen; we can admire the shimmering silver of the olive trees because, at least since 1940 or 1944, we have not ourselves had to take to the weary road, on some collective *Exode.* These were desperate walkers, people dragging themselves forward, in a constant effort to keep just ahead of total ruin and to have at least something to bring home at the end, if only a pocketful of *liards* and crusts of bread, the identity cards of the wandering beggar. Dr Hufton, unfortunately, is a stern witness constantly unwilling to allow us ever to stray from the miry path of heavy-going reality.

This is not to suggest that these migrations were all agony and foot-soreness. If there was one thing that the poor were never short of, that was company. The pedlar did not walk alone, and there must have existed a rough, residual sociability—as well as a crude code of honour (the poor, it would seem, did not rob one another of the little that they ever had to rob) of the mountain path, the river valley and the highroad. There did of course exist a brutal and dangerous competitiveness in these wandering crowds, just as, in the last years included in the author's study, we note an even more brutal competitiveness of sheer misery, with ever-increasing armies of unwanted babies crowding the aged and infirm out of the minimal shelter afforded by the *hospices*. There was also strength in numbers: the stopping places, when not barns or stables, or in summer a ditch or a stack were probably filthy inns, but they would offer companionship and, above all, a great deal of useful information, the stock exchange of vagrancy.

We have referred so far to masculine migrations, because, in the family unit, which is throughout the author's basic measurement, it was the man who would be the most likely to take to the roads, for part of the year (and the longer, the better) or who, when hard pressed, might even opt out altogether, never to return. But he was often accompanied by children, his own or borrowed; and there were less spectacular, shorter, but none the less regular itineraries of female migration: the girl from the Forez or the Dombes who goes to Lyon as a *servante*, the Picardes, the Flemish and Alsatian girls, the Cauchoises, the Beauceronnes, the Briardes, the Wallonnes and the Flamandes, the constant overflow of Versaillaises who follow their brothers or their male cousins to Paris, and who, *filles de la campagne*, or girls from Nancy, Strasbourg, Thiers, or Tournan, provide the so often pathetically easy recruits to the uncountable hosts—as the author frequently reminds us, the sinking and wandering world of the very poor defies statistical evidence—of the pregnant, at once dismissed and, with a small child on their hands, temporarily unemployable.

Although her book is mostly about the family and, therefore, about mothers and children, it was the male members of the family who could always command the widest spectrum of alternative skills, and who were the less encumbered in terms of mobility. There was little for the country girl, once in the town, other than domestic service, work as a laundress or in textiles and silk, at the very lowest and most unhealthy levels of those trades. Death would be the most obvious limitation on mobility; but whereas, for the *servante*, the *fille de salle*, the *blanchisseuse* and the *revendeuse*, the first pregnancy would represent the journey's end, for a time at least—and a pregnant country girl would do anything rather than return to her village—or the descent into part-time, then perhaps full-time prostitution, dependence on the *mouches*, followed almost inevitably by disease, culminating horribly in creeping physical decomposition, shut away in the hospital; for the male, if the worst came to the worst, there was always the Army, the official one, and the unofficial one, *l'armée roulante*, that of banditry, or first the one, then, as a deserter or discharged soldier, the other.

Both the resilience and the elusiveness of the poor are thus best illustrated in this expandability of forms of employment. It is a theme that the author encounters at the very outset of her study, when she sets about the difficult task of attempting to define the poor in contemporary terms and from the very different viewpoints of the ecclesiastical authorities and those concerned with public order. For the poor, in a country like eighteenth-century France, are as evasive of overall definition, and represent hosts as wide or as narrow according to the optic of one's vision, as that later group, the much-disputed *sans-culottes,* an accordion that, as one pulls it out or compresses it, will emit very different sounds, becoming the object of a variety of moral, as well as social definitions.

As leisure comes only after work and may indeed be considered the reward for work, if one can pay the physical price that popular leisure imposes on the participant in a *fête* or even in an ordinary Sunday's entertainment; and as in the most favourable circumstances—rare indeed then in the years after 1767—the maximum working year for the male members of the rural poor might be calculated as about 290 days, with as many as sixty feast days (and considerably less for the female, especially the *servante*), it is now time to consider the second outstanding theme of this beautiful book : the modesty of expectation displayed by the general mass of the poor. There would be no question of long-term planning, though the country girl in urban employment would make desperate efforts, generally defeated by loss of work or a pregnancy, to save for her dowry; it was a matter of getting over the dead season, of not being a burden on the family unit of five or so, say between May and October, by "eating away". The future was the period just over the walker's horizon, and it could be envisaged, as in the words of one of the old songs, in terms of *A Pâques, A la Trinité* or *A la Saint-Michel,* an extensible future, like everything else in this humble world of Little Expectations, but not extensible beyond this year or the next.

Old age and their accompanying infirmities were disasters that would only bear thinking about in the extremely unlikely event of their ever being reached. There was a normal age span for which one might indeed plan, running from about twelve years to approximately twenty-eight, that is from the time one might be expected to earn the price of one's daily bread (or part of it), till an age when disease or physical accident were likely to cause partial or total incapacity, or at least a dangerous, and eventually fatal, slowing up of a variable programme of occupations. Early marriage was a necessary component of an economy so tight that it would have to depend on the prospect of the tiny supplement to be derived from the capacity of small children to earn something from as early as five. The author has some fascinating passages on the employment of toddlers for the purposes of salt-smuggling between Brittany and Maine. The line of division between habitual want and total indigence was so narrow that the least extra might tip the balance in favour of a respite. Pauperisation was not at all as Taine depicted it— a sudden, irreversible, dramatic process, like a man walking on the bed of a river who all at once loses his feet in an invisible water-hole. The day of reckoning could be delayed again and again, thanks to a series of increasingly desperate expedients, though it was likely enough that it would come to most of the rural poor after a lease of from ten to fifteen years, as a result of one of the periodic harvest crises, the overproduction of wine or a recession in the silk and textile trades.

Meanwhile, there was a multiplicity of temporary makeshifts, whose variety in fact makes it impossible to assess the economic expectations of the very poor in statistical terms. They ranged, according to the season, from part-time or semi-disguised forms of begging (it would be as well to be seen carrying the tools of a respectable trade if one were an itinerant in fact primarily dependent on alms), to petty theft of objects like wood, scrap iron, or luggage tied to the roof of a stage-coach; or the varied opportunities for smuggling generously provided by a fiscal system that penalised the circulation of certain primary necessities like salt, leather, wines and spirits (in this form of indirect relief, the old régime was far more considerate to the more resourceful of the very poor than its successors); appeals to an increasingly exiguous charity, or the elaborately calculated use of the extended family network. There were many, if not "fringe benefits", at least temporary, negative preservatives available to the more travelled and experienced of the very poor. In much of the South, it would be possible to economise on the price of a night's lodgings by sleeping outside during the spring and summer months; even in Paris, if one had a relative who was a groom (and many provincials, especially Lower Normans, would be so provided) one might temporarily share a corner of the stables with the horses. For similar reasons, it would be a great advantage to have a relative who was a baker, someone who could provide both a crust and a little warmth at night, even if one slept on the pavement. For an itinerant from Savoy, the Alps, or the Massif Central, gifted with a lively imagination, or provided with a convincing hard luck story (a cottage burnt to the ground, a maiming as the result of a fall from a roof or a burn, an epidemic, a whole range of Acts of God, often attested to by a complaisant Auvergnat *curé,* anxious to help his parishioners on their stony way to Paris), or experienced in the use of the *vielle* or the fiddle, or in the exercise of dancing animals, there were plenty of ways of cadging a bowl of soup, a night under cover, and possibly even a few *liards*. The author offers plenty of evidence that semi-beggars of this type were often positively welcome to farmers and their families, owing to their good humour and their reputation for (relative) honesty. It was felt at least, no doubt as a result of past experience, that such people would not abuse hospitality afforded to them by scouting out the interior, with a return visit in mind. At the other end of the scale, especially in the areas of extensive farming, were those who begged in numbers and whom it would have been unwise to turn away from a night in a barn.

The calendar of the poor would be compressed, for practical purposes, into very brief periods of human experience that, through at least a small dispensation of mercy, would disguise from the potential victims the impending effects of the successive crises detected by such historians as Labrousse. Some awareness, however, of a general deterioration must have been transmitted to the majority of the population through the palpable and openly-expressed manifestations of governmental fears. The impression that one retains from the present study is that, in its relations to the general mass of the poor, the old royal government was becoming increasingly unsure of itself. During the 1780s, the *Lieutenant de Police* busied himself with a series of restrictions on the movements of itinerants and on the exercise of most urban skills. No doubt the authorities had good reason to be afraid, for it is apparent from this relentless account that, for as much as a third of the population, conditions were getting progressively worse from 1763 to 1789. Indeed, so gloomy is the scene described that it would seem impossible that there could be any room for further deterioration. Yet, if the author were to extend her chronicle of suffering into and beyond the revolutionary years, it is certain that the poor would be revealed as even more vulnerable, and far more subject to the repressiveness of authority, than during the last twenty-five years of the old regime, when so many escape routes had been available to those *au fait* with the complicated geography of evasion and survival. Indeed, the most important effect of the French Revolution was to bring at least the awareness, if not the presence, of Government, to the village, and repression down to the level of the poorest town-dweller, exposing him or her to a judicial code far more effective, uniform, automatic and invasive than the clutter of rival jurisdictions that had characterised the old system, at the same time killing the spirit of charity and drying up the few resources still available to charitable institutions.

The plight of the very poor, especially women, was considerably worse in 1794 than it had been in 1789. Perhaps that is another story that, it is to be hoped, Dr Hufton will take up in her next book. For the eighteenth-century poor could not have a better historian, if only because she has taken such infinite trouble to penetrate places where no contemporary other than a few *curés* had ever gone, and to explore the semi-secret world of the desperate with the help of a code understandable only to them.

The author has done a great deal more than develop these three themes. She sketches out the general history of formal and informal relief throughout the century, outlining the effects of the collapse of the Law System in the 1720s, the crises of the 1740s, and the worsening of the financial position of hospitals and *hospices* from the 1760s. She concludes her account of a walking population with those to whom it would be denied even to toddle, much less to walk, with those for whom it would be the end of the journey at the very threshold of life : the dead infants, the murdered children, the principal victims of a brutally competitive society that had little time or sympathy to waste on these innocents. Her last chapter, entitled "Parent and Child", makes horrific reading, though, even on this grim subject, one feels there is room for hope.

The author is an artist, as well as a social historian uniquely qualified to tackle the problems of the feminine poor. She is unwilling to leave her readers in the presence of the dead infant. After death, life, and life at its most rumbustious, most vigorous, most brightly painted : the stamping, screeching, gymnastic leisure of the very poor, the enjoyments of the weekend *guinguette* and of the village or urban fair, the jumping, somersaulting, cartwheeling evolutions to the reedy accompaniment of fiddle and *veille*. She reserves her postscript for the use and abuse of leisure, the noisy violence of Sunday brawls, of interparish vendettas, of the Saturday night priest-baiting, the destructive sorties of *les jeunes gens*, the village bachelors who, though they might not all be young, were all violent, the geography of leisure and sociability, the meeting places of the poor after work, the moral commitment offered by *la Promenade*. The postscript would suggest an option on the future, perhaps pointing out the direction to be taken by her next book, one that will be awaited eagerly by all those who have read the present brilliant and sensitive study of the lost world of the very poor, but not of the utterly hopeless, nor of the totally unhappy, a study indeed that is as full of limited hope as it is of the author's boundless charity.

7

The education of Louis XVI

Historians of the pre-revolutionary period, more especially of the last reign in it, are faced with one almost insuperable difficulty: the King of France, the centre-piece and *agent moteur* of the whole system—and Louis XVI had particularly inflated views with regard to the place of the Monarch in French government and society: he was much more of an absolutist than his grandfather—largely defies historical analysis and has almost entirely defied historical documentation. Specialists, with very little indeed to go on, apart from court gossip, most of it malevolent and entirely inaccurate, much of it put out by the Austrian ambassador, or by the King's brothers, find themselves reduced to interpreting "les silences du Roi", an enterprise of great sophistication, but unlikely to yield positive or very rich rewards.

Louis XVI, it is true, made silence an instrument of government; he was not, as has so often been suggested, shy to the point of being tongue-tied; he deliberately kept his own counsel, in order to increase the aura of mystery that surrounded his office and to preserve his high position from the effects of gossip. In the many political histories of his personal reign, while Marie-Antoinette, Provence and Artois, Madame Elisabeth, Orléans and Conti appear well-chronicled, the personal role of the King remains elusive, as indeed no doubt it was meant to be. Long before historians, his ministers were to be the victims of a laconicity that often bordered on insensitiveness. When d'Ormesson was obliged to tell his royal master that he had not completed his *travail*, because he had been up all night with his dying son, all Louis would say was: "C'est fâcheux." He cannot have been an easy or a pleasant person to deal with; and historians have not found him an easy or a pleasant person to deal with. Like many contemporary witnesses, like Madame de la Tour du Pin, who, at eighteen, in 1788, became a lady-in-waiting to the Queen, and who described the King as a sort of fat peasant, his clothes thrown on anyhow, propelling himself along on his uneven course down the corridors, historians have fallen back on clichés: his lack of dignity, his obtuseness, his deviousness, his limited intelligence, his lack of education.

So *L'Education d'un roi* is a very important book indeed.* What Mme

*P. Girault de Coursac, *L'Education d'un roi: Louis XVI*, Paris 1972.

Girault de Coursac has done is to prove that, in fact, Louis XVI does not necessarily go unaccounted for from the point of view of historical evidence. She is not so much concerned with Louis XVI, as with the young duc de Berry, from birth to the age of fifteen. But—and this she illustrates with great success—at fifteen, the future King was already fully formed. In her study of the child's and the adolescent's education, she has drawn on a number of sources never previously used, including the family papers of the Spanish Bourbons and of the Habsburgs, in Madrid and Vienna, the publications of the duc de la Vauguyon, the man most responsible for the child's schooling, and the papers of the Ministry of War. The result is quite startling: the future King acquires human proportions—some might object superhuman ones, for the author is inclined perhaps to overemphasise the scholarship, the intelligence and the perspicacity of her pupil; her readers at times will be tempted to think of him as rather priggish—and we are given, in the child, as seen by his tutors and in his contacts with them and with his brothers and sisters, a key to his personality and his future behaviour in the position for which he received such a minutely careful, burdensome and exacting training. She has stripped away the mystery and the rippling *zones de silence* that previously surrounded this recalcitrant personality.

The earliest experiences of the child were with death; and, throughout his childhood, death was never far away, hovering in the wings, ready to make yet another incursion at court. It is altogether fitting that the first portrait to come to us of the child should be in stone, on the funeral monument of his father, in Sens cathedral. Dying was something he had to take the measure of almost before he could walk. And, whatever one's opinion of Louis, one has to concede that, when facing up to the business of his own dying, he displayed a calm resolution and an unostentatious piety, as well as a sort of unhurried, almost routine approach to this terrible moment, that impressed even his enemies.

His father, the Dauphin, was born in 1729. He was only seventeen when he lost his first wife, the Infanta, in 1746. He remarried the following year; his second wife was Marie-Josèphe de Saxe, the daughter of Augustus III, then aged fifteen. Their first child, who was given the title of duc de Bourgogne, was born in 1751; a second son, the duc d'Aquitaine, was born in 1753; the duc de Berry, the future Louis XVI, followed in 1754. Provence came in 1755, Artois in 1757. Aquitaine died almost at once, but the duc de Bourgogne, Louis's adored elder brother, lasted ten years, dying of tuberculosis in 1761. His death had a particularly shattering effect on the seven-year-old child. The death of his father, the Dauphin, followed in 1765, when he was eleven. His mother lasted two years, succumbing to tuberculosis in 1767. The young Dauphin noted in his diary, for 13 March: "Mort de ma mère à huit heures du soir." At thirteen, he was an orphan and the eldest of his family.

His father emerges as an unattractive, priggish, prudish young man, if not a Jansenist, then "jansénisant", fat, inactive, lazy, conceited and much given to reading moral lessons to his mother, to his brothers and sisters. For him chastity was the cardinal virtue, Marie-Josèphe de Saxe was equally strait-laced and, after her husband's death, subjected Louis to an appallingly rigorous programme of moral constraints. Her educational role was almost entirely repressive and she remained deaf to the suggestions timidly put forward by the boy's tutors, the sensible de la Vauguyon and the admirable Soldini, that a little physical exercise and an occasional break in a massive working day would not come amiss.

At the same time, she instilled in him a somewhat exalted interpretation of French history : Louis IX and Charles V were to be his models, nothing less would do. She sought to encourage in the child a sort of morbid religiosity that, to some extent, defeated the work of his teachers, who, while keeping him well aware of the horrors of irreligion, corruption and vice, of the dangers inherent in the works of the *Philosophes,* attempted to steer him from the excesses of the *parti dévot.* (In this they were in fact successful, but only after his mother's death : Louis, who was determined to be his own master, had no intention of being the instrument of a clerical faction; he would defend the Church, but it was *his* Church.)

While his mother was alive, he was not allowed to take riding lessons, and it was only later that he was to learn English—a language in which he was never to be as proficient as Provence and Artois. Generally speaking, the influence of his mother undoubtedly contributed to casting a rather priggish gloom over the rest of his life. She had told him that a Prince in the direct line of succession should not be allowed to remain young for long. Certainly, at fifteen, Louis had all the characteristics of an adult immensely imbued with his responsibilities and his duties. The author makes much—perhaps too much—of the fact that in his writing, the verb most favoured by the Dauphin was *devoir,* the adjective, *absolu,* the adverb, *absolument.* Be this as it may, Marie-Josèphe had formed a prodigy who was never to take things lightly; there is no hint of frivolity, and indeed very little of humour, in this ponderous, serious, hard-working (*de l'application* is a recurrent theme in his tutors' reports) child and adolescent. Nothing could be further from the truth than the myths that Louis was easy-going and lazy; he did not find the going easy and he was far too conscious of the awesome nature of his future functions ever to neglect his work.

He was a man of few words, not so much from any natural diffidence —he was always able to captivate his personal servants, including the jealous and difficult, but devoted, Thierry, and those who helped him in his workshops, by speaking to them from the heart—but because he did not believe in using ten phrases when he could use one. He tended to dispense with adjectives altogether, and, in his writing, aimed at extreme precision. There are some remarkable examples of this in the précis that he did of passages set him by his tutors in each of which his version gains in clarity over the original; and he insisted on precision in the reports which ministers were to submit to him and which he read and annotated with great care. He himself wrote well, and if economy is one of the jewels of a good French prose style, he came in a high class. He was anxious both not to waste time and to avoid any possibility of contention in the interpretation of his instructions. He was not so much devious as economical (in words as in expenditure). Verbosity and verbal fireworks he left to the gossipy, malicious and amusing Provence and to the rather frivolous Artois. Louis XVIII was to leave a number of *bons mots*. Louis XVI was content with remarks such as "c'est bon", "c'est bien fait", "c'est fâcheux". His diary never gives any hint of personal feelings. This does not mean that he was hard-hearted, thought he does often appear unimaginative and pedestrian.

He was undoubtedly extremely well taught. At fourteen, he was a mathematician and a geographer of talent. After his mother's death he was able to extend his terms of historical reference: to the Saint Kings were added Henri IV and Louis XIV (but *not* Louis XIII, the instrument of a minister). He also took in Hume's *History of England*, a book that would accompany him to the Temple. But his salient characteristics—his horror of vice, of libertinage, of corruption, his simple and unostentatious piety, his ability to make his servants happy (and his ministers miserable), his generosity to the poor, his charity, and his rigorous economy (the author is too kind to say he was on the mean side) —all these he seems to have fashioned without much outside help. He had never had much fun. Compassionate he certainly was, in a paternalistic way, but he did not think highly of the French ("On dirait que la plainte et le murmure entrent dans l'essence de leur caractère"—a pre-*Gaulliste* statement very much on the theme of "la rogne, la hargne et la grogne"), but he died forgiving them.

Mme Girault de Coursac disposes of a number of other legends. It is clear from her account that Louis was deeply attached to his grandfather, even to the extent of attending intimate supper parties in the Petit-Trianon with him and Madame du Barry. He congratulated Maupeou on the abolition of the Parlement: "Vous avez remis la couronne sur la tête du Roi." He never failed to commemorate Louis XV's death and he took with him to the Temple his grandfather's shaving set. His attachment to Maurepas—in so far as he was ever attached to *any* minister: he regarded ministers as superior servants, but did not treat them as he treated his personal servants—had an educational rather than a political origin. All his teachers, including the well-loved de la Vauguyon and the wise and gentle Soldini, had been protégés of

Maurepas. He was more—far more, not less—intelligent than Marie-Antoinette, who, at eighteen, was still so illiterate as scarcely to be able to write a presentable letter. He was not opposed to *all* forms of pleasure : he grew to enjoy cards, and had an endless appetite for Molière. He was frugal in his eating and drinking habits. He was *not* short-sighted; many of his contemporaries thought he was because he had his mother's rather globulous blue eyes, rather than the sharp, dark eyes of his father and his brothers. We learn nothing at all of his sex life, save that he conveyed to his grandfather, at fifteen, that he was anxious, even eager, to marry. He was a better scholar than Provence, far more painstaking, though he probably did not have his brother's natural intelligence, and certainly not his wit. He despised wit.

This excellent book is also a tragic one. So much application, an education so perfected to his future functions, so many unostentatious virtues, such high notions of his future office, a private life above reproach, a deep concern for the welfare of his subjects, a physiocratic idealisation of the rural virtues, a horror of vice, a distaste for luxury, a sort of general worthiness : all this to end where it did in January 1793 ! At least, thanks to the author, the bumbling, apparently clumsy, man has been given human proportions, virtues (she is short on vices and unwilling to use the word *pimbêche*, though it may occur to readers), so that we can better understand what was to happen during a reign for which he had been so carefully prepared and for which, above all, he had prepared himself with the dedication of a seminarist. He was, as she says, an adult at fifteen. His mother would have approved of him.

The author does not use the word *jeunesse*; the title is *L'Education d'un roi*. It is an educational record almost as stifling as and even more exacting than that of the wretched Emile. Nothing was left to chance; even sleep was accounted for. The child, the adolescent, was allocated eight hours a night; as an adult he was to reduce this to five or six and the Revolution would cut into it even further. Marie-Josèphe favoured the question-and-answer approach, whether on the subject of Piety, or on Vice, Chastity or Monarchy. The child never shirked his homework and his letters to Charles III, his godfather, his first known writings, show a regular, neat and applied penmanship. Poor chap ! No wonder he always seemed a bit solemn, save to his servants and to his children, with whom he was completely unaffected, simple and *bonhomme*.

After this initial work, no one could be better qualified than Mme Girault de Coursac to rewrite the history of the reign itself. There are hints, in this first-rate and pioneering study, that this is what she intends to do next. She has already rendered an inestimable service to all historians and students of the long-neglected political history of eighteenth-century France.

8

English historians of the French Revolution

Miss Hedva Ben-Israel's book* is a study of peripheral English historians of the French Revolution, from contemporary witnesses like Young and anti-Jacobin propagandists like Playfair, to Stephens and Acton. The author states as her purpose, at the beginning, that the historians with whom she is concerned form a school and that, as such, they merit a study in their own right.

They did indeed form a school; they were all insular, all of them observed French affairs from a purely English viewpoint, they were all admirers of the British Constitution, most of them made judgments on "the faults of the French national character", they were all obsessed with the particular problems of the French monarchy, often to the exclusion of any other aspect of the history of the Revolution, most of them wrote with moral fervour and for a moral purpose. With the exception of Young and, occasionally, of Croker, none of them attempted to judge France in French terms or to make the mental effort necessary to recreate contemporary French assumptions about the permissibility of violence.

It never seems to have occurred to them that such an effort was even worthwhile, which is perhaps not surprising, since only two of them had even spent any time in France—the others apparently believed that French history could better be written from the reassuring seclusion of a college in Cambridge or a house in Chelsea—and none of them had ever set foot in the French records, at a time when these were accessible and already well classified.

They had other points in common too; with the exception of the early witnesses like Young, they were all more interested in the historians of the French Revolution than in the history of the French Revolution, they all believed in the compelling force of ideas and thought that history should be, above all, about ideas. They were a school, too, in a negative sense: if one excepts Young, none made a single important discovery or added in any significant way to the sum of knowledge about the Revolution; none ever did any original work; all were, very properly, ignored on the Continent.

* Hedva Ben-Israel, *English Historians on the French Revolution*, London 1968.

The author helps her case regarding the unity of the "school" by her own method of selection. She has excluded all dissonant voices, including the English radical historians and pamphleteers of the 1820s, 1830s and 1840s, who, unlike Dr Ben-Israel's classy team, occasionally had something interesting to say about the Revolution. The picture, too, might have been very difficult if she had extended her period beyond Acton. J. M. Thompson would, of course, have fitted admirably into her club, for he too judged France in purely English terms, never set foot in the French records, and went to Paris only once, in 1937. But A. Goodwin, J. McManners, George Rudé, Norman Hampson and Gwyn Williams would not have gained admission to this rather exclusive establishment. Whether her "members" are really worth a book all to themselves is another matter. They are certainly not very inspiring as historians; if her book has any interest, it is as a study of insularity and of the inability —or rather the unwillingness—of a certain type of Englishman, over the ages, to understand the French. Most of the present team altogether disapproved of the French, writing their books to illustrate their moral failings and their political errings.

Never having themselves acquired any new material, confining themselves to secondary sources, they argued endlessly—and futilely—on the basis of a limited number of facts about the purely political history of the Revolution. It was typical, for instance, that they should have been obsessed by the Flight to Varennes, even to the extent of going over the ground themselves, on foot, or on horseback; Oscar Browning did it on a tricycle. They wrote exclusively for an English public (but not a working-class one) and in terms that such a public would understand. Some of them were a great success, holding the field, in the case of the ponderously silly Alison, for more than half a century.

Part of their success must be attributed to the basic assumption, implicit in their approach, of the superiority of English political traditions and behaviour over those of the French. They did not all condemn the Revolution lock, stock and barrel, and save Burke, who was not a historian, none of them was a counter-revolutionary *à la Barruel* (in this too they revealed their insularity); most of them approved of the early period of the Revolution, which was the one in which political developments seemed to give the promise of an English-type political structure, and most of them disapproved of the later stages, when developments drew further and further away from English example. The line of division might be 1791, 1792 or 1793, according to choice. None of them could find anything to say in favour of 1794 (save to suggest that Robespierre may have been a scapegoat), and none seems even to have been aware of 1795. It was apparently for them a non-period not worthy even of a moral judgment (yet what thundering moral judgments they might have made of Thermidorian class-selfishness and lack of compassion !). All their histories were thus reassuring to the English middle-class reader; for accounts of so much violence, of so many errors, and of what they deemed to be so many crimes, brought home to him, by contrast, the stability, the continuity and the relative quiescence of the English domestic scene, as well as the enormous differences between the histories of the two countries.

However "Englishly" they wrote about France, there was no hint in their various messages that France could ever be like England. In this they may have over-stepped themselves, for two at least, Smyth and Croker, with their attention riveted on the new industrial towns, were convinced that it could; both, in the early 1830s, believed in the imminence of a revolution in England. And Smyth devoted his lectures at this time to the French Revolution with the intention of preventing an English one. But the other historians included did not share fears which, to judge from recent research on the period, were not unreasonable. Alison's approach, following the July revolution in Paris, was different. He was so obsessed by what he saw as the "cyclical pattern" of the French Revolution, from constitutionalism to centralism, from monarchy to Republic, from war to Terror, from Terror to popular government, that he was convinced that events would follow a similar succession; he gave the 1830 Revolution four years to develop into Terror. And in 1834 he crossed to Paris in order to see his predictions fulfilled; he was not entirely wrong, for he got his blood, but the blood, in 1832 and 1834, was that of the artisans of the cloître Saint-Merri and of the *canuts* of the Croix-Rousse, not that of respectable people.

At least most of the historians under review possessed one great English virtue : they did not admire intransigence, they could not abide violence, and they refused to condone crime and murder, even when they were dressed up in the impersonal robes of historical "inevitability". So they were not prepared to accept the Terror as a necessity to the survival of the revolutionary regime, as something that could be condoned, however disagreeable, because it aided in some way the development of democratic principles, the assertion of popular sovereignty and the march of history. They condemned the Terror on moral grounds; they could, of course, have argued that the Terror was unnecessary and inexpedient, that the Republic could have survived without it and that the Terror, with the consequent elephantine growth of a revolutionary bureaucracy, in fact destroyed the Jacobian regime. But they did not know enough about 1794 to argue in such terms, and their condemnation of violence and murder is, inevitably, politically slanted, for they seem to have been quite unaware of the White Terror of 1795–8, or even of the Thermidorian class Terror. So they identified Terror with popular rule and popular excess, forgetting that there was plenty of violence that was not of popular origin and that was directed against the common people. (Mary

Wollstonecraft and even Croker had the further merit of perceiving that violence had not been invented by the Revolution and that it had been conditioned by the severity of repression under the old regime.)

For their condemnation of the chilly "inevitability" of Quinet and Mignet, even more of the sanguinary militarism of Thiers, one must then be grateful. Mathiez, too, would have been given short shrift. There is much to be said for their moral approach, and even if they all tended enormously to exaggerate the role of individuals, to the exclusion of natural disasters and the tiny accidents out of which a revolutionary situation may so often arise, to the surprise as much of participants as of victims, at least their concentration on personalities prevented them from "dehumanising" the revolutionary crisis and from constructing "models" to fit any occasion. One is even grateful for the quavering Smyth when he criticised Guizot on the grounds that "great principles tended to breed inevitability and that general principles dispose of vice and virtue". And however much Acton achieved against historical research, there is something to be said for a man who wrote: "For the purposes of history, murder is the worst crime." Alison, it is true, believed in a "pattern of revolution". But most of the others would not have felt the need of an Anatomy of Revolution, for they had only one Revolution in mind, and even after 1830 and 1848, they thought of these as footnotes to an original revolutionary crisis.

Their obsession with the history of history rather than with history itself had at least the advantage that it made them aware of the weight of historicism on French nineteenth-century politics; they knew, from what they read, that French historians contributed to the survival and the actuality of the Revolution. And, in condemning "inevitability", they had in mind the rehabilitation of violence, in the service of revolution, that could be read into contemporary French historical writing. They at least wished to dispose of the Revolution by reducing it to human proportions. Carlyle, it is true, wrote of the Mob as of a wild, primitive force, both Hero and Monster, the instrument of the incalculable will of God; but it still had, however vaguely recognisable, human features. He never went as far as some of the Thermidorian pamphleteers in suggesting that the *sans-culottes* were a species of tropical beast and that they subsisted on the flesh of other men. Most of these historians, in contrast to the French, were remarkably free from historical prejudice, whatever their political beliefs; and Smyth and Croker were arch-Tories. Perhaps there was no great merit in their political neutrality, for it too arose from lack of imagination, the absence of any sense of involvement: the French Revolution was not *their* Revolution, any more than the history of the French Revolution was *their* history. Burke might weep buckets of tears over the misfortunes of Marie-Antoinette and of other high-born ladies (it helped him to think that he belonged, by right, in such exalted company); it would be hard to imagine Alison, Smyth, Croker or Stephens responding emotionally to the *Chant du départ* or to David's *Marat*. Carlyle alone was capable of making such an imaginative breakthrough.

In this sense, there was strength in the fact that they were so *un*-French, as this made them equally severe on all sections of French society and preserved them from a sentimental attachment to the *ancien régime* or a Burkian ham-acting gallantry. If most of them—Carlyle and Croker, however, were not fooled—had a soft spot for the arrogant and silly Girondins, it was in the widely held, but entirely mistaken, conviction that they were a sort of honorary Englishman. They condemned the *ancien régime* on pragmatic grounds; there must have been something very wrong with it for there to have been a revolutionary crisis in the first place. And no sympathy was to be lost on a government that could not govern. So, unlike the French right-wing historians, they did not need to fix on to a "plot" theory of a "contrived sedition" to explain what happened in June–July 1789. They were often severe on the duc d'Orléans, and exaggerated his importance, as they did that of Mirabeau, but they were hardly likely to fall for "English gold", free-masonry and Protestantism. This could be left to the *Dublin Review*.

What was wrong with most of them (not Alison and Stephens, who were prolific) was that they were lazy. They wrote reviews of other people's books, spent much time and a little energy (though this is not a word to apply to Smyth) in fussing over points of detail or in playing the amateur detective, in order to catch out a French historian lying (*on se console comme on peut*). They prepared lectures to put across limply a languid moral purpose or, like Kingsley, to illustrate, in three hours, the compatibility between the French Revolution, chemistry and the Ways of God. Smyth preached feebly against the dangers of Revolution at home; he cannot have sounded very convinced. A few delved, rather unsystematically, and in order to prove some trivial point, into the enormous printed collections of primary sources pouring out of France. A few of them talked of going to the sources, even planned vacations in Paris. Oscar Browning took his tricycle across and sent back postcards to impressed pupils; but none ever found his way to the rue des Francs-Bourgeois. And when they talked in terms of the original research they never did, they were thinking of biographies, memoirs and reminiscences, ministerial correspondence, the jotted notes for a parliamentary speech.

Even after Tocqueville, it never occurred to them that there was more, much more, that both the *ancien régime* and the Revolution piled up mountains of paper on every imaginable subject, and that every revolutionary institution save the Committee of Public Safety kept detailed minutes. (Carlyle, who was curious about the marching of the Marseillais—goodness knows what there was curious about it—had a glimmering hint that the "Marseilles Council Books" might throw some light; but it was only a glimmer; the records of the Municipality exist from 1790–6, there are thirty volumes of them.) Their excuse might have been that records of this kind did not exist in England. But, after Tocqueville, they could not plead ignorance. It would be unfair, of course, to accuse them of having neglected provincial and local sources, of not having had the urge to write the history of the Revolution in Villeneuve-sur-Lot and of having thought exclusively in terms of Paris. For their French contemporaries suffered from the same centralist myopia and believed that everything had been won or lost, had begun or ended, in the capital. Most of the *érudits locaux* did not emerge till the last decade of the nineteenth century, urged on, up and down France, by the need to commemorate, in however modest a form, the centenary of 1789.

Croker, it is true, was always going to write a general history of the Revolution. (Most of them spent more time talking and writing about what they were going to do, than doing it; there were always hints of great works to come, to such an extent that the author, when assessing their contribution to the history of the French Revolution, often has to make do with little notes jotted down on scraps of paper as a guide to future investigation. These people were about-to-doers, not doers, what the French call *velléitaires*.) Croker spent a life-time accumulating material for that purpose. But he never produced the finished article, he was more a seeker after *curia*, a collector of autographs, than a historian. At least he went to France to get the stuff, bequeathing to the British Museum the finest collection of printed material in existence. He was even aware of the Sections, the *sans-culottes*. And he did much more for the future of revolutionary studies than any of the others. This is why he is very properly given an important place in the present book; the author's chapter on the man, the politician, the collector and the collection is by far the most valuable.

Most of the others never bothered to cross the Channel. Those who held chairs in Cambridge were clearly too fixed in their ways, too embedded in their comfortable colleges even frequently to make the journey to London. Smyth, who emerges as the arch-sloth in a collection of rather idle men, spent sixty years in Cambridge. No wonder he was an important figure there; the author writes that he had great influence on his pupils, while admitting, rather ruefully, that his work was little known outside Peterhouse. He was a don, not a historian; he loved music, lyrics and entertaining. Perhaps in these parochial terms he was, and still is, an important figure. (He gets a chapter to himself, though one suspects this may be an example of Girtonian piety rather than a recognition of merit.)

Among its other merits, Dr Ben-Israel's book is a valuable, if peripheral, contribution to the history of history in nineteenth century Cambridge.

There must be some consolation for present holders of Regius Chairs and hope for future ones to discover just how bad, how indolent, how wrong-minded and how feeble some of their predecessors have been. No one could ever fear of falling below the standards of erudition and productivity set by Smyth, Stephens, Kingsley and Seely. Of Acton Dr Ben-Israel observes, perhaps regretfully, that "one must conclude that he conducted no original research". No wonder that, under such a "genteel tradition" (these are the author's words), English historians fell so far behind their French and German colleagues in the nineteenth century.

Yet from laziness, donnishness and lack of imagination, what opportunities most of these historians—Carlyle was an exception—missed! They might quaver at the sheer bulk of material stored away in the Archives Nationales: but at least they had the enormous advantage of being able to consult contemporary witnesses of the Revolution. There were still plenty alive in the 1830s and 1840s. They might have followed the example of Michelet, but few did. At best they consulted a few rather seedy *émigrés*, or the son of Mallet du Pan; Croker had long talks with Louis-Philippe in exile. It never occurred to them to seek out former members of the Committees, in Brussels, or, after 1830, back in France.

These people were not unknown; perhaps they were dismayed at the prospect of meeting "monsters", regicides, terrorists, even in their old age; or perhaps they were afraid that, when confronted with a silver-haired, frail old man, they might be induced to see the terrible Jacobins in a more favourable light. More probably they were shy about revealing their schoolboy French. And yet retired revolutionists, like exiled monarchs, love to talk, and Barère lived till 1842. A visit to Tarbes, even to Macaulay's "idea of consummate and universal depravity" might have been well worth while. It remained for a twentieth century American historian, Leo Gershoy, to make the journey and to talk to a very old man who had actually *seen* Barère, in his eighties, as a small child.

The trouble with most of them was that they were gentlemen, and gentlemen amateurs at that. Or, like Burke, they tried to be gentlemen. They could only conceive of history either in terms of reasoned ideas or of respectable political leadership. Save for Croker and Carlyle, they did not have an inkling of popular grievances, they knew nothing of poverty (save possibly in terms of potential sedition) and could not perceive irrational fears. Even Carlyle referred to Dark Forces rather than attempt to explore the assumptions of a submerged popular mentality. They liked Tocqueville because he came clean and put the blame squarely on all the French, because he recognised the superiority of English institutions, admired the English landed classes, emphasised the differences between French and English political development, rejected theories of 'inevitability', and insisted on the importance of administration; but they rejected him when he suggested that the Revolution did not constitute a dramatic break in French history and because he played down the role of personal leadership.

They criticised Louis XVI severely, but all believed that the monarchical form of government was the best. Apart from Young, who does not deserve to be associated with the "school", only one of them had ever heard that there had been a famine in 1789, none that there had been one in 1795 (and *that* they might have known, for there had been one in England at the same time). They knew about the *Physiocrates* and the *Philosophes*, but they did not know about grain prices, *taxation populaire*, and popular hostility to internal free trade in grain; it was not the sort of thing to get into the *Edinburgh Review* or the *Quarterly*, the forums of so many of their gentlemanly disputations. And, save for Lecky, they never looked properly to Ireland; if they had, they might have been much better historians of the French Revolution. Some of them *did* look to Ireland, but as a contemporary problem, either to prevent the danger of sedition by repressive action, or to promote home rule. But it did not occur to them that the nineteenth-century Irish peasant might have anything in common with the eighteenth-century French one.

The lowest down they ever reached was the prissy, *petit-bourgeois* level of Robespierre, and, however much they disliked him—one or two had a word to say in his favour—he was a sort of gentleman and dressed like one. They had little use for Marat, for he clearly was not, had never wanted to be. They had heard vaguely of the *hébertistes*. The *enragés* are never mentioned in their works. It was not surprising that they all failed to appreciate the originality of Louis Blanc and to connect his history with his socialism. They were far less perceptive historians of the French Revolution than Bronterre O'Brien, Harney, Roland Dutrosier, and other English republicans and radicals.

History for them was an amiable off-shoot of *belles lettres* or a form of sermonising. They thought research rather vulgar; it was all too professional and unimaginative, and could best be left to German and French specialists. It was their right to debate, to sit in judgment, to lay down the law, while others, over the Channel, did the hack work. They were lightweights but, like J. M. Thompson later—and his career has so much in common with theirs—they were much admired by their contemporaries in Cambridge and London.

A point of view so insular naturally did much to invalidate the judgment of most of the historians and critics who are the subject of the present study. We find in Marsh the extraordinary statement that the Jacobins were "illiterate anarchists"; it is difficult to establish the paternity of the reference to "the ordinary half-educated people of the *Tiers État*", though it may be the author's own contribution to the debate. Alison describes the Jacobins as "Fifth Monarchy men" and dates their assumption of power from 10 August. One does not know what is meant by the phrase that Croker "now learnt that [Custine's trial] was an act of private vengeance"; Vincent was not a private man, and the General had openly and repeatedly defied his Minister. Macaulay, predictably, talks nonsense about "the French character" and romanticises about the Girondins. Acton is only interested in "outstanding personalities" and in "the history of history".

Even so, in such an uninspiring field, there is something to be garnered, and one is all the more grateful for the example of an acute judgment in that it is so occasional. In this respect, witnesses like Young and the earlier historians like Croker have the most to offer. Young was the first to perceive that the Terror represented the total mobilisation of all the nation's resources, in manpower, in raw materials and in transport, and that it was the very contrary of anarchy. Southey was the first to think that Robespierre had been hard done by by historians and contemporaries, and he was the only man in his time, years before O'Brien, to express interest in the Babeuf Plot. Even Smyth occasionally lapses into acuteness; he argued that historians "have to do with human beings" and warned against the tendency to observe groups in terms of a social class, when groups were so often under the control of individuals —a strangely modern qualification, and one that could well be applied to Soboul's tendency to underplay the part of militant minorities in the *sans-culotte* movement.

Carlyle, unlike so many of the others, was not taken in by the Girondins, who were patronising about the masses, narrow and barren. And there is a glimmer even in Macaulay when he writes that the three who perished (Robespierre, Saint-Just and Couthon) were better than those who survived. O'Brien showed sense when he wrote that the Girondins would have kept the working classes down. He described them, very acutely, as "lawyers, bankers and babbling literati who, jealous of the nobility ... sought to swindle the Government ... into their own hands", a much better description than that proposed by Croker; but he was a victim of his own political illusions when he said that Robespierre embodied working-class aims. There is a surprisingly penetrating remark from Walter Scott, of all people, on the subject of the importance of envy and social frustration as recruiting agents to revolutionary commitment, especially among middle-class barristers and lawyers. But the most original observation comes from Stephens when he insisted on the bureaucratic centralism of the Terror, contrasting it with Thermidor as the revolt of the provinces (the Thermidorian regime was above all that of each *députation*).

Flashes of insight of this kind are, however, very rare. Some must have been the result of intelligent guessing. In the long barren spaces that separate them, the going is heavy and almost entirely unrewarding. Some of the historians mentioned have some interest in illustrating

contemporary English attitudes to their neighbours across the Channel:
Acton observes that *les Deux Amis* have this in common: that we can
do without them. It is an impertinent remark, for their book, though
prejudiced, contains many accounts of events experienced first hand.
He also writes off Prudhomme as mendacious, yet his enormous *Histoire
des crimes* contains a wealth of accurate information about the impact
of the Terror on the Departments. Acton was not interested in provincial
history; he would have regarded it as banal. It is Acton that we can do
without and most of the other historians admitted into the "school".
For the author herself is hardly convincing on their value as historians
of the Revolution. Her own knowledge of the actual history of the
Revolution is often shaky, and she appears incapable of assessing the
value of their work as a whole.

It is her subject that is the trouble; for having decided to write a study
of English attitudes to the history of the French Revolution, she can no
longer pick and choose and is obliged to let in almost anyone who has
written about the subject (though she omits most of the republicans).
The result is, on the whole, a hotch-potch of mediocrity. Nor is she over-
strict about her conditions of admission, for she includes sections on both
the Christian Socialists and the romantics, who, she admits, never actually
wrote about the French Revolution, but merely expressed their dis-
approval of it. Her book reads too much like a university thesis which,
no doubt, it was. Year by year, and rather laboriously, all her historians,
critics and reviewers are trotted out, with little attempt at relating them
to one another, save in terms of date: some come after others, but some
pop up all over the place, outside their own chapters and after they
have been formally dismissed and we have, rather gratefully, taken
leave of them.

Dr Ben-Israel's book appears to have been written some years ago,
for it takes no account of recent work on the impact of the Revolution
and its historians on the development of the popular movement and
of a working-class culture in England. There is no mention of either
Edward Thompson or Gwyn Williams. If she had read their work, her
book might have acquired a new dimension and taken life. As it is, she
is only concerned with the dull dogs who wrote with their slippers on
about events that, far from moving them, left them with mixed feelings
of moral superiority, disquiet, and tempered, languid indignation.

9

Robespierre

Robespierre's most fatal weakness as a revolutionary leader was that he seldom appeared either to be saying what he meant or meaning what he said. His speeches were always long, repetitive, and boring; and they were delivered in a feeble monotone (one of his earlier critics described them as "canticles", and there is indeed something priest-like about his litanies on the subject of Things to Come). They tended to be placed in the future tense, but it was a future that was only just round the corner, and they were always heavily larded with the first person singular, whether in the future—"Si le sacrifice de ma vie peut servir à établir le régime du bonheur, je le ferai avec joie"—or in a revolutionary past—"Dès le début de la Révolution, je consacrais mes jours et mes nuits à combattre les ennemis du bien public"—that got longer and longer as the Revolution proceeded, and as the orator went on writing testimonials to himself. All these were certainly grave faults in a politician who relied on his speeches, even more than on his newspaper, to assert his political influence over the Assemblies, the Jacobins, and the country as a whole.

But even more dangerous was his proneness to think aloud, to ask himself questions: What should we do next? How can we best ensure the survival of the Republic? Will my death strengthen the foundation of *la Vertu*? Questions which he would then fail to answer. It was as if he were throwing himself on to his audience, engaging with it in a public moral debate, something like a Quaker meeting, asking what the next step should be. He was always dropping hints, generally about his own impending death; a theme to which he returned, with morbid repetition, from very early on in his career as a revolutionary politician, at a time when even the most zealous agent of Artois would hardly have thought it worth hiring an assassin to do him in—at this period his speeches were still provoking ripples of laughter among members of the Assembly—till the terrible summer of 1794, when his immolation must indeed have appeared to an increasing number of his fellow deputies almost as a necessary preliminary to some sort of settlement of an impossible political situation.

When it was not death—his own, or that of unnamed but still vaguely recognisable Enemies of the Republic—when it was not Plots—Standard,

Prison, Foreign, Military, Food, Atheistical, Pitto-Coburg, Ultrarevolutionary, Agricultural, Red Shirt, Lubomirska, Dillon, Batz, Dubarry—then it would be the Golden Future Time, always just round the corner, rather like Thorez's *les lendemains qui chantent*, now long over-due: one more little purge, only a very little one, and we will be there. For Robespierre is also a seer, ever peeping into the crystal ball, catching the vague outlines of a Republic of tented Spartans, the boys and girls in clean white robes and sandals, Fraternity lying down with Purity, Modest Contentment with Serious Intent, Moderation in Drink living it up with the *sans-culotte* Arts and Crafts: Roofmaking, Bricklaying, Shoemaking, Haymaking, Modesty trying to get on with Maternity, Respect for Age laurel-crowned by Grateful Youth. No wonder so many of his contemporaries either found him a bit of a bore, or could not make him out, or simply could not abide him—"Robespierre," wrote Choudieu in old age, "était imbuvable"—no wonder his colleagues on the Committee were perpetually asking themselves how they stood with him, what they had said or done to upset him, cause him to sulk or walk off in a huff; no wonder parliamentary journalists became increasingly afraid to publish his speeches *in extenso*, for fear that people might try to read between the lines and get the answer to the riddle wrong, or, worse, right.

Robespierre has always been a Problem. In his lifetime, he was not merely a theoretical or historical one. His deliberate evasiveness seemed to point in several directions at once, leaving far too many people guessing. But the problem became even more obscure after his death. At least he was dead. At the time, most people were mightily relieved at this, though a good many were to change their minds in the next weeks or months. The myths started at once: Thermidorian pamphleteers depict Robespierre being welcomed cordially, and in excellent French, by Cromwell, in a well-heated, if somewhat overcrowded residence. And they have gone on ever since. His most recent English biographer, John Laurence Carr, likens him, in a book written in 1972, to Jesus Christ; and about the only claim that he does *not* make for His Holiness is that he could walk on the water, which is fair enough, because Maximilien had never been to the seaside.

Norman Hampson, in his biographical debate,* has not only set out to cut through the accumulated layers of 180 years of myth-making, in order to reduce the man to proportions that are at least recognisably human; he has also used him as an opportunity to discuss the nature of historical evidence. To facilitate this bold enterprise, he has adopted a method that only a historian of his great literary gifts, imagination and skill at debate could have pulled off. While taking the part of the narrator

* Norman Hampson, *The Life and Opinions of Maximilien Robespierre*, London 1974.

who, in alternating chapters, gives the reader all the known facts, he has also multiplied himself by three—or is it four?—creating fictional characters to whom the debate is then thrown open. One is a civil servant, sardonic, suspicious, and generally extremely hostile to Robespierre; the second is a Party member, who is above personalities, and shows evidence of being a Wykehamist. The third, a clergyman, attempts to see things from Robespierre's point of view. Inevitably, such a method, even in such skilled hands, has its dangers; and one is occasionally reminded of a WEA discussion group, with all the chaps puffing away at their pipes, and saying: "Well, I grant you that, but . . ." But, in fact, we soon get used to "Mac objected", "Ted queried", or "Henry observed". It is, however, important to get the three identities straightened out from the start, so as to avoid having to turn back and discover who is who. Two further identities remain shrouded in mystery: the one, "J.S.", who, one suspects, is a fourth version of Hampson himself, the other, the bovine, bald figure, staring sightless at us out of a sea-green background on the dust cover, and claiming, most improbably, for it appears to have a firm jaw, to be Robespierre's face in death. Poor Robespierre! Now given someone else's head, after losing his own, and after all those other posthumous mishaps!

It would be unfair to the author of this detailed and closely argued study to suggest that he has at last disposed of his recalcitrant subject, has laid him once and for all in his unquiet and much-trampled on grave, has said all there is to be said about the man. If anything, at the end of the book, he emerges as even more elusive, changeable, contradictory and given to double-talk than when we are first introduced to him as a grave, rather solemn child, old before his time, weighed down with the responsibility of bringing up single-handed his sister and younger brother. And this is as it should be, for he is no Danton, no Mirabeau, no rugged figure hewn out of a single block, with an enviable appetite for life; on the contrary, he is at all times a mass of quirks and of conflicting rancours, an enigmatic composite of the pleasant and the detestable, the considerate and the implacable, of deep calculation and suicidal temerity, a puritan, who nevertheless enjoyed food (in reasonable quantities) and feminine company. The only simplicity about him was in his tastes, in the relative modesty of his material demands, a modesty that, far from being a propaganda stunt, was quite genuine.

Some of the more contradictory facets at once spring to mind: the private Robespierre—so woefully secret, so apparently incomplete, and so jealously guarded from all save perhaps the faithful Duplays and the Vaugeois, for whom the curtain to the inner sanctum might be slightly pulled aside (there was probably not very much to reveal)—and the public, Most-of-the-Time Robespierre, so diffuse, so verbose, and

generally so implacably boring (all the more credit to the author for
having ploughed through all ten volumes of his speeches and writings).

Then there is the provincial Robespierre, the pre-revolutionary neo-
physiocrate, who had written a prize essay denouncing Paris, the dangers
of centralism, the corruption of great cities, and extolling the simple,
healthy and modest enjoyments of provincial life : an essay perhaps too
in self-persuasion by a man who, having been educated in Paris, found
himself condemned, by his lack of wealth, to live in Arras. Without the
terrible temptation offered by 1789, he might indeed have remained
provincial, have followed the semi-rural precepts of his essay, might
have married—according to his sister, he was teetering in that direction
at the time of the calling of the Estates General—might thus have completed that atrophied, terribly bare private life, might never have been
heard of outside Arras. And, on the other hand, there is the Parisian
Robespierre, the deputy for Paris, rather a strange animal, for although
so much of his political influence was firmly Paris-based, although he
never committed the terrible mistake, in the midst of civil and foreign
war, of denouncing the capital and its inhabitants, he always remained
deeply suspicious and rather fearful of the place, shunned its cloying
corruptions, choosing to live almost on the doorstep of his public life,
rue Saint-Honoré, not only in order to save time, but also, it would
seem, so as to have to walk as little as possible, to cut down to the minimum the exposure to the gaze of the open street. No *boulevardier,* this
man; not for him the varied temptations of the Palais-Royal, catering
for every vice. It is tragically significant that the longest journey that he
ever seems to have undertaken within the confines of the city was when he
was being carried along by events already beyond his control, from the
Convention and the Pavillon de Flore eastwards, first to the Mairie,
then to the Hôtel-de-Ville, and back again, over much the same course,
already half dead, to the familiar home quarter and to the place of
execution. How he went on the outward journey we do not know; we
do know that the return was made in an open cart, exposed to the
mocking of the onlookers in the street and in the windows. That scrupu-
lous historian Paul Saint-Clair Deville himself went over the whole course,
not in a spirit of reverence, but, with the help of a pedometer, in order
to time the succession of events.

It is, then, easy to understand why Robespierre was so much more
relaxed when in his weekend rural retreats, at Choisy or Créteil. Living
in Paris, he was carefully insulated from the noise and bustle of the great
city, in the muffled quiet of the Duplay household, surrounded by
terracotta busts of himself. Just as de Gaulle was in the habit of taking
occasional strictly rationed dips into the fraternity of the crowd, Robespierre's evening visits to the Jacobins might be seen as carefully rehearsed
contacts with the People, after which he would retire, to wash his hands,

rue Saint-Honoré. Professor Hampson has a wonderful passage on the subject of the Feast of the Supreme Being, when he depicts Robespierre's feeling as to the contrast between the applause and enthusiasm of the virtuous spectators and the vicious mutterings and malicious remarks reaching him from behind, from Tallien, Bentabole, and others. The People, he would reflect, had Understood Him. Yet, of all the deputies of Paris, he seems to have been the one who had the least physical contact with the Parisians. Maybe this was why he felt himself at such a marked disadvantage in his relations with Marat. If, throughout his brief political career, he always tended to think in national terms, and took so much trouble to organise his publicity in the Departments, it was no doubt because he never became a full convert to Parisian imperialism. Not for him the coarse language of *le Père Duchesne*, whose creator was also a provincial. Not for him the priorities of poor Jacques Roux, who knew about hunger, and who lived among the very poor, in the filthy, overcrowded Gravilliers; to Robespierre, Roux seemed merely a troublemaker, voicing the grievances of the ignorant and the illiterate on the subject of food, heating, cold, and overcrowding. One suspects that, in Robespierre's tidy mind, Paris was as much a disembodied concept, preferably to be referred to in some clumsy phrase like *le bercail de la liberté*, as his own idealised *le Peuple* (guaranteed *inodore*). Both were ideas, rather than the one being a place—and for most of its inhabitants, a very smelly, stinking, uncomfortable one—and the other, real people, those very ones who mocked him on his last journey. Professor Hampson shows how, in his choice of informants and of trusted advisers he showed a marked preference for people from his own part of France—fair enough—and also for other provincials, from Lyon, Valence, Montpellier, le Havre, Tonneins, Moissac, and so on. The Duplays were probably the only native Parisians with whom he maintained close contacts. Morally, at least, he was almost as much a "federalist" as the Girondins.

Then there is the well-publicised contradiction—the late Professor Cobban made much of it—between Robespierre-Out-of-Power, and Robespierre-in-Power, the former a starry-eyed idealist, the latter a pragmatic, prudent politician and war leader, the man in the middle, in a collegial system of government, who could generally be counted on to get his priorities right. It is of course not just a matter of contrasting situations, it is also one of time. Robespierre, as a member of the Committee of Public Safety, was more mature than the idealist from Arras; he was also more aware of the immediacy of the threats to the survival of the embattled Republic. Nor is there any reason why Robespierre should be singled out to illustrate what might appear to be a betrayal of previously strongly expressed principles. Almost any of his colleagues could be marched to the same tune. Barère, for instance, in the course

of the Revolution, had pretty well run through the whole gamut of the
political spectrum, while the stern Saint-Just had, on the eve of the
Revolution, written a pornographic poem, as long and as boring as his
later public statements.

All these apparent contradictions and the obscurities in which almost
every event of his public or private career is enveloped are discussed with
great sensitivity and imagination in Hampson's *livre-débat*. Perhaps one
of the most striking general impressions that one retains of Robespierre's
evolution as a journalist, orator, and politician is that of gradualness.
However fast events might be moving, he was generally careful to move
behind them. It was only in the last few terrifying weeks, when pretty
well every member of the Revolutionary Government, and indeed every
member of the Convention as a whole, was looking over his shoulder at
his potential assassin or victim, and when all the leading protagonists
were frozen into attitudes of quivering immobility, like children playing
at a You May Not Laugh game, for fear of putting a foot wrong, or of
showing their hand, or of saying anything at all, it was only then that
something very peculiar, completely baffling, seems to have happened to
this deeply cautious and calculating revolutionary tactician, to drive
him at last out into the open to act with demented temerity, forcing a
whole series of issues and setting in motion the implacable machinery of
his own destruction. Even Hampson and his little team, when faced with
something so entirely out of character, so unlike the way that he had
previously behaved in times of crisis, are driven back on such explanations as illness, loss of nerve, physical and mental fatigue, depression or a
desire to see an end to an intolerable situation, whatever the consequences.
Or, of course, he may have, for once in his career, taken a calculated
risk, and lost. Hampson certainly shows that, up to the very last moment,
everyone was groping in the dark, as in a hideous game of blind man's
buff between grown-ups, in which the life of each one was at risk, not
knowing who was friend, who was enemy and who was still uncom-
mitted. It might so easily have worked out quite differently, for Robespierre, up to the last, held some very strong cards; and, if almost every
politician had been expecting some sort of violent political crisis, no one
could possibly have predicted, even a few hours ahead, its sudden and
definitive outcome. 9 Thermidor will always be the most fascinating of
the revolutionary *journée* because, hour by hour, it could have gone
either way and was indeed such a very close thing.

Another general impression to be retained from a debate which is both
about the nature of historical evidence and about that of a man not easily
given to revealing himself and with whom or against whom generations of
historians have identified, is that of moderation and common sense. It is
very hard to see why, historically, Robespierre should always have exercised such a powerful appeal to the immoderate, the intransigent, the

whiter-than-driven-snow, the hundred percenters, the romantic "im-possibilities". Several of Robespierre's own colleagues, the steely Billaud, the cruel Saint-Just would be far better candidates for such veneration. Indeed, enthusiasm of this kind would appear to be the cruellest of historical betrayals, for Robespierre, in power, had his feet very firmly on the ground, and was always concerned to round off the sharp edges of possible contestation, and to appeal to the uneloquent occupants of the middle ground. No one perhaps has ever got Robespierre more out of focus than J. S. Talmon, for, once a member of the Committee of Public Safety, he put his *rousseauisme* away in a drawer, revealing himself, in all his political decisions and interventions with his colleagues very much as a "possibilist". He was a "possibilist" in religious matters, being anxious to reassure Catholic opinion.

The Cult of the Supreme Being may well have been an indirect invitation—very much in line with his normal deviousness—to reopen the churches; in any case, it was taken as such in many rural areas and even in a number of towns. It was the same with foreign trade, "il ne faut pas tuer le commerce", the neutrals had to be kept happy, and he realised that government purchasing commissions abroad and in France could best be run by bankers, grain importers, and Protestant international traders. It was due to his intervention that the crew of a Danish frigate, arrested by an officious Norman *comité de surveillance*, were rapidly released, with apologies. By the spring of 1794, he was prepared to slow up on the literal application of the *maximum* legislation and on requisi-tioning, because he realised that the regime could not survive if it were to continue to wage war on the whole of the countryside. Like his brother Augustin, he was quick to use the word "ultra-révolutionnaire" and to detect and denounce "exagération" in some of the sillier interven-tions of both *Représentants en mission* and other roving commissioners. He was suspicious of the paper *le Père Duchesne*, not only because he found the crudity of its language offensive, but because Hébert seemed to be hitting out in every direction at once, thus earning for the Republic a maximum number of potential enemies. He rightly regarded the idiotic Cloots, the first of the professional "Europeans", who took up the time of the Convention by trundling out before it delegations of Oppressed Peoples clad, like communist dolls, in National Costume, as a tiresome buffoon, though he flattered him when he saw in him an agent of a foreign plot. It seems quite likely that, by the summer of 1794, he was prepared to put out feelers towards peace talks with England—and there are also indications that the British government thought that he was worth talking with—and that suspicions of such intentions may have antagon-ised some of the more *jusquauboutiste* members of the Committee. He condemned atheism not merely as unvirtuous and aristocratic, but also as politically imprudent.

For a man of virtue, he was often surprisingly indulgent towards weakness and vice. In one of his most fascinating chapters, Norman Hampson suggests that Robespierre was understanding enough on the subject of corruption, regarding it as inevitable in many politicians. Private corruption could be disregarded. What he saw, however, as a major threat to the regime, was the revelation of public corruption, particularly at the parliamentary level. For what could the enemies of France now hope for? They lost the battle militarily. Their only remaining weapons would be either to have the leaders of the Republic assassinated, or publicly to discredit the Republic of Virtue by exploiting the revelation of a network of scandals, sowing suspicion over the whole political spectrum. In short, one could live alongside corruption, so long as it was kept quiet. In the whole, murky affair of the liquidation of the *Compagnie des Indes*, his principal concern seems to have been to hush up the extent of the scandal. Again, he was taking a political and very pragmatic stance. He might wander on, for hours and hours, on the subject of a very impavid *Vertu*, but, faced with the reality of an immense scandal, his reaction was political rather than moral. He was of course completely honest himself, and no doubt fully earned his nickname; but *l'Incorruptible*, like so many other descriptions of him, is a gross over-simplification. However self-righteous he might appear in his public statements, he could in fact be remarkably indulgent towards other people's weaknesses. Of all the members of the Committee, it was he who was the most reluctant to sacrifice Danton. What is more, it is very clear, from the author's careful analysis of various elections, that Robespierre was something of a manipulator when it was a matter of marshalling votes, and that *l'Incorruptible* seems to have known, almost from the start, most of the tricks of revolutionary machine politics. He certainly did not believe in leaving anything to chance, preparing the ground with great deliberation and well in advance. The only time that he did leave things to chance was 9 Thermidor. "Popular sovereignty" was all right as a concept, but politics had to be *managed*, so that the right choices were made, the right people came to the top. And he had never any doubt that he was one of them.

Norman Hampson is especially well prepared to bring a ray of light, the cool stare of his naval eyes, into the many murky areas of revolutionary politics, rigged trials, plots, real or contrived, bribery and corruption. He has gone over all the ground once explored by Mathiez, but, unlike Mathiez, not in pursuit of an indictment against Danton and his alleged friends, but in an effort to discover something like the truth. He more or less believes in the elusive, yet apparently ever-present Batz, and he does not wholly discount that Hébert may have been bribed by Marie-Antoinette, or by the comtesse de Rochechouart, and that he may have been involved in an obscure plot to rescue the Queen from the

Conciergerie. This is not only very exciting stuff; Hampson undoubtedly succeeds in giving it some credibility, though it does appear that he may have mixed up Boulogne, just outside Paris, with Boulogne-sur-Mer. It was in the former place that Batz was said to have had many agents and friends.

His description of the manic weeks, heavy with fear and suspicion, preceding the crisis of 9 Thermidor, is both brilliant and extraordinarily dramatic. We can sense through it the panic that seized each member of the Committees, each deputy, as he asked himself, each morning, whether he would end the day in his own bed, or, indeed, in any bed. And he illustrates the groping ballet steps of half-perceived alliances, as the revolutionary leaders, with extreme prudence, sound one another out. Hampson sees these agonisingly prudent comings and goings, not in terms of class or of social conflict, but of terrified people, of men anxious merely to survive.

Suitably, in his debating team, it is Henry, the clergyman, who is the most prepared to give Robespierre the benefit of the doubt; Ted, the civil servant, never does. Mac, the Party man, is just not very interested in the man as a man, seeing him as a tiny object caught in the whirlwind of uncontrollable social forces. If it had not been Robespierre, it would have had to have been someone else. Leave the name blank, leave the date blank, fill both in later. But 9 Thermidor, or whatever, *had* to be. Henry is the man we should follow the most readily, if only because he understands Robespierre as a moral being, is aware of his contradictions, his weaknesses, his ordinariness, and is deeply compassionate on the subject of a fate far too awful, far too dramatic, for such a fumbling, prissy, routinal, comfort-loving, vaguely ridiculous, prickly little man, a sort of revolutionary Widmerpool, Maximilien-Isidore, not named then for martyrdom, but for modest respectability and provincial pretention, no outstanding genius, a consistent winner of second prizes, a lover of oranges, sugar cakes and canaries, very clean, very careful of his dress. With Henry, as with Carlyle, we feel for that blue coat, dirty and blood stained, and for its half-dead wearer, lying on the table, and we think, with a sort of horror, of the unoccupied room, with its many busts and *fusains* of the neat man, the unslept-in bed, on that terrible night, when only the very humble, the very poor, old people, children and women—but not the wives or sisters of members of the Commune—could afford the tiny luxury of sleep, because they were below the level of politics, though even they may have turned over uneasily at the sound of the 3 a.m. thunderstorm. It is all such a very long way from the provincial scholarship boy (*beaucoup d'application*) and from the small-town barrister who turned out pretty, but conventional, *pastorales*. If only it could have ended more reassuringly.

"I will tell you, I said, all about Robespierre." And indeed, Hampson does. He brings no single answer, for there is no single answer. And he leaves us perhaps more confused than when we set out with him. And that, too, is as it should be, for Robespierre was as complicated and contradictory a human being as any of us. His book is a formidable achievement, and should be read not only by those rightly fascinated by Robespierre, but by all who are concerned with the nature of historical evidence.

10

Robespierre and the Year II*

The poet Prévert once remarked† that he did not think very much of the *branche légitime des Bourbon,* for what was one to make of people who were not even able to count up to twenty? The historian, like contemporaries, must be equally puzzled to know what to make of the Year II. For here was a system of counting that began with *two,* and ended with twelve. There had never been a Year I, though it was given a retrospective identity in order, as it were, to bolster up and afford a sort of respectability to the prestigious Year II of the Republic One and Indivisible. Those who had participated in the September Massacres in 1792 cannot have been aware, as they went about their business, that they were operating on the very brink of the new era: perhaps a suitable inauguration to the new order of things, in which killing, in one cause or another, was to be one of the few consistent features.

There was no doubt, however, about the reality of the Year II. It was designed to open with the autumn equinox, on 22 September, at that sad time of the year when British Public School boys and girls are making the journey away from home and family. It also coincides, as the name of the first month, Vendémiaire, implies, with the normal beginning of the wine harvest, at least in northern France. It was rather as if the new revolutionary year should begin with a hiccough; and, indeed, the vinous image is maintained throughout Vendémiaire, the honour of naming the very first *décadi* (the rest day of the new ten-day week) going to *Tonneau.* But a year which thus opens in bacchic celebration ends on a suitably serious note, with a moral prize-giving, in a strange clutter of five *jours complémentaires,* known, at least in the Year II— but not, of course, in the Year III, or in any of the following nine years of the New Age—as *les sans-culottides.* It is rather as if, at this stage, the year had run out of breath, or the authors of the new calendar had run out of flowers, animals, minerals, vegetables, and useful objects. The first *sans-culottide,* 17 September 1794, is consecrated, it must be admitted rather optimistically—for, as it turned out, it was to fall well

* Public Lecture given in the University of London on 25 November 1974.
† See page 1.

over a month *after* the death of Robespierre, and well within what has come to be known historically as the Thermidorian Period—to the *fête de la vertu*. Other prizes round up the dying year: *Génie* (18 September), *Travail* (19 September) (though this might legitimately have been awarded to *any* day, other than a *décadi*, of a year spelt out in a 'nine-day week'); *Opinion* (20 September), an aspiration rather than a reality, though, as it was to turn out, in the early days of the Thermidorian Reaction, opinion would at least acquire some negative forms of expression, as a revolt against the dreary demands of Virtue and Austerity. The year ends on 21 September with the ultimate, rather grudgingly awarded prize, *La fête des récompenses*. I am not sure who is supposed to get this, but I cannot help thinking it may be a consolation prize for women, otherwise totally unrepresented in the new calendar (*belle-de-nuit*, *sextidi*, 16 Vendémiaire—7 October 1793—is a *plant*, and not what you might think) though it does include a few female animals, such as *Vache* (*quintidi*, 15 Pluviôse—3 February 1794) but even the "friendly cow all red and white" has to wait her turn until after *Taureau*, granted the first *quintidi* of that rainy month.

I should not delay you further with the no doubt unpremeditated bizarreries of a succession of days that recalls, at one moment, a seedsman's catalogue, at another, the stock of a fashionable grocer, or of a well-patronised florist (marked down in *Inter-Flora*), or, finally, a child's First Reader—a rich and varied collection from which you may choose, at random, *pomme de terre, tomate, pomme, orange, topinambour* (Jerusalem artichoke, a faithful standby in hard times), *endive, turneps, brocoli, chiendent, épinard, violette, narcisse, pâquerette* (Easter daisy), *asperge, lilas, pensée, myrtille, fritillaire, rhubarbe, acacia, jasmin, rossignol, poule, abeille* (the bee, not, I should emphasise, the shoe polish), *pigeon, lièvre, chien, cochon, oie, dindon, charrue* (plough) or *pelle* (shovel), lest you should think that I have set out to make fun of solemn revolutionaries who believed that they were thus offering to a grateful and worthy population of Republicans the cornucopia of modest plenty (*une honnête aisance*), while at the same time daily underlining the complete break with a recent, but shameful, past. I can, however, appreciate why the Thermidorians, in the course of the Year III, which, both in France under its new name and in the rest of Europe under that of '95, was a year of acute distress and famine, should have felt the need to abandon altogether a nomenclature of days that would have seemed a mockery.

Instead, as the Year II must always seem so closely associated with the life, the death, and the memory of Maximilien Robespierre, I would like to draw attention to the terrifying disparity between poetic intention and public reality, both in the calendar of the Year II and in Robespierre himself, as well as to remind you of some of the more ironical consequences of a new measurement of time invented for the needs of a New Man, born again in the pristine innocence of republican virtue (there was to be no thought, however, for the New Woman). It seems to have escaped the attention of the two inventors of the new calendar that the Year II both began and ended on a Sunday, or on what had been a Sunday (Ier Vendémiaire and 5me *Sans-culottide*), as if some impish spirit had intervened to force the Year of Regeneration back into the wicked old pattern. The Year III was to begin, less compromisingly, on a Monday. It was not lost on contemporaries that 10 Thermidor also fell on a Sunday. In this manner, despite the most patient efforts to paper over the traces of the past—to the benefit, among others, of the wolves of France, the wolf traps having had to be withdrawn as bearing the emblem of the *fleur-de-lys*—the old calendar was thus liable now and then to peep through the opaque new measurements, rather like the heavily embossed V.R.s on Dublin letter boxes painted over in green.

Let us briefly look further at the widening gap between the often undoubted beauty and reassurance of the intent, as expressed in the words used for the new months and the new days, and the sordid, bloody horror of the reality that they so often attempt to cover. Who would know that the word assigned to 9 Thermidor, in the Year II a Saturday, is *mûres*? It is, perhaps, consoling to reflect that, all over the countryside, on that day, hordes of schoolchildren would be going from bush to bush, their mouths showing spreading areas of mauve, picking blackberries, and that they were certainly thus better employed than all those armed men waiting about in uncertainty in Paris. Perhaps, if we are in search of a Sign, we should look elsewhere : for instance, in the column of the *Almanach National de l'an II* devoted to the phases of the moon, we learn that the new moon would come out at eleven minutes past ten on the night of Friday the 8th. 10 Thermidor is devoted to the cooling *Arrosoir* (watering-can), perhaps designed to wash away the fresh blood in the middle of the much-used Place de la Révolution. And who would have detected in *tulipe* the day (4 Germinal) on which the first batch of the *hébertistes* were to be executed; or who would have been able to predict that Fabre-d'Eglantine, an indifferent poet and the principal author of the calendar, should unwittingly have assigned to the date of his own execution, 14 Germinal Year II, the innocent *laitue*? Even more heavily disguised, under the soothing beverage *camomille*, an old-fashioned remedy for sleeplessness, is 22 Prairial, historically commemorated as the date of the most hideous piece of legislation of the Terror period. Few would detect in the gentle-sounding Germinal the true beginning of the high-level judicial murders; while Prairial, with its promise of fertile fields, and daily illustrated by such agreeable fruit, trees, and plants as *angélique, fraises, acacia, tilleul* (lime) and *jasmin,* politically spelt out the great panic resulting from the Admirat murder attempt and the consequent acceleration of the Paris-centred Terror. The promise of the following month, Messidor (from Latin *messis,* harvest) the bloodiest of all those of the Year II, is echoed at least indirectly in the title of its first *décadi, faucille* (sickle), for, by that date, the Terror had already started downhill on its final, precipitant course. Poor Fabre, who had put both thought and poesy into his new measurement of hope, abundance, and renewal, would die many months before the day whose title he had chosen to add to his name, *églantier*, the climbing rose, which falls on the safe side of the Thermidorian crisis, on *primidi* 21 Fructidor.

There were other limits, too, on the effectiveness of the new measurements of time, work, leisure, and sleep. Saints could be drummed out, *anniversaires* could follow, for in the Year II people as well as days were taking on the names of fruit, vegetables, trees, and plants. But the firmament, with its gods expelled, could still refuse to conform to the dictates of revolutionary orthodoxy. Ventôse was expected to blow, but it was often becalmed; Pluviôse had to rain, yet in many places in the Year II it was remarkably dry. Brumaire, certainly foggy enough in the confused and quarrelsome minds of the political leaders in Paris, men already ranged between *citras* and *ultras*, moderates and partisans of endless, limitless repression, rebelled with a succession of clear skies and reminders of the proscribed Saint Luke. Floréal did at least oblige with flowers, as well as with plenty of executions, especially in the Vaucluse; but Christmas, which fell this year on 5 Nivôse, was warm, with no snow on the ground.

L'Almanach National de l'an II, the repository of so many hopes, and, like any calendar, revolutionary or unrevolutionary, of so much popular wisdom, offers further guidance as to the predictable course of the future days: that on 9 Thermidor, the sun would rise at 4.22 and set at 7.3; that on the 10th, sunrise would be at 4.23, sunset at 7.37— still very long days, then, for protracted uncertainty, hesitation, and doubt, the opportunities for so many changes of decision, even if the days of the dying summer were already getting shorter.

Even in the pace of events, which were to rush so much more precipitately than the new, slowed-up clock—running now in hours of a hundred minutes—as well as in the often pathetic contradiction between events and the names of the days on which they occurred, as though some sick humorist had given careful and macabre thought to the relationship between the two, there is thus an increasingly marked discrepancy between the political calendar as we have come to know it, and the official one contrived by the optimistic authors of the new measurement of time, the one to be guillotined in the Year II, the

other to commit suicide, appropriately *à la romaine*, in the pretty month
of Prairial in the Year III. For, as we know, the so-called Thermidorian
Reaction begins on 10 Thermidor; indeed, such is the obsessive significance of 10 Thermidor that it requires a certain effort of imagination to
realise that the Year II still had not run its course, that there remained
another twenty days of Thermidor, thirty days of Fructidor—a name
that, to us, must seem more closely associated with one of the animal
characters in *Les Albums de Babar* than with intense heat—and the
five dangling *jours complémentaires*; that, in fact, there were still fifty-
five irrelevant days to go before the Year II could be wound up and
put away lovingly in the moth-balls of historical myth and memory. At
least the politically-motivated would now be able to see out what
remained of the summer in undisturbed sleep, and even face the on-
coming autumn with a sort of equanimity. All that was left of the once-
prestigious Year II was the memory of recent panic, and an immense,
rather selfish, sense of relief. It is 10 Thermidor, and not the official
calendar, with its pseudo-rural optimism, that is the great divide, not
so much because it is that between the living and the dead Robespierre,
as that between all-embracing, manic fear, and dawning reassurance.
Though summer still technically had some time to go, at least to the
end of Fructidor (culminating, incongruously, for that useful article
would have been much more in demand in Thermidor, in *panier*), that
particular mad, hot summer, the summer of *les Dieux ont soif*,
came abruptly and quite unexpectedly to an end on that bright
morning.

The Revolutionary Calendar was heavily subjected to the sort of back-
to-the-land physiocratic nonsense, a purely urban fantasy, that had been
so fashionable in educated city circles in the 1770s; Fabre and Romme,
as well as all their colleagues who enthusiastically adopted the new
measure of days and months, displayed themselves as late-eighteenth-
century romantics, as they walked carefully in the revered steps of *le
Promeneur Solitaire,* in a revolutionary crocodile on an outing to Mont-
morency and Ermenonville, or wept with the weeping willow, as it leant
protectingly (and to the dictates of the urban engraver, rather than to
those of the prevailing wind), over an urn, half-ruined, though built only
a year previously, and fully armed with all the sad funereal plants that
clutter up the month of Pluviôse, which is also that of the anniversary
of the King's death: *buis, if, cyclamen,* and the dreary *peuplier,* later
for some reason such a favourite with the iconography of the Year II,
the straight ranks of beribboned poplars disappearing into a distant
perspective offering the ideal forward marching area for Unanimity and
Enthusiasm, as they walk hand in hand down flowered avenues, towards
the horizon of *le bonheur commun.*

The Calendar offers a fantasy trip, a fairground journey on a garishly

painted scenic railway, past haunted castles, the quaint ruins of seign-
eurial towers and turrets, the humble thatch of the toiling countryman,
seen at the plough or tending his vine (*Guerre aux châteaux, paix aux
chaumières*), past hillocks topped with windmills, streams and canals
dotted with busy barges pulled by sturdy horses, past now bell-less
church towers, surmounted with stiff tricolors, flying out straight in the
wind of Unanimity, the discreetly ruined tombs of many Martyrs of
Liberty and Friends of Humanity, partially hidden by cypresses on
little islands, and surrounded by fishermen, fishing for the community,
and not for their own satisfaction. Yet, if no doubt derided by the
worthy *cultivateur*, who must have been equally unresponsive to the
patronising and useless advice offered to him by other urban and
revolutionary do-gooders such as Collot's own *le Père Gérard*, this rural
scene of papier-mâché ruins and contrived waterfalls, as far removed
from reality as Marie-Antoinette's *Hameau*, was nevertheless to be the
ideal living abode of many *Conventionnels*, most of them as land-locked,
as little-travelled, as unobservant as Robespierre himself. The authors
of the new calendar were very much aware of the force of words and
symbols, and in their unbounded optimism there were almost equal
elements of realism and dream. To acquaint the population with the
often bizarre aspirations of the new regime, and yet to present them—
in the manner of the election posters of Indian political parties—in the
familiar terms of the barnyard, the market, the back garden, the woods,
rivers and fields, was, in fact, both a stroke of genius, an act of faith,
and a tremendous vote of confidence in the future. Clearly most of them,
and none more than Robespierre, genuinely believed that if they called
days new names, they would be new days, months new names, they
would be new months, if they invented new years, over a new span, then
they would be new years. And from this it would follow, such were the
limitless virtues of example, education, and habit, that the people
privileged to live within the new measurements of time would be people
reborn. The calendar did not stand alone; Frenchmen were no longer
to be described as of an average height of 5 *pieds 4 pouces,* they would
no longer drink *pintes* but *décilitres.* And so, they believed, they would
no longer think in terms of the week, would abandon the deplorable
habit of "Mondaying", would slip out of the habit of religious worship,
because they would soon lose track of the recurrent *ci-devant dimanche.*
It was a bold bet.

A bold bet indeed, but one that did not take into sufficient account
the power of rural memory, the frailties of human nature, the pulls
of ambition and greed, and the realities of political rivalries at the top
level of government. There was probably no member of the Revolutionary Government more aware than Robespierre of the chasm—and all
the evidence of the summer months suggested that it was a widening

one; that Vice with streaming hair, and Old Corruption, financed suitably enough from across the Channel, were in the process of chasing from the revolutionary temple, its cardboard Mountains and sphinxes spewing out the pure waters of Reason as a background, the white-clad figure of Virtue and the blue-clad figure of Purity—opening, day by day, between the vision of *le Bonheur commun,* and the crude realities involved in running a country for war.

Most of his colleagues on the Committee of Public Safety had specialities, just as each of his colleagues on the Committee of General Security had assigned to him a specific area of France. The Fleet was safe with Jeanbon, Carnot had all the required military and organisational skills, knew too whom to appoint, the two Prieurs knew how to get huge armies supplied, Lindet, who had a farm, knew how to get the urban markets supplied, Saint-Just would have been an able general, Hérault, before the discovery of his involvement with two foreign ladies (twins whom he had taken on both together) had known about diplomacy. Cambon, from outside the Committee, looked after finance. Collot and Billaud had acquired useful practical experience in mass killing. Couthon knew how to draw up decrees, was a patient negotiator and mediator. Only Barère seems to have been quite as much a general spokesman as Robespierre, though, unlike poor Maximilien, he possessed too the politician's ability to be many things to many men, whereas Robespierre could only appear as a petrified figure draped in rectitude. He did at least know about the importance of the neutrals, and had notions about the organisation of foreign trade. He also had a lot of friends in the north-east, and was not easily fooled by what was said to be going on there. But he found most such matters unworthy of his careful consideration; and if he were prepared at least, while still attending the Committee, to give up some time to signing arrest warrants it was merely in order to prevent his colleagues from multiplying them even further.

If anyone needed the fantasies, the artifices, the Potemkin Village scenario provided by the Revolutionary Calendar, as reassuring, as highly coloured, and as innocent as the *Calendrier des PTT*, if any revolutionary leader felt the insistent need to turn living people into concepts, so that even soldiers would become porcelain figurines, as emblematic as all the terracotta busts of himself that gazed at him from all angles, and would be suitably addressed, not as soldiers, but as *défenseurs de la Patrie,* if any man in the Year II was entirely given to a double talk that consisted in never calling anything what it was— I am sure the word *guillotine* never passed his lips, he would have used a complicated circumlocution such as *le glaive de la justice*—it was Robespierre, a man who, even as a public figure, always had to live at one remove from reality, insulated in the quiet of his study, in the steady adulation of the Duplay family, themselves so exemplary as to be some-what unreal, with his visitors pre-selected and carefully screened. It has often been remarked upon that Robespierre was at least accessible, and that he received his visitors with an open amiability. But he was no Marat, to be seen in a towel. There had to be plenty of written introduc-tions beforehand; and, indeed, it was in his dealings with people that Robespierre was to display his most atrophied vision. He took a great deal of trouble with establishing and maintaining written contacts all over France—there was a *réseau Robespierre* that has not been suffici-ently studied and that is at least revealing of the extent of his informants —but he was readily the dupe of the first-comer. The mere fact that a man from the Departments wanted to see him indicated that he must be a good man, could be believed, trusted, and should be satisfied. For instance, in the ancient running quarrel between Rouen and le Havre, a quarrel to which the circumstances of the Revolution added further acrimony, the Havrais had the sense to get in first, obtaining an inter-view with Robespierre in late Brumaire. Having put their case to him, they got what they wanted; for the rest of his short life, Robespierre remained convinced of the revolutionary tepidity of the Rouennais, a selfish, unvirtuous commercial lot. Well, they had not *bothered* to get in touch with him! And all those in whom he placed implicit trust—men like Bertrand and Gravier, Aigoin, Payan and Jullien, Dumas and Herman—had gone out of their way, first of all to write to him, then to obtain an audience with him. No wonder those who feared and (in private) mocked him, after having been refused an audience—always a bad sign—called him *le pape Robespierre*!

It is not so much that he did not understand about people, as that he could only form an opinion of people in the context of their relations to himself; they did not exist in their own right. It was a partial blind-ness highly dangerous to a politician, who, in an exceptionally long revolutionary past, had given proof of prudence, even cunning, an ability to march behind events (and crowds), to manage elections, and pack institutions.

Of all the accusations subsequently made against Robespierre, the most improbable is that he and his côterie (and there did exist a côterie, people selected for their rectitude, rather than for any visible political capacity) were aiming at personal power. People who are aiming at supreme power do not generally run away from such power as they do possess. The truth seems, on the contrary, that he had got thoroughly sick of power, and of the mounting tide of terror and repression that gave to Prairial, Messidor, and the first decade of Thermidor their hideous significance. If anything at all is clear about the tangled events leading to 9 Thermidor, it is that Robespierre was eventually destroyed as a suspected moderate, because he seemed a semi-silent threat to the ultra terrorists, Collot and Billaud; that he had become appalled by the renewal of the Terror in Paris, and that he may have been preparing to appeal to the *côté droit* of the Convention to solicit their help in bringing it to a halt (as, indeed, he did, in his speech of 8 Thermidor). I am not suggesting that Robespierre was not, or never had been, a terrorist—he was as capable as any of his colleagues of sending even his best friend to the guillotine, though in his case only after publicly wrestling with his conscience till it was induced to come out for death—but that by Prairial, or, more likely, Messidor, he had become convinced, on grounds of political expediency, that the regime simply could not afford any more purges in high places, any more trials of members of the Convention.

Why then all the fuss? Have I not suggested that he was unattractive, unimaginative, that he liked to hide from realities, that he had no practical experience of "revolutionising", that he was remarkably uncurious about the details of government and administration, that, a member of a Committee, he was anything but a Committee man, that, on the whole, he was boring and petit-bourgeois? What then would be missing in his absence? The answer, I think, is *ideology*, a moral purpose, moral definitions of the aims of the Revolution, the moral justification of the revolutionary dictatorship. Right up to Floréal, it was Robespierre who had always provided the much-needed high moral line, explaining why popular sovereignty had to be put away in the frigidaire—temporarily, and *temporaire* is a dangerously familiar adjective of the Year II vocabulary; in Lyon it went on for enough time to effect the killing of thousands. Every time the Committees decided on a course of action that was bound to be unpopular with the common people, it was Robespierre who would do the explaining, pointing out that it was all in their own interest, that it hurt him more than them, and so on. Moral guidance was what was expected of him. He had such a funny name that most people would know it. But it was a name without a face. He was like a sort of moral juke box; you made your choice, and out came Virtue, Sin, Corruption, Purity, Plots, Plots, Plots, Imminent Self-Immolation (on this or that altar), *je, je, je, mon, mon, mon, ma, ma, ma, moi, moi, moi,* as though the needle had got stuck.

Probably it was too much to ask of any man. For, at least up to Germinal, he had been able to combine his usual practical skills as a political manipulator, as the man in the middle, with the numerous contents of his own private pantheon. But, by the summer of the Year II, the gap between pretty words and brutal realities had become too great, he had been overcome with disgust, doubt and a sense of the unattainability of everything that he had preached so zealously. Perhaps he had begun to realise that he had been the principal victim of his own words, that his colleagues had been merely using him as a *marchand de rêves*, to be discarded when no longer needed. The deep and permanent tragedy of Robespierre—including a disproportionately hideous end for a man who should, by every right, have ended up enjoying retirement in a *bicoque de banlieue,* its garden decorated with scallop shells arranged in neat patterns and with wooden swans—is that, in his curiously contradictory personality, he represented, in word, in manner, in intent, the terrible duality of the Year II. Robespierre liked pretty things; he had still not got very much further than the pretty versifier of Arras days, he was attached to pretty words, believing even that the grim face of the Terror could be given a reassuring disguise, a floral foliage. In the long, dreadful wait for death, lying, filthy and soiled, on a table, he may have had plenty of time to reflect on the consequences of *not* putting away childish things, and to wonder what would become of all the cherished objects with which he had surrounded himself, as privileged companions to his foreboding musings about the future of mankind.

11

Provincial terror

Colin Lucas's study of the institutions and personnel of the Terror in the
Loire following the federalist crisis of the summer of 1793, is a brilliant
pioneering book* combining meticulous and exhaustive research, even
down to the level of several hundred municipal and village records, with
rigorous analysis, a light and pleasing style, a sympathetic and direct
understanding of groups and individuals, a constant awareness of the
bitter persistence of provincial rivalries, a general grasp of the whole
history of the Terror throughout France, and, above all, a wonderful
feeling for place. The choice of the Loire, a Department formed quite
accidentally, but corresponding nonetheless to a much older unit, during
the period of the high Terror, is a particularly happy one, since it includes
an area of recalcitrant contrasts : mountain and plain, some communications and virtually no communications (especially from West to East),
a very mixed economy, opposing dialects, with undoubtedly the most
colourful of all the Terrorists, a group not, however, lacking in
individualists.

One could hardly go wrong with a personality as extravagant and as
untamable as that of Claude Javogues, a man who could surely claim
a leading place in France's long line of *grands exaspérés*. Since Javogues
is much the most important single character in the book, his impossible
and unpredictable behaviour lends to what might otherwise have been
rather an austere work on the interrelations and proliferation of institutions, a totally human and often attractive dimension, as well as a sort
of bizarre, wild unity. For, if Javogues nearly always behaved unpredictably, his mood changing almost from hour to hour, there was at least
a predictability, a weird coherence, in the fact that he could be relied
on to behave either badly or worse.

Very occasionally, and totally unpredictably, he would lapse into a
sort of boisterous affability. A number of *Représentants en mission*
appear to have been fairly impossible people, vain, touchy, *protocolaire*,
loud-mouthed, but Javogues is in a class quite of his own. Whether receiving the members of a municipality, at midday, in his bed, between his
two female "secrétaires", or throwing nuts at a delegation, or pulling the

* Colin Lucas, *The Structure of the Terror*, Oxford 1973.

hair and stamping heavily (he was a huge brutish man) on the feet of petitioners, while pouring out a flood of drunken abuse and murderous threats, in dialect, or suddenly displaying a bluff compassion for someone whom he had threatened with death the previous day, Javogues is never dull.

Indeed, the sudden emergence of a temperament both incandescent, totally intransigent, swinging wildly from protestations of friendship to semi-coherent abuse, obtuse, largely unaware of danger, is perhaps the most puzzling problem posed by the book. Here was this blustering *bellâtre*, foaming and roaring up and down his native Department, even biting people, the veins sticking out of his enormous, bull-like forehead, shaggy eyebrows, a revolutionary giant, nearly always with food in his mouth, frightening women out of their wits, pinching their bottoms and making coarse references to the size and spaciousness of part of the female anatomy, apparently living in an almost permanent state of rage. And yet there was little in his earlier life to give so much as a hint of such violence, wildness and foolhardiness. He had not hit anyone at school and he had led an obscure existence in a fairly affluent legal community. Indeed, once back in Paris, he seems to have been remarkably mild, prudent and even quiet, at least during the rest of Robespierre's red summer and much of the Thermidorian period.

Dr Lucas wisely refrains from too many comments on the subject of his extraordinary central figure, allowing the man to reveal himself in his expletive proclamations, in his wild, meandering, often unfinished letters, or portraying him through the eyes of others, of those who, in fear and trembling, had been ushered into the terrible presence, and who left accounts of occasions remembered over a lifetime, often in the heightened colourfulness of the Forézien *patois*. The man was clearly not totally mad, not completely unbalanced, and sometimes he could even pause, in his precipitous path towards political and personal disaster, to display something like calculation and cunning, in order to win a point or to come to the rescue of one of his favourites, the rather unpleasant Lapalus and the mysterious Duret. But he does seem to have been drunk much or most of the time. There are frequent descriptions, some of them from political allies, fellow terrorists, some of them containing too a *soupçon* of admiration for the man's sheer, animal capacity, of the number of empty beer and wine bottles rolling about on bedroom floors or in committee rooms (he was clearly a man best avoided in the morning) tripping up the unwary petitioner, as the Représentant bellowed, throwing himself about like a wounded bull.

Javogues was "une force de la nature". There was no limit to his foolishness. He thought nothing of defying the Committee of Public Safety—the Terrible Twelve—which took his screaming letters so mildly, nor of denouncing one of its members, Georges Couthon, who belonged

to the hated Auvergne, as a counter-revolutionary. Much of the correspondence that he received from Paris, from Lyon or even from Saint-
Étienne, went straight into the bin; his "secrétaires", one of whom was
apparently an illiterate peasant girl, were there for other purposes. Here
was a single individual defying, over a period of months, what has so
often been described as the strongest government that revolutionary
France was ever to know, and, for a long time, getting away with it. Here
he was invading the territories of other *proconsuls*, arresting their agents
and denouncing them as counter-revolutionaries.

Of course, there had to come an end, but it was surprisingly long in
coming. The Committee of Public Safety preferred not to take on such
a bull full-face, warning him obliquely by having his two favourite
agents guillotined. He did eventually return to Paris. Not unnaturally,
he lent the power of his iron lungs to attempt to shout down Robespierre
in the Jacobins on 8 Thermidor (what would Robespierre have made of
such a splendidly untamed Savage?) and rejoiced at 9 Thermidor. Later
he subscribed to Babeuf's paper, and, once more, conformed to type,
predictably getting himself shot in 1796 as a result of the so-called
Grenelle Conspiracy.

Dr Lucas is thus unencumbered with the undramatic details of retirement, exile, family life, political turning of coats and adjustments
to changing circumstances. No other Représentant of the Year II vintage
comes anywhere near Javogues's intemperance and tempestuousness.
Carrier was extremely prudent in his dealings with the central government. Le Bon was a boring, scraping bureaucrat of Terror who killed
people administratively. Dartigoëyte, once off the theme of the Bible
Story, could be quite reasonable. Even Taillefer could hear the warning
bells. It is easy to see why Claude Javogues should have had such an
insistent appeal to one of his descendants, Georges Javogues, a retired
and impoverished schoolmaster. There was certainly nothing petty about
such a specimen.

It is this happy combination of man and place—Javogues was one
of the very rare Représentants to have been sent to his home area,
though, oddly enough, this did not make him any more effective as a
terrorist—that makes *The Structure of the Terror* so highly readable. Dr
Lucas writes of places that he has seen; there is probably scarcely a
commune mentioned in this long book that he has not visited, and his
old Citroën made him far more mobile and adventurous than many of
the revolutionary *gendarmes*, who would have thought twice before
risking their horses in snowdrifts and mountain passes. The place-names
roll out like poetry; he has been to Saint-Just-la-Pendue, Saint-Just-en-
Chevalet, Saint-Romain-en-Jarez, Saint-Symphorien-de-Lay, he has
been over the top, on the old highroad from Lyon to Paris through
Roanne, and he has patiently followed the torrentuous course of the

Upper Loire. He has even acquired a liking for Saint-Etienne, its rue Longue, its *crassiers*, its clanking trams and its inward-looking Stéphanois, and he has penetrated the various *patois* of a region situated right on the great linguistic divide.

Talking with present-day Foréziens, he has recaptured their deep and traditional hostility to the neighbouring Auvergnats, and this awareness of ancient regional antipathies has given him an extra sensitivity to the political alignments of an exceptional period. His first chapter is a marvellous example of historical geography, comparable, though of course on a much more intimate scale, to Raymond Carr's memorable introduction to his history of Spain. It colours, lends life and purpose to, the rest of the book. Dr Lucas has not written merely from the protective serenity of libraries and *dépôts*; nor is his vision limited to the eighteenth century (there is a telling quotation from *Le Monde* on the subject of the threatened closure of a branch line). It would be hard to find a more eloquent example of the absolute need for historians to go out and see for themselves.

The rest of the book generally manages to live up to the promise of the first chapter. That on Javogues could not fail to be lively and interesting. It is revealing to learn that this arch-terrorist came of a comparatively well-to-do family. There was no rancid poverty to explain, as it would in the case of Robespierre, his commitment to militancy. He certainly found it natural to give orders, even though most of these were either incoherent or contradictory. Some readers may not be entirely convinced by Dr Lucas's claims for Javogues as a coherent political thinker—it is hard to think of him being coherent about anything at all—and as a firm partisan of what he repeatedly refers to as "the Democratic Republic". And it is perhaps rather silly to suggest that his order for the collection of gold and silver was derived from his aversion to these base metals, as obstacles to the realisation of that Never-Never-Land: it was, as everywhere else in France, part of government policy, and was dictated by the urgent needs of economic mobilisation.

Javogues spoke much the same language, uttered the same threats and adopted the same emergency measures as the general run of the more energetic *Représentants en mission*. His originality was in the bellowing tone and in the wildness of his statements. Although he was in an area far removed from the war zone, one is not really convinced by the argument that his decisions were in some way more political than those of most *proconsuls*. Nor did his conception of political and social democracy go any further than pious invocations to the virtues of poverty. His *taxe révolutionnaire*, like those adopted elsewhere, was a practical measure to raise funds for the Terror programme, not a consciously conceived effort at social levelling. Dr Lucas is reading backwards : Javogues might read Babeuf in 1796, but he was not thinking like Babeuf in 1793–4.

As is the tendency with first books, this one often appears to make too many claims for what in fact closely follows a general pattern common to most of revolutionary France. This is particularly true of the rather long drawn-out chapter on the "sociétés populaires". It was not just in the Loire that they were seldom very active before the summer of 1793, it was not just in the Loire that attendance began to fall off in the spring of 1794, it was not just in the Loire that they proved themselves primarily concerned with the problem of provisioning their own markets and, more generally, acting like revolutionary *syndicats d'initiative*, in the defence of local interests and as instruments of "communalism".

And Dr Lucas is perhaps pushing his evidence too far when he asserts that these clubs—or some of them—were obsessed with the problem of creating social harmony and social justice. He seems to be much nearer the truth when he points out that individual members tended to exploit them in order to promote their own trade or professional interests. It was, for instance, useful for a painter to be a *sociétaire*, for he might thus obtain the job of repainting the church or hall in which the club met. Dr Lucas is sometimes too prone to spot ideology where self-interest would be sufficient to explain things, and to take the orthodox language of unanimity and egalitarianism at its face value, when, so often, it was merely an *exercice de style* and a harmless expression of conformism.

He is solid and extremely well documented on the other instruments of the Terror : the *comités de surveillance*, the *armée révolutionnaire,* the *commissaires*, the *Département*, the *Districts* and the municipalities, and the Revolutionary Tribunal. In the Loire—and this may come as a surprise to specialists of the period—the normal authorities, especially the municipalities, seem to have been rather more effective than the exceptional bodies (*autorités révolutionnaires*). He also gives detailed accounts of their proliferation, composition and activities, though in this last respect, one would have liked to have heard a little more on the subject of the role of the Revolutionary Committees as instruments for the repression of the habitual crimes of the very poor, for, in other parts of France, the Terror was to weigh particularly heavily on the habitual lawbreaker at the lowest level of society. Indeed their crimes and misdemeanours often came to be interpreted as "crimes contre la République", that is, as thefts at the expense of the community.

Dr Lucas has a fine chapter on the Terrorists. Here we are far removed indeed from the rocklike and rigid collective definitions that Albert Soboul applied to the Paris *sans-culottes*. Dr Lucas is well aware of individual as well as of collective pressures, as motivations to militancy.

Within an urban context, he takes into account family and professional ties, friendship, shared experience, common tastes in leisure, common schooling, the fact of living in the same street or the same quarter.

What is more, Dr Lucas reveals that most of his militants, like Javogues himself, were relatively wealthy men, not the wealthiest, but very much in the middle ranks of a comfortable *aisance*. Nothing could be more unlike Soboul's *sans-culottes*. Students of the French Revolution will find this chapter on militants, on individuals, the most original and the most rewarding of this remarkable book. Dr Lucas combines perceptive historical "impressionism" with a firm statistical basis of tax rolls and *taxes révolutionnaires*. He probes much deeper than Soboul, while, at the same time, he is not a man to attempt to make his documentation say more than it actually says. His reluctance to go even a little beyond the strictest bounds of his evidence may also be explained by the fact that the present study closely follows the sequence of a doctoral thesis. He is now so experienced an historian of the revolutionary period that in his future work he may be more willing to risk hypotheses which cannot be entirely sustained by archival evidence and that he will allow himself occasionally to hazard "I think it must have been something like this". This is not "prophecy", but enriching conjecture. The worst that can happen is that the conjecture can be proved wrong.

The chapter dealing with the recall of Javogues—and what a job it is to get the impudent, angry fellow back to Paris!—is of general interest both in the context of the application of the Decree of 14 Frimaire and of the bitter political disputes of Pluviôse and Ventôse. The recall of Javogues is not an event in a void, though it could have been justified at any stage of his utterly turbulent mission. Lapalus and Duret were to be executed as "ultra-révolutionnaires" and "hébertistes", just like Vauquoy later in the summer. Lyon, it was claimed, was a centre of "hébertisme"; and, in the club there, there was a violent offensive by the "locals" against the "strangers" (Parisians and Nivernais), just as there was in the Loire against the Auvergnats. There are many direct parallels between the dating of the recall of Javogues and events in Paris, in Lille and in Lyon. Grimaud, too, when he got back to Moulins from Lyon, was hounded as an "ultra" as well as an Auvergnat. Thus Dr Lucas has added yet a further dimension to the many proliferations of the Ventôse crisis. Javogues was lucky. The anger of the Revolutionary Government was deflected from his person on to those of his two henchmen. But he had to eat humble pie and to apologise to Couthon. Couthon could wait.

Dr Lucas, who has worked for so long—almost ten years—in the Rhône and in the Loire, as well as in Paris, is well placed to perceive the extreme complexity of the rather static life of eighteenth century provincial France. He is aware of the particularities of such differing centres as Saint-Etienne, Saint-Bonnet, Boën, Montbrison, Roanne, Feurs and Charlieu, and he is an old hand at the terrible administrative squabbles between rival *chefs-lieux* and rival Departments (one can see why Charlieu should have been so anxious to get itself included in the Saône-et-Loire). So his description of "federalism" is both acutely perceptive and complicated. He is certainly right, too, when he emphasises that, even at the height of the Terror, the last word would be with the rural *maire*, secure in his ignorance, in his ability to cover up, and in his *attentisme*. The Loire was no exception in this respect.

Nor was it in that of the greater permeability by revolutionary ideas and institutions of places on the highroads and in the valleys, *lieux de passage*, than isolated mountain villages. In the Loire, *la montagne* lived largely out of reach of the Terror. Elsewhere, in the Mont-Blanc parts of the Hautes-Alpes and the Isère, it was often the other way round, with the mountain villages giving the lead in militancy, with large attendance at the club, especially during the winter, while the plainsmen, with travellers to cope with, had less time to give to "saving the Republic". In the Alps at least, it was often stated, in the nineteenth century, that the mountaineer was also likely to be more literate than the plainsman, if only because education would offer the easiest means of escape from the isolation of a mountain community.

Dr Lucas is certainly well placed to insist on the uniqueness of the Loire. But, of course, each Department was unique, and the Terror in it unique. His book is so good that one feels like imploring him not to run after false gods, but to stick to the Loire that he knows and loves. There must be a follow-up to this splendid book. Who better than Dr Lucas to pilot us through the Thermidorian Marshes and the Directorial Badlands, in this wonderfully evocative Department?

12

Mary Wollstonecraft

The best and most convincing of causes can be compromised, for a time at least, by unattractive, tiresome, or silly advocates. The cause of the rights and grievances of women was given its most vigorous expression by Mary Wollstonecraft, though, much to her annoyance, there were one or two others in the field at the same time as herself. It was a most unfortunate advocacy, for Mary was always silly; she was almost always egotistical; and she was generally envious, rancorous, and meddlesome. In other ways she was less consistent. She undertook, in sudden spurts of enthusiasm, many projects, and finished few of them; this was no great loss, as what she did finish was mediocre and ill-written or appallingly gushing, polemical and hysterical. Claire Tomalin, in her fascinating biography,* writes extremely well; and her book is of current as well as of historical and literary interest, for Mary Wollstonecraft, like Robespierre, represents a type of intransigence and unremitting seriousness that, unfortunately, recurs with each generation.

Mary Wollstonecraft was born in 1759, a year after Robespierre, whom she outlived by four years dying in 1797, at thirty-eight. She was never in fact to meet Robespierre, but loathed him from afar. This seems to have been the result of a mixture of indoctrination and misinformation, for the two had more than age in common, though Mary was neither cruel nor bloodthirsty, and she was never in a position to do harm on a national scale; she merely wrecked most of the people with whom she came in contact. Like Robespierre, she seems to have been born with a sense of grievance, and this increased with time. She felt that she had been done out of her grandfather's money, and she nurtured a lifetime of rancour towards her brother Ned, probably because he had the sense always to keep well out of her way and to see that his children were out of reach of their aunt. Another of her brothers ran away to sea. Her sisters were less well-placed, though they did eventually get away to Ireland, but only after having sustained lasting damage. She seems early to have persuaded herself that she had been the victim of an unhappy and misunderstood childhood.

Much later in life, she was to embellish her childhood with references

* Claire Tomalin, *The Life and Death of Mary Wollstonecraft*, London 1974.

to walks in the wild woods and to imaginary conversations with angels and woodland spirits; and she generously provided herself with a testimonial for an early social awareness that she can hardly have possessed : in Beverley, she would later claim in conversations with her London set, living in Yorkshire in her father's house as a teenage girl she had already become acutely and painfully aware of the degradation of eighteenth-century poverty, especially that of women and mothers of large families, as well as of the road to prostitution, and of the humiliation and exploitation of female domestic service. But she was probably thinking backwards. Certainly, much later, she was to write some of her most eloquent passages on the subject of the pitiful condition of women servants, dismissed, once pregnant, without a reference. She herself, despite chronic shortage of money, never seems to have been without a maid, though the author of her life suggests that she always tried to treat each one in turn as a human being—not, of course, her intellectual equal, but even so to be reasoned with intelligently—even ordering them to take their meals with her (an order that would have been most unwelcome to any eighteenth-century maid, thus cut off from the relative freedom of retreat to below stairs, and especially unwelcome to any of *her* maids, thus held captive to a meal-time *exposé* of her views on such matters as the education of girls, or the right way to wean babies). She certainly managed to get through a great many of them, though in most cases, we can only guess at the cause of this—even by eighteenth-century standards—unusually rapid turnover. She also claimed to have been very clearly aware of her parents' "inadequacies".

What is certain is that, at fifteen, she was already displaying a fine hand at self-pity and moral blackmail, in a prolonged and furiously jealous row with the first of a long line of female intimates, Jane Arden, who eventually got fed up, failed to respond, and managed, unlike many of her successors, to get clear away. The next person she latched on to, Fanny, did not. After trying to persuade her not to marry, and, when she did, pointing out that her husband was unworthy of her, she managed at least to get in at the death, turning up in Lisbon to be at Fanny's bedside—the poor girl was in no condition to suggest that there was no point in her coming—when her friend was in the last stages of consumption. She seems to have much enjoyed the trip, taking in all that she saw around her, writing to her friends about the dirt, squalor and fanaticism of the unenlightened Portuguese. It is likely that the widowed husband had to pay for her trip back.

But, two years earlier than this, in 1784, when she was twenty-five, she had achieved a far more considerable success, having managed both to break up her sister Eliza's marriage—she had married a boatbuilder, a fact so shameful that Mary had attempted to keep her brother-in-law's trade secret from her intellectual friends—and, better still, indirectly to cause the death of her infant niece. She had insisted that her sister abandon both her husband and her baby, who, in the prolonged absence of its mother (under full-time indoctrination from Mary) had fallen ill, had not been properly looked after, and had died. This was not a *tiercé*, but it was a considerable double triumph. She never quite managed to score so high again, though not for want of trying.

Her next wrecking operation took her to Ireland, as a governess in a noble household. Predictably, she did not get on with *les aristos*—or at least she got on only too well with the male one, but could not abide his outspoken, sharp, and intelligent Countess. She condemned the latter as frivolous: she had lap-dogs on her bed, talked about fashion, and took a pride in rank. And when not sulking in her room—her Ladyship had "patronised" her by giving her one of her old dresses, and it was only after prolonged negotiations that she finally agreed to come down and make an appearance in the drawing-room to meet the old Earl—she was either talking of visiting the "cabins" of the poor tenants on the estate (there is no evidence that she ever actually got inside one of them) or stoking up the flames of domestic disharmony, indeed with some success, for the Kingsboroughs divorced shortly afterwards. One of their last instances of agreement was to have Mary dismissed: their error, not to say crime, was to have attempted to be consistently kind to her. She paid them back, again doubly. She had been quite successful in pointing out to the eldest daughter that her mother was both unworthy and frivolous; it was a long time before the girl resumed relations with the Countess. And the latter Mary placed, in an unfavourable and silly role, in one of her bad novels—a poor revenge, for it was not the sort of thing that the Countess would ever have been likely to read.

It was time to move on. She had been hopeless as a governess. She was even more hopeless as a teacher: she disliked the children, and she disliked the grind of lessons. On the other hand, she was apparently quite good at managing the servants and looking after the domestic arrangements. She left most of the actual teaching to her sisters, whom she had forcibly embarked *dans cette galère*. While they taught, she wrote about how to bring up young girls; she had read *La Nouvelle Héloïse*. Her sisters soon got fed up, and left her to set up a school of their own, at a safe distance from London.

Unfortunately, she was not yet done with puericulture. So she adopted an orphan called Ann, in order to "model" her, try out on her her educational theories. But Ann proved disappointing and unreceptive, so that she became bored with this enterprise, as she had been with so many others, and sent the child back where she had come from. Ann at least made a good getaway and did not suffer any permanent damage. It was the same with her friendships, which she would take up with gush and passionate enthusiasm, and which, sooner or later, she would drop, in

spite and rancour and protestations of deep unhappiness. Much of
the spite would then be saved up, later to be embalmed in her unreadable
novels as a sort of delayed, but ineffective, revenge. For her spite was
quite untalented and totally devoid of humour.

In her relations with girls and women, things would nearly always
turn sour, after she had barged in, again and again—for she was not
easily shaken off, once on the scent of trouble—hectoring, doleful, or
displaying her wounds. She had only to turn up for everything to become
addled. At one time, for instance, she had been very keen on the Blood
girls; but later she was to write them off with bitterness, as unworthy
of her interest and efforts; they had been a disappointment to her, and
had been only concerned with frivolities like fashion and clothes. She herself did not care what she wore—though, at one time, she appears to
have favoured a severe-looking *amazone* outfit—or what she ate or drank,
but she certainly stoked up on tea, occasionally laced with laudanum.
The sight of joy, happiness, contentment or even moderate enjoyment
was more than she could bear, and was regarded by her as a deliberate
manifestation of aggression. Any promise of unhappiness or disaster, on
the other hand, would bring her running fast, so that when she moved
closer those in the proximity could expect the worst. "Mary to the
Rescue" had a distinctly sinister ring about it. Yet she seems to have been
surprised when those whom she had been methodically haunting did not
welcome her with opening arms. Wrecking was not enough for its own
sake. She expected to be thanked for it as well.

But it was not until she had been taken into the coterie of the radical
publisher and bookseller, Joseph Johnson, that she was able to give her
full measure. Up till then, she had mainly been a private nuisance,
especially to all those with whom she came in contact or who befriended
her or tried to help her. Now she could become a public nuisance as
well, and soon an international one. For one thing, she was henceforth
relieved of the necessity of having to work for a living, whether as a
sulky governess or as an impatient schoolteacher. Now she would have
all her time to write about education and to set herself up as a mono-
polistic champion of women's rights. Johnson was a prudent entrepreneur
with a sound business sense who made a good living, in the 1780s and
1790s, dealing in mild sedition, promoting radical causes and gingerly
treading the path to semi-treason, while encouraging more open treason
in others. He seems to have been a singularly unpleasant figure, and it is
with some relief that one learns that, despite all his precautions, he did
eventually receive a sentence of six months' imprisonment—not nearly
enough. He can hardly have taken Mary on for professional reasons, for
he was an astute judge of literary talent. It must have been something
else: her infinite capacity for unhappiness, her voracity for *amitiés
amoureuses*—a game at which Johnson played with as much skill as at

timid treason—even her craving for a father-figure (her own father having, like so many other people, been proved unsatisfactory).

Anyhow, if Johnson did not make her, he certainly completed her, providing her with an audience, the company of misfits, cranks, dreamers and Dissenting radicals, and enabling her to expand to the full maturity of silliness in a set that was as self-satisfied, as arrogantly intellectual, as intolerant of anyone "ordinary", and as disorganised as herself. They were mostly an unpleasant crowd who seem to have felt the need to herd together out of common hostility to most of mankind (and woman-kind as well) and to the vast majority of their own countrymen and countrywomen (though some of the most consistently treasonable were in fact Scots). It was typical, for instance, that they should have felt the need to latch—for most of them shared Mary's own leech-like propensities —on to tame foreigners. How, a decade or so earlier, they would have welcomed in Jean-Jacques! As it was, they had to make do with rather a bargain-basement *philosophe*, the disagreeable Fuseli, one of the few people ever to have escaped the cloying clutches of Mary both unscathed and unrepentant. With these went what they liked to regard as tame foreign countries. Almost anywhere would do, so long as it was not England. At one time, it was the American Dream, at another, Irish rebels or Scottish traitors, a little later, and after Mary had been admitted into the Heavenly Band, the French Revolution, or what they believed the French Revolution to be. And the French revolutionaries were to follow their dictates, and to be honoured by visits from them; some of these were even returned.

This was where people like Brissot, quite as silly as any of them, and the other Girondin Golden Boys would come in, and where Robespierre, who lacked such international contacts, being mainly concerned with keeping neutral opinion happy, and Marat, who had experienced the English Dissenters, did not. Mary would presumably have gone for the idiotic Cloots, but she seems somehow to have missed the Prussian buffoon; however she did, predictably, go for the two most publicised, and silliest, female revolutionary trapeze artists, Olympe de Gouges and Théroigne de Méricourt—surprisingly, she does not appear to have heard of the Enragées women, Claire Lacombe and Pauline Léon—as well as for the equally idiotic Babeuf. And she at once recognised a sister figure, or rather a kindred spirit (for she treated her sisters abominably) in Madame Roland; the two could commune in social rancour—Mary had suffered kindness from an aristocratic household, Manon Phlipon had been slighted by being sent to the kitchen when on a visit with her mother as a child—as well as in priggishness and exclusiveness.

So Johnson and his set made a grab at the French Revolution, not for what it was, but for what they imagined it to be, and, like nearly all the English and American radicals, they got it all completely wrong. Increasingly isolated in England, they must have discovered by the end of 1792 that they did not in fact possess any effective audience in France either, and were thus not in a position to affect the internal course of the Revolution in any way at all.

Mary and others of the set had planned to visit Paris in the summer of 1792 and see the Revolution for themselves. Their visit was long overdue, as they had been preceded by many other foreign tourists on that fashionable trip in the course of the previous three years. Not to have witnessed the Revolution at first hand by 1792 was almost shaming. Unfortunately they were unable to get to Paris this first time, because their projected visit coincided with the always unpredictable calendar of the revolutionary killing-season, which might be in the winter, but more often favoured spring and summer. They had reached Dover when news either of 10 August or of the September Massacres caught up with them through travellers; reluctantly, they had decided to return to massacreless and unrevolutionary London. Shortly afterwards, driven desperate by Fuseli's indifference towards her, Mary called on the painter's actress wife, telling her that she was going to have to give up her husband, as she Mary, had decided to marry him. The woman failed to appreciate the force of this argument, and shut the door in her face. This was both an unpardonable insult on the part of the woman— Mary had only wanted to point out to her that she was quite unworthy of Fuseli—and also indicated a total lack of imagination on Fuseli's part. London was henceforth unbearable. And, in December 1792, she decided to go to Paris on her own.

Mary, who throughout her life, from earliest childhood, had always tended to relate public events to her own private needs, grievances and preoccupations, had by now developed her own views about the true purpose of the French Revolution. They were at least original: the Revolution had been contrived as a form of therapy to enable her to recover from her private sorrows resulting from the treatment that she had received from Fuseli's wife. A cold and wintry Paris, as it prepared for the King's trial, was to be her convalescent home. It was as if she had confused the whole city with the fashionable *maison de santé* of Dr Belhomme.

Having crossed over via Calais, she turned up, unannounced as was her wont (her own immediate needs were always so imperative that it was in the proper order of things that all those privileged to have known her were to be constantly available to meet them), at the house of some wealthy friends—the set rather went in for affluent connections—in the rue Meslay, Section du Temple, near the King's prison. But the family had gone away to the country, leaving only a few servants; and these were ill-natured enough to claim not to be able to understand Mary's

French, which must have been excellent, for had she not translated Necker? It was a bad start. The house was huge and unheated, the servants were surly and unhelpful; the therapy was not going to work. Brought at last face to face with a Revolution, Mary did not like what she saw; and what she saw was fear, envy, cruelty, rancour, and what she felt was the presence of death. She wrote to Johnson :

> ... once or twice, lifting my eyes from the paper, I have seen eyes glare through a glass door opposite my chair, and bloody hands shook at me. Not the distant sound of a footstep can I hear ... I want to see something alive; death in so many frightful shapes has taken hold of my fancy.—I am going to bed—and, for the first time in my life, I cannot put out the candle.

We do not know what Johnson made of such unfashionable sentiments but, for Mary, this was a great change from her earlier, rather theoretical, dismissal of violence as an appropriate instrument of political change, in the course of conversations with members of the set. Talking about the Revolution in pleasant houses in North or West London was one thing, but being in a vast, silent house, its rooms shrouded in dust-covers, in Paris in December 1792 and January 1793 was quite another.

Now Mary was really frightened, and fear sharpened her perception —so often in London sadly lacking—and her sense of compassion, of which, when sufficiently moved, especially by the evidence of her senses, she had always been generously endowed. She even felt bitterly sorry for her near neighbour, the King, hoping, like Tom Paine, that his life would be spared. In fact, the therapy *was* working, but not at all in the way that she had hoped. The Revolution was not proving a diversion, a vast *divertissement* laid on for her benefit; it was actually changing Mary, revealing to herself, and no doubt to her surprised and disapproving correspondents, an awareness of others, and a feeling for other people's sufferings, even for those of monarchs and *ci-devants*.

This unprecedented escape from the narrow confines of obsessive self-pity may have been further helped by the fact that she had taken up with Madame Roland and her friends, who, by the spring of 1793, feeling themselves physically threatened by the new direction taken by a Terror that they themselves had joyfully and confidently initiated in the previous September, had begun, somewhat tardily, to preach the virtues of the Rule of Law. Having only one source of information about what was happening in the highly confused situation that eventually erupted in the violence of the *journées* of 31 May and 2 June, it is unlikely that she ever had any clear understanding of what was at stake in the conflict between Gironde and Montagne. As was her habit, she would have seen it in purely personal terms : her friends were being persecuted, hunted down, their lives endangered, by cruel fiends, by men who betrayed their education and intellectual and social origins by appealing to the predatory violence of the Crowd (about which entity she would probably not have been so coolly analytical as the historian George Rudé, for she had indeed *seen* the Crowd, and had trembled at the evidence of her own eyes).

In fact, her long stay in revolutionary Paris, and her experiences of the spring and early summer of 1793, seem to have done much more for her political education and for her development as a sensitive human being than all the previous years of utopian musings and *palabres* of escape over the teacups in London private gardens. Whatever judgment we may make on the last three years of the poor woman's life, there is no doubt that she had at least acquired the ability to explore beyond theory and to appreciate the human realities involved in violent revolution. Two years later, when travelling in Norway, she was to be upbraided by some local liberals for having been unfair to Robespierre in what she had written about her experiences of the Revolution. They, of course, knew better. It would be nice to know what she said to them. Whatever it was, she would have been speaking from the heart, and from bitter experience. No doubt they would have easily disposed of her protestations by saying that she was prejudiced, because Robespierre had killed her personal friends.

In May, the family with whom she had been staying, who had returned to Paris some time earlier in the year, decided to leave once more, and in June Mary was offered a refuge in a small house in the village of Neuilly, a place which, throughout the Terror, was to be the favoured retreat of members of the former nobility. We do not know what Mary thought of her many *ci-devant* neighbours; but it is likely that she may even have begun to consider *les aristos* as ordinary human beings, as much exposed to suffering as others less well-born.

Neuilly turned out to be an effective retreat from the violence of the times in more senses than one. For here she experienced one of the very brief periods of complete happiness—a happiness rendered all the more intense by the constant threats from without, for even Neuilly contained its zealous minority of informers and spies—in her generally unhappy existence, as a result of having met the American trader, Gilbert Imlay. Henceforth, she was to develop the most potent antidote to an increasingly universal Terror, as a result of having to live to the dictates of the most intimate and inexorable of private calendars. Some time in August 1793, apparently still in Neuilly, she became pregnant. The couple seem to have spent the rest of the summer in Neuilly, though Imlay's movements are always confusing. Anyhow, they were back in Paris, possibly in the Faubourg Saint-Germain—a dangerous place for foreigners—in the early autumn. The course of her pregnancy thus coincided with the setting up of the Revolutionary Government, the bitter conflicts between *citras* and *ultras*, and the great political crisis of Ventôse, Year Two. At about this time, too, Mary's private calendar

was given a serious jolt. Imlay had apparently had enough. It was the
old, apparently inevitable, pattern, only this time it was much worse.
Whatever the reason, claiming business engagements, Imlay left Paris
some time early in 1794, and went to Le Havre, suggesting that she
should follow him there when he had made the necessary arrangements.
But for weeks she was left without news, and she eventually took the
coach there some time in the spring.

On 25 Floréal Year Two (14 May 1794), she gave birth to a girl,
Fanny. In the *état-civil* of Le Havre, a source discovered by Mrs Tomalin,
Mary is described as the wife of Gilbert Imlay, and Fanny as their
legitimate child. The Jacobins of Le Havre, though extremely effective
terrorists, seem not to have been over-scrupulous in checking on the statements of the couple. They may also have believed that Mary, like her
husband, was an American. What is clear is that the deception was
deliberate. Indeed, on her return to England a year later, Mary went
on describing herself as Imlay's wife.

The birth of Fanny, whose life was to end tragically, is not only one
of the rare bright spots in Mary's own chronicle of failure and wretchedness; in more general terms, it represents a tiny affirmation of life in a
world of death, during that terrible summer of mounting terror.

In the circumstances, it is hardly surprising that, though living in Le
Havre, Mary should have completely missed the significance of 9
Thermidor, though, in the port, she must have been aware that a number of the English residents who had been imprisoned during the Terror
began reappearing in the course of the early autumn. Her world
was now reduced to a world of three : herself, Fanny, and a maid—the
first one either proved incompetent or could not abide Mary's command-
ing ways, and had to be dismissed, and the second, Marguerite, proved
eminently satisfactory. But Imlay had disappeared, claiming that he
had business to complete in London. Some time in the autumn, the trio
moved to Paris, where much of the Thermidorian Reaction was lived out
amidst doleful complaints of abandonment and lengthy epistles on the
subject of Imlay's behaviour, as well as energetic sponging in perhaps
the most unfavourable circumstances of the whole century.

The fact that Fanny survived at all might have owed something to
the loving care of Marguerite, a sensible Norman who had certainly never
read Mary's various treatises on the bringing up of girls; but it also
illustrates Mary's own supreme ability to dun people for financial and
material assistance even in the most desperate condition. England and
France were still at war, the French Republic was undergoing a famine
of unprecedented dimensions, while the French political scene was
increasingly dominated by the politics of vengeance. Yet Mary and her
infant contrived somehow to cling on, in a bitterly cold Paris; Mary
herself appears at all times to have been able to get news of herself

through to her friends in England. She was also no doubt beginning to become lonely; most of her English and American expatriate friends, as usual misjudging the evolution of the political situation within France, had decided to get out, leaving her without an audience to listen to her grievances and to admire her in her new role as devoted mother (though Marguerite was doing most of the work).

But her main concern still was to pursue Imlay—she had always been best at pursuit—and for this purpose she needed to be able to harry the man from near by, rather than from across the Channel, now Imlay's main protection. She had to be in London, in order to confront him personally with what she regarded as his imperative responsibilities. This she somehow managed to do—Mary had an engaging way of defying the facts of war and history—in May 1795. Perhaps she was able to use a contact in Le Havre. Anyhow she landed in Brighton the same month. Imlay was not there to meet her, but she soon caught him in London. Imlay, a very weak man, was full of promises, but evasive. Worse, as Mary learnt, he was busy pursuing other girls. Mary had a rather unconvincing try at suicide, making sure that Marguerite had been forewarned. Imlay, in order to remove her temporarily from the London scene, where presumably she was making a maximum nuisance of herself with his own friends in the set, suggested that she might like to undertake a business trip for him to Scandinavia.

So, within a month of her return, she had set off again, this time for Sweden. The worthy Scandinavians were expected to take note of the fact that Mary, an unmarried mother, and a shamefully abandoned woman, was travelling alone with her baby. But, in fact, with her usual capacity to get it both ways, and to lie to herself as well as to the world, she seems to have left Fanny behind with Marguerite in the port of Gothenburg, where all three had landed, while she went on to admire the waterfalls, fjords and forests, and the simple habits of the Scandinavian peasants, on her own, or in the company of her hosts. She even managed to get a book out of her tourism in northern parts. It does not seem to have been an unpleasant trip. "Towards the end of July she settled in Tönsberg for a while without Fanny and enjoyed walking, riding on horse-back, rowing, and sea-bathing." Six months later, we find her writing to Hamilton Rowan: "... and I live but for my child —for I am weary of myself...."

Refreshed, she returned to London to confront Imlay who, by this stage, had added insult to injury by openly setting up with an actress. It was the Fuseli pattern all over again, but much worse, for, as Mary saw it, Imlay had exposed her to social humiliation as an unmarried mother (she persisted, however, in calling herself Mary Imlay), a grievance that seems surprising when coming from the most strident contemporary partisan of women's rights. Something had to be done, and done it was.

On a rainy day in October 1795 she set out on foot for Battersea Bridge, but this would not do, so she went on, following the Boat Race course, to Putney Bridge, and jumped in. This might have been the end of it, but, of course, it was not. Some boatmen had seen her jump, and she herself, borne up by her Dark Avenger's outfit—a long black skirt, a black blouse, boots and stockings—was carried along by the outgoing tide towards London. The boatmen were able to fish her out, taking her to "a none too respectable" pub called The Duke's Head on the Fulham side, where the arrival of the wet and clammy female Radical must have been the subject of pertinent non-intellectual comment. The boatmen do not appear to have been thanked for their pains. But she was out to make the most of yet another botched-up suicide.

No sooner cleaned up and in dry clothes, she was once more moving in, changing her lodgings, this time to Finsbury Place ("so as to be close to Mrs Christie"), writing round and talking about her injuries at the hands of Imlay. "I have been treated brutally; but I daily remember that I still have the duty of a mother to fulfil", she writes, having, of course, left Fanny with the patient Marguerite. Fanny, one suspects, was merely an additional article in her standard Avenger's kit, a poor little living doll, to be taken up when Mary was doing her rounds, posturing still as Mrs Imlay. Imlay, sensible fellow, meanwhile had taken off to Surinam, so that Mary's moves momentarily became purposeless, as she, her child and her French maid wandered across the face of London, in search of a base from which she could, without having to walk too far (especially if she were carrying her moral blackmail kit with her), haunt one or other of her friends among the long-suffering members of the set. At this stage of her life in the spring of 1796, her movements take on the apparently incoherent, busy, buzzing criss-crossing of a large and angry blue-bottle. But as it turned out—and experienced Mary-watchers should have been able to predict this—she was in fact coming down to land. In April 1796, she had moved herself, her maid, and the rest of her props, from Finsbury Place—no longer worth haunting, as the long-suffering Christies had cleared out (having Mary in the neighbourhood may have accelerated the decision)—to Cumming Street, off the Pentonville Road. This was in easy haunting and hovering distance from Chalton Street, Somers Town. She was moving in on William Godwin.

By August 1796 she had become the mistress of that self-righteous cold fish. They were indeed an awful pair. "You do not know how honest I am", he wrote to her. "I am not well—I am hurt", she wrote to him. By letter and by word of mouth, each carefully explained to the other on what conditions they should live together, what would be the frontiers, the forbidden zones, the areas of co-operation. In March 1797 they got married; Mary, on this occasion, described herself as a spinster.

Now at last she had got what she had wanted; but that was the last thing she would ever have wanted friends in the set to think. Of course, being no ordinary couple, neither could admit to an ordinary marriage. In her letters, Mary was at once adopting a deprecatory tone, laced with her usual fantasies ("I have had it in my power, more than once, to marry very advantageously"), and, as always, she could not express unqualified satisfaction, suggesting that she had not really wanted marriage and that she had only done it for the sake of Fanny.

And then, at last, came a moment, in fact over a week, of dignity and fortitude, unexpected and all the more moving for that, redeeming so much of the silliness, pettiness, myth-making, self-pity, "miserabilism", egotism, obstinacy, inability to cope and inability to deliver the goods, that had characterised all the previous life of this muddled intellectual. Some time early in 1797, she had become pregnant for a second time. On 31 August, she gave birth to a second daughter, called Mary after her mother. But, during her labour, she had not wished to have a male doctor in attendance—the birth of Fanny had been attended only by a midwife—so that, when a doctor had finally been called, the after-birth had already gone seriously wrong : part of the placenta had remained inside the womb and septicaemia had set in. She died ten days later, on 10 September 1797, in great pain, without complaining, and apparently faithful to her husband's profession of atheism.

Mrs Tomalin comments : "There is something peculiarly horrible about this third death of Mary's, buzzed about by doctors and well-meaning intellectuals, painful, long drawn out and lacking in peace or dignity." Yet it was not lacking in dignity. And, rather than in the myth-making work of her husband, or in the posthumous debate among rival feminists and their historians as to her significance, her happiest monument is this daughter, the cause of her death. Mary Godwin grew up a surprisingly sensible person, especially on the subject of the education of her son, Percy Shelley, "to whom she determined to give as conventional an education as possible. When it was urged that he should be taught to think for himself, she exclaimed : 'Oh God, teach him to think like other people', and sent him to Harrow and Trinity College, Cambridge" —certainly the first sensible remark to be quoted, and the first sensible decision to be referred to, in this long account of much silliness and meddlesomeness, occasional good intentions (generally misdirected), persecution mania, touchy conceit, and semi-intellectual arrogance.

Although he was a professed atheist, Godwin had Mary buried in the cemetery of St Pancras, with a bold, simple headstone over the grave. A few years later, the bodies of the comte d'Antraigues and his mistress, both of whom had been murdered, in mysterious circumstances, by the comte's butler, were interred a few yards away. Poor Mary never seems to have been able entirely to escape from the company of *les ci-devants*.

The final victim of this sad story was to be Fanny Imlay, who in 1817 committed suicide in a Swansea inn to which she had travelled alone, at the age of twenty-two, after Godwin and his second wife had made life intolerable for her, and after Mary's sisters had refused to do anything to help her.

No doubt when she originally set out on her biography of Mary Wollstonecraft, Mrs Tomalin had in mind primarily the political radical, the pioneer of women's rights, and the compiler both of travel books and of treatises on the education of girls. But what she has in fact produced is something far more interesting. Mary's claim to public recognition tends to be pushed into the background, and what we read is a fascinating account of a twisted and difficult personality. Mary often tries the author's patience very hard—though perhaps not so hard as at least this reader's—and, every now and then, she is unable to conceal her irritation at the antics of the woman. Yet, too, time and again, when confronted with the latest round of "Mary to the Rescue" (meaning just the opposite), or the latest manifestation of "The World Unfair to Mary", she pulls back from open condemnation, to ponder on the pitifully few choices available to an independent-minded, muddled, semi-educated, penniless woman, very conscious of her breeding, as well as of her rights, in late eighteenth-century England.

There was, of course, an awful lot that Mary, single-handed, could do little or nothing about; *la force des choses* was heavily stacked against her. But the author is perhaps a little too kind to her, a little too indulgent of her very trying ways, and certainly much too generous in her assessment of her literary talents. For there was an awful lot that Mary *could* have done something about, and what she generally *did* was to cause the maximum amount of damage, both to herself, and to her friends and acquaintances; and, unfortunately, she was no stationary nuisance—she got around, indeed never nearer a sort of contentment than when doing so. Perhaps she cannot be blamed for having been totally devoid of humour; and so it would be uncharitable simply to write her off, as did, shortly after her death, some of her principal rivals as *maîtresses-ès-féminisme*, in the characters of "Bridgetina Botherim" and "Harriot Freke". She had always been a bit of both. But there was more to her than that. Altogether, it is a very sad story, with only one real heroine : the sensible and devoted Marguerite, who, as soon as the opportunity occurred, removed herself from the messy scene of these English intellectuals, and went back, prosaically, to Le Havre. There is certainly no hero.

In her postscript, Mrs Tomalin mentions, *en passant*, that one of Mary's many lodgings—for one could not scatter blue and white plaques over half of London—is going to have a tablet. She reflects—with a touch of bitterness perhaps, or is it merely nostalgia, or the proper desire to see a person who has taken up so very much of her own time and patience officially commemorated?—that there exists no educational institution, no college, that is named after Mary Wollstonecraft. As it has always been customary thus to commemorate those who did the most harm to education, or those who, understanding the least about it, wrote the most about it, someone in high places should certainly take heed of her plea. Mary's very surname has about it an unmistakable ring of crankiness, ungainliness, and discomfort, a promise of puritanism and serious intent. Surely we can think of a suitable candidate for "Wollstonecraft College"?

13

The Neo-Jacobins

The Directory is one of the most unmanageable periods in French history. It defies almost any kind of generalisation; and its sheer difficulty may account for the fact that many historians, save in the past five years, have either dismissed it altogether—as a historical irrelevance, a sort of hiatus, a "between" period stretching dismally and darkly from the inglorious fading-out of the Thermidorian regime to the definitive settlement of Brumaire—or have condemned it as a time of anarchy, selfishness and extreme individualism. Anarchical it certainly was, and this is perhaps its attraction; for it illustrates, often in an extreme form, the regional antagonisms, personal polarisations and tendencies towards total decentralisation that had been latent throughout the revolutionary period.

It is a period, too, that becomes almost totally meaningless if studied from the exclusive angle of the capital. Like the Thermidorian regimes— for they should be declined in the plural—there were a number of Directories, up and down France, their nature varying almost from Department to Department, and in as wide a measure as the relative innocuousness or the relative brutality of the White Terror. There were even some more or less law-abiding Departments, though endemic banditry prevailed in much of the area north of the Loire from 1795 almost to the end of the regime; while in the Midi there were some Departments where there were no political murders. As Professor Mitchell has shown in his study of royalism during these years, the likelihood of a restoration coup could only be appreciated in regional terms; while the spread of royalist cover organisations, like the Instituts Philosophiques, corresponded to regional patterns previously dictated by the accidents of the religious settlement, by the existence of pockets of religious minorities, or by the presence or absence of strong forces of popular royalism. However one may judge the regime and the period, they are not easy to write about; and they largely defy analysis in national terms. This is perhaps no bad thing, as anyone who thinks it is possible to write about *any* period of French history in national terms will soon run into trouble. The Directory should be an object-lesson in historical caution and humility.

Professor Woloch, in taking up more or less where Dr Tønnesson left off in his rather drab *La Défaite des sans-culottes*, has helped to fill in one of the most important gaps* : that concerning the personnel, aims, organisation and spread of the "neo-Jacobin" movement during these bleak and, above all, chaotic years. The interest of the subject had previously only been hinted at in articles written ten or fifteen years ago by Soboul and by Cobb, which only came to the most tentative conclusions. The present author has given us what is likely to be the definitive *bilan* of the personnel of the neo-Jacobin cadres all over the country. *Jacobin Legacy* is a fine, scholarly, pioneering work for which both students and, above all, future researchers, who seek to tackle the subject at a more localised level, will be extremely grateful. Nor is Professor Woloch an imprudent newcomer into this intractable jungle; he is well aware of the difficulties, having previously worked in depth on a single neo-Jacobin community, that of Metz, during these years. It is a very good instance of getting one's historical priorities in the right order.

Jacobin Legacy might also be described—and this is in no way to decry its value—as a historical aftermath, an extended footnote about a group of people who were largely irrelevant to the realities of the French political scene between 1796 and 1799, about militants who were but the shadows of what they had been in 1793, and in the Year II (or even, in some cases, in the Year III). For if the Jacobins and the so-called *sans-culottes*, in their prime, were somewhat larger than life, the neo-Jacobins and neo-*sans-culottes* are little more than figures from the past : names on a monument to those who are not yet quite dead, people concerned above all to survive, not so much for themselves as for a Republic which they considered *they* above all could best serve— an objective that was not always easy to attain under the anarchical conditions of the White Terror, though Professor Woloch has nothing to say about this purely negative aspect of neo-Jacobinism. The neo-Jacobin "movement"—and the author is not entirely convincing when he maintains that the disparate, tentative and sporadic efforts of small groups of ill-attended and scattered clubs can merit quite such a title— weighed down with historical nostalgia was above all concerned to gain some measure of respectability and recognition from a very conservative government : hence its insistent, almost strident attachment to the Constitution of Year III—an attachment that became more querulous as the Directory showed more disregard for the instrument out of which it had itself been born. The "movement" never acquired respectability and only passing recognition, and that not on any merits of its own but for the uses to which the Directorials could momentarily put it.

This then is a good, sad book about sad, drab and largely unsuccessful people. The ultimate tragedy of the story that Professor Woloch has to tell is that people who, in five years, had achieved so little should have

* Isser Woloch, *Jacobin Legacy*, London 1971.

been punished with such extreme cruelty. Most of the surviving members
of the group were deported, in a matter of days, as the result of the
iniquitous *sénatus consulte* of Nivôse Year IX. That is almost the end
of the story, for few of these ever returned. This reduced the "movement"
to a handful of ageing men who had, for some reason, been left behind in
France or who had had the good fortune or the good sense to take an
early refuge in the safety of the civil and military bureaucracy outside
France.

The present volume is above all a study of personnel, along the rather
limited and unimaginative lines that Soboul and his pupil, Tønnesson,
have followed for the investigation of the cadres of collective militancy.
Indeed, a criticism that might be made of *Jacobin Legacy* is that the
author attaches too much importance to lists of membership of short-lived
clubs, to elections, to newspapers and to pamphlets. The people that form
the subject of what he significantly describes in his title as *Jacobin
Legacy*, are permanently figures in their own recent—recent in years,
but an immense gulf in circumstances—past (Year II, Year IV); they do
not appear to have budged an inch since then and their popularity, in so
far as they enjoyed any, was based on memory rather than on any
present achievement—what *could* they achieve in any case in the con-
stricting circumstances of the Year VIII?

One has the impression that most of these named militants go on doing
the same thing, whether pouring out a drink while stationed behind the
comptoir, or writing pamphlets and apologias, or organising the republican equivalent of church fêtes, as if they were afraid to step out of those
repetitive lists in which the author has patiently, but definitively, set
them—following often in the wake of the police, who had a similar
inclination for lists aligned in neat columns.

Certainly, they never come to life as individuals; and the only case
of mobility, over a period of five years, is that of the ubiquitous and
resourceful Diochet. The author has further contributed to this impression
of immobilism, irreality and isolation by omitting to take into account the
crippling effects on neo-Jacobinism of a vast civil and military bureaucracy outside France. A great many of the potential leaders of such a
movement were safely ensconced in jobs in Italy or the Rhineland as early
as the Year III. Professor Woloch has established a no doubt comprehensive dictionary of Yesterday's Men, but only of those who had obliged
the police, the author, and future students of the period by staying in
France and indeed, in quite a remarkable number of cases, in their own
towns, their own quarters. For neo-Jacobinism is almost as locally rooted,
and as much dominated by *l'esprit de clocher*, as had been the *sans-
culottes* of the Year II. Most of the personalities with whom Professor
Woloch is concerned are local men, operating in their own towns, and
no doubt owing what little influence they seem to have enjoyed among

their own people to long residence and to a wide network of friendship and acquaintance.

The result is rather wooden. Too often one has the impression of reading a mere list of names in *vacuo*, detached from the brutal realities of everyday life. This is partly because the author has not investigated the pre-revolutionary careers of his subjects and has generally relied on secondary sources—mainly Soboul and Tønnesson—to sketch in the details of their period of militancy in 1793 and the Year II. As neither historian has ever been concerned to describe individual militants "in depth" over a long period of years, and in the more sophisticated context of quarter, marriage, friendship and leisure, it is inevitable that so many of these people, taken thus at second hand, are almost totally lacking in relief. Professor Woloch's lists are hence mainly of use in identifying the hard core of neo-Jacobin activists in Paris and in the former centres of ultra-Revolution. We learn nothing about them as individuals, though, judging from their writings, men like Dubreuil, Lefebvre, Satur, Lenglet and Touquet were very dull fellows indeed, tedious moralisers and bargain-basement Robespierres. The author always accepts without question the class and trade categorisations that Soboul and Tønnesson have imposed, often rather mechanistically, on their collective personnel.

It is not his fault that this book was written before the highly intelligent and infinitely more human studies of local militants, seen within the topography of their quarter as well as in the framework of their collective militancy, by Colin Lucas (for the Loire) and by Richard Andrews (for Paris), had been made accessible. With their examples to guide him as regards methods of approach, his book might have acquired a sophistication and a vitality that it lacks. One can hardly blame him for not having extended the scope of his investigation to reach farther down, for he had to set some limit to what is a pioneering work covering the whole of France.

So we get little more than political attitudes and public statements. It is both tantalising and frustrating. In most instances, for example, we do not even know how these survivors of the militancy of the Year II supported themselves; though one of the most interesting of the author's discoveries is that a number of the less affluent of the group—people like Marcellin, who had long had vague contacts in this sphere—especially in Paris, were either employed directly by the police or were at least paid intermittently by them, for services that are not specified but the nature of which one can guess. This was particularly the case during the brief ministry of Sotin at the Police Générale. A few more were brought for a time into the bureaucracy, especially when Bernadotte was at the Ministry of War, in an effort to balance any predominant influence on the part of the royalists. They were, however, almost totally excluded from the judiciary; and all those of *sans-culotte* origin must have been bitterly hit by the trade recession of the Year IV. Certainly, many of those about whom Professor Woloch writes were men with private means, especially the most persistent pamphleteers; while Félix Lepeletier was a millionaire, able to finance a whole group of neo-Jacobins huddling around him in Versailles.

Thus we are informed about their activities above all in the preparation of elections. Elections, however, were not the only reality of life under the Directory, even though, under that amazing Constitution, they were never very far off. By concentrating entirely on one side, on what was never more than a minuscule group of hardy or lucky survivors, the author gives little hint of what they were up against and how they were threatened; for the White Terror was a more permanent reality than elections. It went on all the year round, at least in the Midi, though it always became more sanguinary in April—at the time of the convocation of the *assemblées primaires*—and was in fact a much more effective instrument of electoral influence than the rather timid and generally legal efforts of Professor Woloch's neo-Jacobins. By the Year IV, the White Terror had acquired unofficial institutional status. *Jacobin Legacy*, in this respect, is rather like a study of the Front Populaire and of anti-fascism without fascism and the *ligues*, or of ultra-royalism in the absence of ultra-revolutionism.

The politics of the Directory, like those of Thermidor, were dominated above all by considerations of vengeance and by murder used as a political weapon. It would be interesting to know, for instance, how many of the names identified as militants of the south fell victim to the gangs between the Year IV and the Year XI. For the activities of these people were above all *defensive*; they were defending the Republic as a means of defending themselves. This is not to say that many of them were not pure idealists and very brave men. But they had lost *élan* as a result of the appalling experience of 1795, and their ephemeral clubs were more remembrance societies than organisations working for the present. Whereas the *sociétés* of the Year II, at least up till Ventôse, had been concerned with real issues, both local and national—but above all local, the neo-Jacobin clubs of the Directory did not even have the initiative to press for the construction of a new road or of a bridge, confining themselves to pious appeals to the instincts of charity and to expressions of egalitarianism little removed from a purely moral concern for philanthropy. They seem almost totally harmless. Perhaps they knew all along they were doomed and were concerned above all to design for themselves a decent funeral monument. The funeral was provided for them, in 1800, by the Government; the monument was erected in 1802 by one of their number, the architect Lefranc—a tough man with an astounding capacity for survival—not in France but, of all places, in

Zanzibar. It may still be there. Professor Woloch, too, has provided them with a decent interment.

The accent throughout, then, is on political programmes, electoral tactics and doctrinal consistency. We are never allowed to forget that the neo-Jacobins were consciously harping back to a coherent policy of social welfare which the author, like his subjects, attributes to the Committee of Public Safety of the Year II. Thus demands for fiscal reform are interpreted as a highly original initiative in favour of a progressive income tax, while a concern for the pensioning off of old soldiers and a general bid for the support of the Invalides—one of the likeliest pockets of neo-Jacobinism in Paris—is taken as representing a concern for *le bonheur commun*. The author cannot be blamed for reading too much into his material: it is something that often happens with a first book. But sometimes his zeal takes him beyond the limits of common sense. In his case-history of Evreux, for instance, he makes far too much of what seems to have been a small local quarrel, a clash of personalities involving very few people. Touquet is as shadowy a figure as his adversary, Crochon; their rivalries may be explicable merely in terms of personal antipathies or in the context of the politics of vengeance. As we know nothing of their Year II roles, we are unable to judge between them. And the "programme" with which Touquet, a sort of Directorial Homais, is credited is little more than a restatement of *sans-culotte* moralism and of moral egalitarianism; it is more of a "climate" than a doctrine.

These people were small-town puritans whose resentments—moral, personal and social—Professor Woloch has promoted into significant political attitudes, in terms of neo-Jacobinism and Directorial conservatism. They do not seem to have been particularly significant, even in the context of 1798. The Evreux club was a tiny one; the local neo-Jacobin paper has little of interest to say. Behind all this moralising there is no doubt a reality of persistent personal feuds and friendships. If the author had read more deeply into the minutes of provincial *sociétés populaires* of the Year II, he would have been made forcefully aware of the fact that personal quarrels counted for much more than revolutionary unanimity or *la trompette guerrière*. And if this had been the case at the height of the Jacobin dictatorship, how much more would it be the case under Thermidor or the Directory—both highly individualistic regimes in which personal resentments were given full play and, indeed, dominated local politics. The author, who has spent a great deal of time with his "clubistes", his "exclusifs" (this is an admirable description of these rather prissy democrats), is over-eager to take them at their face value. But there is more in these polarisations than mere ideological or political conflicts.

The remarks at the end of the book are extremely important and need repeating. Thermidor had in fact left many options open; it was not, as it has so often been represented, especially by *robespierriste* historians, the last act, nor was it a regime that can be defined in narrow class terms. It is in fact very difficult to define in *any* terms, other than in those of the extremes of regionalism and of local initiative. The Directory is perhaps easier to define, being somewhat more centralised; but it too had to contend with every form of "communalism" and local individualism. Whatever the score was at any given moment, it was never a very clear one; and in conditions of almost continuous uncertainty, both about the present and the immediate future, winners and losers found it difficult to recognise one another. This is the most important point made by Professor Woloch. The White Terror had destroyed many neo-Jacobins; but it did not destroy neo-Jacobinism, nor did it destroy the Republic, or what was left of it. In this sense—that of strict survival—the neo-Jacobins were right to stick to the letter of the Constitution of the Year III, even at a time when the Directorials were violating it with repetitive persistence, because it was the best that they could get and it would have been fatally compromising, after 1796, to invoke the Constitution of 1793; thus, in the relative modesty of their aims, they were showing sense as well as prudence, and proved themselves far more aware of contemporary political realities than the idiotic *babouvistes*, whom some of the neo-Jacobins were prepared to defend as fellow victims but with whose imbecile programme they did not associate themselves. This was probably the best they could do.

Much of their activities consisted merely of "showing the flag"—a modest "politique de présence". After 1795, there was little likelihood of a massive return to the Terror. Their greatest hopes were to come in the Year V. Even so, their achievement was minimal : for a short time they held positions of limited power at a very subordinate level; and their existence may have acted as a check to the more extreme ambitions of the ultra-royalists. Some of the Directors were prepared to give them a grudging support with this purpose in view; indeed as it turned out in the Year V their greatest opportunity was not of their own making but was provided for them, most obligingly, by the ultra-royalists when they came out into the open in an overall effort to destroy the Republic. This was perhaps the ultimate insult. The *cercles* were little more than counters moved about by others, and it is characteristic that, at one time, the Minister of Police should have been prepared to pay, even to employ some of their members. One even wonders why they were so much feared, if we are to take the Government press at its word. Or perhaps they were not, merely fulfilling a useful function as bogy figures in a conservative arsenal; they could always be used to frighten *les honnêtes gens* into an unwilling support of the political system; and if, in respect to them, there were many reminders of *la loi agraire*, many hints of *néo-babouvisme*, these were to be found in the Directorial newspapers, not in those pious, timid parish magazines of neo-Jacobinism.

Power, even at this subordinate, temporary level, was a highly dangerous gift at any time between 1795 and 1799; if neo-Jacobins were prepared to risk assassination—as *commissaires du Directoire* or recruiting agents, as tax collectors, or as other highly exposed minor officials—there was no reason why their services should be refused. The Directory was lavish with its *commissaires*; officials at this level were expendable. If they were killed, there would be so many neo-Jacobins the less; if they survived and were effective, they could take the local odium for doing the Government's dirty work for it. Men of prudence disdained the cup offered to them; in 1795, 1796 and 1797 it often proved impossible to complete municipal councils or to recruit *maires*. Wise men produced medical certificates to prove their incapacity for public office. Neo-Jacobins might do as a temporary stop-gap, but in no case were they allowed a tenure of office for more than a year. So they remained very much on the periphery of effective political life. While they were drawing up their lists—an act of faith in itself—issuing their electoral declarations, writing their dispirited and boring pamphlets, and gropingly forming the caucus of an alliance between "neo-Jacobins" and "neo-sans-culottes"—a coming together of ghosts—the *hardis gars* and the bold brazen girls of the Bande d'Orgères, and of a hundred or more similar groups of bandits and highwaymen, were getting on with the job of plunder, rape and murder, while the Army took its toll of girls and pillage, in and out of France. There is surely some significance in the fact that the Bande d'Orgères, or at least some members of it, outlasted the poor neo-Jacobins and were back on the roads while the survivors of militancy were heading for the Seychelles Islands or French Guiana.

Neo-Jacobinism, then, was little more than an intellectual exercise, a lot of vague talk, the expression of good intentions, occasional brave words with nothing to back them (the neo-Jacobins were too respectable to resort to physical intimidation and murder, relying only on persuasion—a further example of their isolation from the mass of the population), historical memory affected by hindsight and hence a tendency to idealise the so-called "social" policies of the Year II, an inability too to get the record straight and to decide between "centralism" and *néo-hébertisme*. It was a twilight debate, conducted, one suspects, in the absence of an audience : membership of Professor Woloch's much-vaunted and patiently rediscovered clubs is pitifully low, at least by Year II standards, attendance lower still. They had nothing to offer the common people, other than vague exhortations on the subject of *civisme*, appeals to them to observe the *décadi*—characteristic of these neo-Jacobin sabbatarians—a lot of similar moral uplift, appeals, generally unheard, to the well-to-do to remember the call of charity, much talk about the virtues of poverty and ineffective petitions on the subject of the reorganisation of the *hospices* and the provision of a programme of public works for the *indigents*. Their clubs were more like Sunday schools than relief organisations. They proposed no palliatives, other than moral ones, for the poor; and it is unlikely that people like Félix Lepeletier, Vatar and Dubreuil were even particularly aware of poverty, other than as a subject of academic debate. In this at least, the neo-Jacobins were true heirs of the Jacobins and, indeed, of a great many *sans-culottes* as well. The really poor were in fact more likely to turn to *chauffage*, to White Terrorism and to crime; the *cercles* were as irrelevant to their immediate needs as were the contemporaneous Corresponding Societies to those of English and Irish paupers.

Part of the trouble is the nature of the author's sources. Petitions and pamphlets—the latter apparently with only a very narrow circulation— are only very ephemeral guides; and police reports are dangerously deceptive. For many *observateurs*, neo-Jacobins had to be invented, if they could not be found; they had to have something to report on and the meetings of small groups in cellars and *tabagies* represented an important source of their *gagne-pain*. Clubs could not be allowed to die, *conciliabules* had to be *nocturnes*. The police spies were as dependent on their *exclusifs* as they were on their royalist conspirators; and they could always be relied upon to exaggerate the numerical strength and the effectiveness of both.

Apart from rescuing from oblivion the surviving neo-Jacobin personnel of provincial France and of Paris, Professor Woloch has drawn up a provisional map of the spread of neo-Jacobinism throughout the country. Predictably, it is revealed as an urban phenomenon, with strong roots in the centre, in the east, the south-east and the south-west, rare pockets in Normandy and the west, a few strongholds in the east, almost none in the north-east. Many of its strongholds are in the old areas of ultra-revolutionism and de-Christianisation in the autumn of 1793: this is particularly true of Nevers, Clamecy and Moulins, Mâcon and Autun, Besançon, Tonneins, Moissac, Saint-Affrique, Chambéry and Grenoble, Dax and Mont-de-Marsan. Neo-Jacobin strength in the Loir-et-Cher may be a relic of the *procès de Vendôme*. Its presence in Laval and Mayenne is little short of amazing. The existence of clubs in the Ariège may be due to the influence of the Vadier family, as well as to that of Protestant minorities in Pamiers and Saverdun. Périgueux and other towns in the Dordogne are also revealed as centres of propaganda. Toulouse came to the fore in the Year IV.

Much would depend, in this matter of the survival of neo-Jacobin pockets, on the presence in one place or another of leading local political personalities of the Year II. In the Dordogne, for instance, the former

Représentants still controlled a following, particularly in Périgueux. The strength of neo-Jacobinism in Toulouse owed much to the personality of Destrem, Moissac, Tonneins and Saint-Affrique, Dax and Mont-de-Marsan in the Landes were dominated by survivors of Year II militancy. If Avignon figured prominently in the geography of neo-Jacobinism, it was no doubt due to the influence of the quarter known as la Carreterie, an area that had strongly resisted Thermidorian pressures in Prairial Year III. In Paris the principal centres of militancy, or at least those most often referred to in police reports, were the Invalides, the Petite Pologne, and the Gros-Caillou, the Panthéon and the former Section Popincourt. There was an important club in what had been the Section de la Réunion. But the poor quarters north of the Hôtel-de-Ville do not seem to have been drawn into these activities or even to have been propagandised by the *clubistes*. Professor Woloch has given researchers a very useful indication about the likely distribution of neo-Jacobin groups.

The ultimate merit of this exploratory book is to have emphasised the tragic irrelevance of 18 Brumaire, the most unnecessary and, of course, the most disastrous of the *journées*. Thermidor and even the Directory, as the author states, had kept all the options open. They were not prestigious regimes; but they were the least bad that could be expected in the circumstances. It was on 18 Brumaire that the decisive Counter-Revolution began. The democracy of the Directorial period may not have amounted to very much. It was, all the same, a democracy of sorts, with newspapers and clubs of several tendencies, annual elections —even if these were no less annually busted—a clamour of disagreement, denunciation and counter-denunciation, lack of unanimity that was a sign of political health as well as of regional tribalism, habits of disorder, violence and anarchy that favoured "communalism", the timid and narrowly-controlled survival of a democratic tradition renouncing secret conspiracy and popular *journées*.

It was also a period of great educational opportunity and of consequent hope for the future. Even Professor Woloch's small, isolated groups of already ageing ex-militants realised that the Directory, whatever its shortcomings, offered the best guarantee for the future of a Republic of sorts; and *any* Republic, even that of the Year III, was better than none.

The Directorial regime was destroyed—from within—at a time when it had solved most of the outstanding problems that it had inherited from Thermidor, when even the violence of the White Terror was beginning to recede, and when Frenchmen of very different opinions were preparing to accept a system that at least had the merits of seeming the least unacceptable to most; 1799 could thus have been a year of hope and of reconciliation.

It is a pity that a work so scholarly and based on such patient and ingenious research should be marred by persistent mistakes in French and by an inability to get even the commonest place-names right. We have heard of Dunkerque and of Dunkirk, but never of Dunquerque; Barcelonnette comes out as Barcellonette. We have Chalons for Châlons, Perigueux for Périgueux, Saint-Hipolite for Saint-Hippolyte-de-Montaigu, Paniers for Pamiers, L'Ure for Lure, and, strangest of all, Maçon for Mâcon. All this could have been put right with the help of the *Dictionnaire des Communes*, an *instrument de travail* to be strongly recommended to Anglo-Saxons embarking for the first time on research in French history. One of the principal characters, Agricole Moureau, is wrongly but persistently described as Agricole Moreau. The mistakes in French are too numerous to be listed, but it is clear that the author has a certain difficulty in distinguishing masculine from feminine.

14

The French Carbonari

If any modern French ruler could claim to the title of "roi de la Concorde", it would be Louis XVIII. Once the government in Paris had
succeeded in bringing to an end the ultra-royalist White Terror in the
Gard, the only too brief personal reign of the former comte de Provence
could legitimately be described as the happiest period in the violent and
intransigent history of modern France. The country would indeed have
even been spared the horrors of the White Terror, had it not been for the
dreadful disaster of the Hundred Days, described by the abbé Bertier de
Sauvigny as "the greatest crime ever committed by a single person against
a whole nation". France and Europe were at last spared the horrors of
war : an inflated army and an occupational bureaucracy were success-
fully demobilised, the war debts were rapidly paid, university and
cultural life was resumed after the stifling imposed uniformity of the First
Empire and, save for the dearth crisis of 1816, the conditions of the
common people did not undergo any dramatic worsening.

It was indeed a period of comparative social peace, both among the
peasantry and the urban artisanate. There was no major popular rising
during the reign, the east-central areas of Paris remained quiescent. It
was a period of intense literary and historical production, while, politically, parliamentary institutions were reintroduced, though based on a
narrow suffrage. The press, after the long silence imposed by the rigorous
Napoleonic censorship, at last came into its own. The police and the
Prefects remained, but at least they were not the blind bureaucrats of the
previous regime. And the country was at last placed on a firm basis of
legitimity.

Yet, within five years of Waterloo, secret societies grew up in some
twenty-eight Departments, a series of conspiracies—all of them inept, all
totally unsuccessful—sought to overthrow the Bourbon dynasty, without
displaying any more positive programme than the seizure of power by a
coup de force, the winning over of sections of the army and, inevitably
—for this had been the panacea of every military conspiracy since the
so-called *hébertiste* "military plot" of the spring of 1794—the capture
of the fort de Vincennes.

Even more characteristically, one of the plots was advertised through placards and handbills distributed on the Pont-Neuf, while a students' conspiracy (which won no support whatsoever from the *faubourgs*) took place on a Monday, 5 June 1820. Likewise in the geographical spread of conspiratorial organisations there was more than a hint of the past, Carbonarist cells being most virulent in the Isère, especially Grenoble, in the Meuse, the Vosges, the Saône-et-Loire, the Haut-Rhin and the Sarthe, as well as in Niort, Saumur, Thouars and Parthenay; for this had been the most active area of Isser Woloch's neo-Jacobin clubs in the course of the Directory, though, as we shall see, there were other reasons too for the predominance of the Haut-Rhin in semi-secret conspiratorial movements in the early 1820s.

Old Hatreds and Young Hopes is an unsatisfactory book about men themselves shadowy, lifeless and incomplete.* Alan B. Spitzer's study is in fact little more than a chronicle of names—this is not to deny that these, 244 in all, may be a very useful guide to future historians who wish to study this ephemeral movement in greater depth—and, even as a collectivity, *les Bons Cousins* hardly hold together. This is not surprising, as the group was in fact amorphous, feeding on illusion, delusion, false hopes, an inability to come to terms with reality, and riddled with informers and *agents provocateurs*, who appear almost as numerous as the deluded conspirators. From the little we learn of them individually, they emerge as inflated egotists and cranks, a scatter of "pauvres Bitos", each one shut off within his own fantasy, believing that he, and he alone, was the Hidden Director of a Directorate that probably did not exist other than in the inventive imagination of the political police. Of their individual motivations we are scarcely given a clue, though there is a description of the unfortunate Bories, of the "Quatre Sergents de la Rochelle", that might fit several generations of IRA men, of whatever obedience: "His habits were pure, his tastes were simple, his life retiring. . . . His heart was free from ambition, his most ardent wish was to die at the moment of the people's victory." This is the nearest we ever get to a description of individual motivations.

Socially, too, it is difficult to suggest any coherence in a group ranging from low-ranking officers, senior NCOs, Alsatian Protestant industrialists, law and medical students, a handful of noblemen, professional people and a very small number of artisans; though, in Nantes, we do encounter that familiar triumvirate of Year II militancy and *babouviste* commitment: an innkeeper, a wine merchant and a compositor. Nor is age of very much help. It would be wrong to describe the French *Charbonnerie* of 1820–2 simply as the conspiracy of frustrated youth; though most of the victims, including the unfortunate Four Sergeants, were in fact young. Some of the apparent leaders were men whose careers and ambitions had been frustrated by the advent of the Second Restoration. Boredom with

* Alan B. Spitzer, *Old Hatreds and Young Hopes*, London 1972.

an uneventful and pacific regime was undoubtedly a powerful motivation to engagement in these foolish matters, but it is one that Professor Spitzer does not pause to investigate or even hint at. In nineteenth century France, there were many who, like Lamartine in Tocqueville's splendid phrase, "se sont faits révolutionnaires pour se désennuyer".

Professor Spitzer does rather better when employing regional explanations of positive commitment, though he hardly explains the absence of certain Departments and towns. What of Rouen, Lille, Amiens, Marseille and the towns of the Valley of the Rhône, of Bordeaux and Toulouse? It is easy to explain the presence of garrison towns, especially those of the east and south-east, for all were thinking in terms of a military conspiracy, and there had to be a garrison to win over. All were equally convinced of the necessity of having a general; they did indeed get one or two, including the idiotic Bertin. He could have made Alsatian commitment more intelligible if he had insisted on the nostalgia felt for the previous regime by the economic élites of that province: as Geoffrey Ellis has shown, in a work as yet unpublished, Alsace, especially the Haut-Rhin, had certainly been the principal beneficiary of the extended markets provided to inland towns like Strasbourg and Mulhouse by the Continental System. By 1806, merchants and industrialists from these two cities could look as far as the Leipzig Fair. The fact that the two Alsatian Departments had been the most regular providers of the revolutionary and Napoleonic armies is better known. They would then contain, in enforced idleness and economic decline, a proportionally larger number of *vieilles moustaches* than elsewhere.

Professor Spitzer indicates that the movement, far from being original, was imitative; but he does not indicate imitative of what, as he does not provide a background or narrative of the recent past extensive enough to bring out possible influences. There are the obvious masonic, Italian and Prussian ingredients; the French carbonarists were using language and paraphernalia similar to those favoured, at the other end of Europe, at much the same time, by the future Decembrists. But what indeed of "les survivances de la Révolution", so often referred to? We have, of course, the ineffable Lafayette, the Sartre of eighteenth- and nineteenth-century revolutions (for the Hero of the Two Worlds, to have missed a potential revolution would be like missing Ascot for a socialite), and the stern and boring Manuel. But did any of the activists themselves date back to 1793–4 militancy? Were any of them sons of *sans-culotte* militants or *babouviste* conspirators? We do not know, though none of the 240-odd names is familiar to a specialist of the Revolution and the Directory. The author at least effectively disposes of the egregious Buonarroti—and for this he will earn exclusion from the next annual colloquium on *babouvisme*, as well as an excommunication from Turin and Amsterdam.

Perhaps, owing to the paucity of records that provide little more than lists of names, it was impossible to do any better and to give any semblance of life to these mostly obscure people. What exactly were the motives that drove them into the dangerous, occasionally fatal, path of not so secret conspiracy? We are not told; we can only guess. Boredom has already been suggested. There was certainly also a powerful element of self-dramatisation and conceit. The movement was sufficiently vague for any rancid provincial mediocrity to come to believe that he was himself at the centre, "le moteur caché" of a vast conspiracy. Because of the lack of a formal organisation, to the neglect of the most elementary forms either of discipline or security—this book opens with a quote from Réal : "Le peuple français est, de tous les peuples, le moins propre à une conspiration"—it was open to the humblest *carbonaro* to feel himself the Babeuf of a movement enveloped in the exciting and flattering draperies of pseudo-masonic flummery : skulls, daggers, triangles, suns shining through storm clouds shot through with harmoniously forked lightning. The trappings were more important than the aims. For what *were* these?

Professor Spitzer himself emphasises that none of the conspirators ever envisaged that they might encounter concerted military resistance. The regime was expected to play the game and dutifully to collapse as soon as the tricolour flags appeared on a bridge or in front of the barracks of some wretched provincial hole like Niort or Thouars. The people would, of course, respond; though they could not be expected to be entrusted with such dangerous secrets in advance. For the students involved, conspiracy was a form of self-assertion, a proclamation of class arrogance and a compensation for intellectual vacuity. Theirs was the most despicable form of self-indulgence : for, in their contacts with simple-minded NCOs, they communicated their own urge for action for action's sake to others who, as soldiers, risked their heads, when they took these middle-class café-strategists literally. The poor *Quatre Sergents* had been indoctrinated in cafés behind the Panthéon; they would not have ended so young and so tragically, would not have given their collective identity to two inn-signs in Paris, if they had not previously been in contact with the law and medical students of the rue Descartes and the rue Lacépède. It was they who lost their heads, not the students.

Indeed, for the rare victims of a comparatively mild judicial repression, the biggest surprise must have been their own death sentences. After all, they had only tried to overthrow the Bourbons, call out the garrison, display the tricolour. In most instances, they had never fired a shot; not from a spirit of humanity, but because they did not have the time to. The humbler elements simply stumbled into conspiracy at the instigation of others who, like Victor Cousin (one can think of more recent parallels) preached violence from the safety of his professorial chair and took care to be out of the country (preaching the good word in Switzerland and Italy), when his students, who had taken him literally, proceeded to realise the programme of the Maître. Nor is there any suggestion that either Lafayette or Voyer d'Argenson ever even set out, in their comfortable *équipages*, to any of the prearranged rendezvous of this, that or the other coup : Belfort, Saumur, Nantes, Strasbourg Thouars, and so on. To preach conspiracy was one thing (especially if covered by a *député*'s immunity—and the Restoration was a parliamentary regime), actively to conspire was quite another. Victor Cousin could have earned a chair in California, and from the present account it is easy to understand how unlovely Motier, also known as Lafayette, the man who had deserted to the Austrians once the Revolution that he had embraced had turned against its keeper, was able to survive, to re-enact his Balcony Scene, in July 1830.

As Professor Spitzer shows, the conspirators were 80 per cent middle class; they enjoyed no support from a common people that had learnt its lesson in 1795 (*babouvisme*, too, had not been for *it*, though, of course, it had set itself up as its Moral Tutor); nor, indeed, did they seek it. They believed that action itself would create a revolutionary situation and they took no account at all of the political and social contingencies of the 1820s. They were in fact surprisingly modern, save in one important respect : they believed that no coup could succeed in the absence of a General. So this book, though ill-written (we have such gallicisms as "seized itself of the case", "barricaded himself . . . behind", "cloture" (*sic*), used as an English word, *vindicte publique* translated as "public reprisal", and a style repetitively reminiscent of the question-and-answer method of a Catechism, whether religious or Stalinist) should be read not only by students of history.

This is its principal, and no doubt unsought, merit. For, apart from identifying his rabble of crackpots and *ennuyés*, Professor Spitzer has little enough to offer. He writes a long chapter on justice which might have been summarised in the statement: "political justice is political". Indeed, he rather gives the impression that political justice was an invention of the Restoration regime. The actual narrative of events is both bold, staccato and extremely confusing; but then the events themselves were confusing and confused. For we are not dealing with real coups, or even real attempted coups, but rather with purposeless gallopings through the early hours that do not even have the romantic charm of the flight of another young officer, from a very different and more worthwhile assignment (seduction, followed by passion and death) in *Le Rideau cramoisi*, which is a much better period-piece than all this conspiratorial mumbo-jumbo.

Some of these unfortunates were executed for coups that had gone off like damp squibs, or had merely ended wretchedly, in a few shouts, unheard in the empty morning countryside. One must not be too hard on the author, for it would have been well-nigh impossible to have written an intelligible account of people who were so silly and of events that would have made a Field Day by a Public School cadet corps seem like the execution of the Schlieffen Plan. The soldiers involved in these harebrained escapades were as inept as their civilian counterparts were indiscreet. Indeed were it not for the evident (and quite unwarranted) alarm of the royal authorities, one would be tempted to believe that the whole thing had been contrived by the Minister of Police and his numerous subordinates. No doubt much of it was.

Even so, this is a useful book. Professor Spitzer has been at pains to identify what had previously been a largely nameless personnel, the object of myth, vituperation and romantic hindsight. They were on the whole a silly, seedy lot; and we can usefully be reminded that students are often arrogant fools (even Law and Medical ones—but then we *are* in the 1820s), that Saumurois are often dotty and always very brave, and that university professors who act as university demagogues and preach violence, in an endeavour to make themselves acceptable to the more vociferous (and least representative) among the young, are despicable.

15

The French peasantry 1815–48

Conscription, so unpleasant to those who are subjected to it, is a positive blessing to the historian. A military society, or a government primarily concerned with military needs, seeks to be minutely informed about its potential sources of manpower; and, consequently, about the related problems of public health, prevalence of disease, regional contrasts in masculine physique, housing conditions and popular eating habits. Just as the reports of the late eighteenth-century and early nineteenth-century gendarmerie constitute one of the most varied and, on the whole, accurate sources for the historian of crime and of popular protest, the social historian will find himself constantly having to make the long Métro trip, now on rubber wheels, to the fort de Vincennes.

Jean Vidalenc has shown considerable ingenuity, as well as the archival flair of an old hand at the game, in using the reports of Army doctors, garrison commanders, billeting and transport officers for a comparative study, Department by Department, of the French rural population in the first half of the nineteenth century.* Army doctors, through the "Conseils de révision" and with twenty years of war behind them, had acquired, by 1815, a unique knowledge of the comparative value of recruits, in terms of health, discipline and combativity, from one region to another.

In the process, they had also gleaned a great deal of random information on such related subjects as alcoholism, the prevalence of violence, the age of marriage, sexual habits, the family, and literacy. Equally, billeting and transport officers needed to come by a rough-and-ready comparative assessment of housing conditions—one of the author's more melancholy conclusions is that the recruit was better off in barracks than in billets— the availability of beds, linen, blankets and fuel, the variety of diet and the accessibility of horses, mules and fodder.

Nor were they the only people concerned to amass information of this type. Once the system known as "le remplacement militaire" had, rather grudgingly and hedged in with many restrictions, been established (from about 1798) in the interests of the French bourgeoisie, all those

* Jean Vidalenc, *La Société française de 1815 à 1848: Le peuple des campagnes*, Paris 1970.

marchands d'hommes—many of them were to combine the job with that, previously exercised or carried on concurrently, of *marchants de chevaux*—who embarked on this lucrative, but highly speculative and uncertain trade, would similarly be in need of accurate information regarding the potential sources of available and healthy manpower, the *remplaçant* having to meet the requirements of a generally exacting medical test. If, subsequently, he collapsed, became incapacitated, or fell ill, those considerate parents who had bought his services would have to fork out once more for another mercenary.

The *agences de remplacement*, much exposed to bankruptcy at the best of times, needed therefore to know just what they were buying. Hence, often, a mutually profitable collaboration between Army doctors and these nineteenth-century slavers. Both the Archives administratives de la Guerre, in Vincennes, and the various private collections relating to the activities of some of the larger *agences*, like those of Valence and of Lyon, offer therefore a crude, but useful thermometer of French public health, especially in rural areas, in the first half of the nineteenth century. In this respect, M. Schnapper's thesis* can be said to be the necessary complement of M. Vidalenc's work. Indeed, with regard to standards of health, the two overlap to some extent. But M. Schnapper is more concerned with the operations of the *agences* and the places of origin of *remplaçants* and *remplacés*, so what he gives us is a comparative map of poverty, lack of patriotism, family selfishness and what might be described as "tiédeur militaire". Not surprisingly, he has concentrated his research primarily on the Gironde, a Department never noted for its military ardour.

M. Vidalenc is one of the rare French university historians never to have ceased to frequent the rue des Francs-Bourgeois and the various *archives départementales*—and he is one of the most prolific of contemporary French historians, his books ranging from the *émigrés*, the *demisoldes*, the Eure between 1815 and 1848, to the "Exode" of 1940. In all, he has displayed great ingenuity in tracking down original source material, often in the most unlikely places. Indeed, one suspects that his choice of subject has often been dictated by the previous, often accidental, discovery of an unusually informative series of documents—the right order of procedure for a historian. This is certainly the case in the present work, based as it is almost exclusively (save for provincial *Almanachs* and topographical surveys) on military sources housed at Vincennes.

The method may of course present certain dangers. The military authorities, on whom the author relies so heavily, seem often to have taken rather superficial a view of regional variations; they were in a hurry and their attitude was not unlike that of garrison commanders

* Bernard Schnapper, *Le Remplacement militaire en France*, Paris, 1970.

when they tended to judge a city or a province on the availability, the expertise and the beauty of its women. The result is a picture of almost universal gloom. Everywhere, it would seem, the condition of the French peasantry was entirely unenviable, wretched and stunted; everywhere too it was getting worse. Everywhere, between 1815 and 1846, the pressure of population on the land was becoming more acute, despite a relative slowing up of the rate of population growth; this was due, in part, to the absence of wars and, after 1817, of a major dearth crisis.

Even very poor peasants often went to great expense to purchase a *remplaçant*; the savings thus spent to keep a son at home, on the land, were lost to improvement on the land. Almost everywhere, disease was rife: here tuberculosis, there malaria. Ignorance and superstition are drearily insistent themes. From one end of France to the other, peasant families huddle together on mud floors in windowless hovels, the acrid smoke of peat fires curling out through a hole in the roof; the front entrance is faced with an imposing pile of dung, near enough to induce disease.

Malnutrition is another near universal theme. A few tin pots and pans, a couple of benches and a crude table, sometimes a cupboard-like bed, and little else. It is a Travel Through France much less varied, far more monotonous, than those of Arthur Young. By 1846, the condition of the French peasantry as a whole was far worse than it had been in 1789.

This impression of monotony and repetitiveness is further accentuated by the author's rather unimaginative way of organising his tour. We are taken from Flanders to the Paris region; from the valley of the Loire to the foothills of the Massif Central; from the Eastern plains to the upper Saône and Rhône; the west, the south-west, the Mediterranean coast and the islands are dealt with in separate groups; and we end up with the Alps and the Pyrenees and the mountains of the interior. Departments that border on any of these larger units are often dealt with more than once. Each Department gets at least one mention, often in a couple of paragraphs. M. Vidalenc is an implacable guide; we are not allowed to linger.

There exist, however, many indications regarding provincial particularities that constitute valuable pointers for future research. The author is informative on the subject of rural migrations, whether to the cities, abroad, or to other rural areas. In this respect, the general picture still corresponds closely to the map of migrations within late eighteenth-century France. The Aisne, the Somme, the Aube, the Eure-et-Loir and the Morvan habitually provide Paris with seasonal labour, as well as with domestic servants and prostitutes. Creusois, often travelling along their own semi-secret itineraries in family units, regularly make the long journey to the capital, plying on their way as pedlars or building labourers, and they maintain their provincial cohesion and their professional specialisation within the framework of the city. Most of them eventually return to the Creuse. There is a similar current between the Cantal and Paris.

But, apart from these two groups, there are few migrations from south of the Loire: the *montée à Paris* had not yet become a movement from the Midi northwards, corresponding to the two networks of the Paris-Lyon-Méditerranée and the Paris-Orléans-Midi. After the 1817 famine, there are repeated waves of migration from the Bas-Rhin and the Meuse to New Russia, the Crimea, Russian Poland, and Hungary; the settlement of Alsatians in the Habsburg Empire, especially in Transylvania, seems indeed to have preceded the experiences of 1812 and 1817, but the movement towards Russia appears to have been unprecedented; it may have been organised with the encouragement of the duc de Richelieu. Migrations from Alsace to the Rhineland and beyond had been common throughout the previous century. The Meuse also provides part of the seasonal labour for Burgundy and Lyon. The Briançonnais head for Turin, the Gapençais for Valence and Montélimar, the Jurassiens for Nantua. There is yearly migration from the Lozère to Spain, and from the Pyrenees to the valley of the Garonne (Moissac, Tonneins, Marmande). Child vagrants from the Ariège are arrested in Paris in the 1820s. The foresters of the Aisne, after taking in the meagre harvest in their own area, move to the Brie, as temporary hands to help in a harvest which is a week or ten days later. All these currents illustrate the map of relative rural poverty and overpopulation in the late eighteenth century. M. Vidalenc thus confirms the awful continuity of the history of the very poor, from the *ancien régime* and the Revolution, to the eve of the railway age.

Recruiting officers favour the inhabitants of the Aisne, the Ardennes, the Yonne, the eastern Departments and Corsica, which, they state, provide the best soldiers. The Nord and the Aude likewise receive good marks from them as providing a varied and abundant diet. They refer to the extreme dirt and alcoholism of the Bretons of the interior. The coastal regions round Dunkirk, Calais, Boulogne, the Seine estuary inland from le Havre, the Marais-Poitevin, the oyster beds of Marennes, the lakes of the Landes, the neighbourhood of Sète and the Camargue are identified as areas particularly prone to epidemics. Inland, the Dombes and the Morvan are described as malarial, the Vexin Normand as prone to typhus. The inhabitants of the Orléanais are subject to rickets, those of the Isère Alpine to goitre and lunacy; the poor Solognot is said to be stunted, ill-developed, and brutish.

The habitual centres of banditry and *brigandage* have likewise hardly changed in the course of seventy years. Les Maures and l'Esterel, le Luberon, les Monts du Forez, the wild roads of the Haute-Loire, especially in the neighbourhood of Pradelles, the *route de la montagne* through the Ardèche, on which the sinister *auberge rouge* of Peyrebeilhe is one of many bloody posting houses, the canton of la Fage-Montivernoux, in the Lozère, areas of les Causses, are still good bandit terrain, as they had been during the latter years of the eighteenth century and the first White Terror of 1795 to 1802. By the 1820s, banditry in these parts had often become a family tradition; it was also almost the only economic activity in areas of abysmal poverty. The fruits yielded by the "auberge rouge" were small indeed: handkerchiefs, skirts, poor quality clothing; the bodies of the victims were fed to the pigs (a new form of subsistence farming), and the victims of that lonely inn were themselves generally poor people—who else would travel over that grim road?

There are still *bandes* in the forests in the south of the Eure-et-Loir, a Department much given to rural murders. The Gard too maintains its tradition for crime and violence; the great Beaucaire fair is an annual magnet to robbery and murder. In 1826 there were said to be 400 bandits in Corsica, with an average of 100 murders a year; twenty years later, in 1846, ninety people were assassinated there in three months. The *flotteurs* of the Morvan and the Cure retain their deplorable reputation for tribal violence, while the Marais-Poitevin is a *terre franche*, a refuge for every type of lawbreaker: deserters, smugglers, poachers, wild men, escaped convicts, extreme individualists, hunters. Langres, Melun and Chartres have all witnessed a sudden increase in their population, thanks to the construction of *centrales*; they have also become more recent centres of crime, those condemned to *residence surveillée* having been assigned to these towns, part of the population of which remains constantly in touch with the Paris underworld.

M. Vidalenc is also a statistical guide to popular *mores*. "L'union libre" is predictably commonest in the highly urbanised Departments: Seine, Rhône, Seine-Inférieure: but it is almost as frequent in predominantly rural areas such as the Calvados, the Bouches-du-Rhône, the Loiret, the Pas-de-Calais, the Gironde and the Sarthe. The Eure-et-Loir takes first place for "abandons d'enfants"; infanticide is especially prevalent in the interior Departments of Brittany.

Inhabitants of mountain areas, especially the Hautes-Alpes, are generally stated to be better educated than plainsmen; the highest rates of illiteracy are reached in the Eure-et-Loir, the Indre, and the Breton Departments. The author has compiled a Michelin guide of places better off the tourist routes; it is indeed likely that, save for Stevenson with his donkey, few English travellers can have emulated Young in his systematic investigation of rural wretchedness.

The general impression left by a book given no doubt a somewhat artificial unity from the fact that it is largely derived from a single documentary source—and Army officers are not the most original of writers, nor the most imaginative of observers, though they had the benefit of an unparalleled comparative experience gained in the course of long years of garrison service—is one of immobility. Nothing much had changed in France, so far as the lower orders were concerned, between 1789 and 1846. What change there had been was mostly for the worst. The countryside was even more overcrowded, the landlords more rapacious, escape more difficult. The urban population of 1815 was much what it had been in 1789. By 1848 the ratio between urban and rural population had changed, if anything, slightly to the advantage of the countryside.

There had been no improvement in food, clothing, and housing, nor in agricultural techniques. Smallholdings had tended to become smaller. Ignorance, superstition and apathy were still the guiding lights of the poorer peasant. There might never have been a Revolution at all. The commentary made by a landed proprietor of Rémusat could, according to this gloomy chronicle of immobilism, have been extended to almost all the rural population : "La révolution avait fait dans ce pays peu de bien, peu de mal; elle y avait laissé peu de traces."

So much for the French peasantry in the first half of the nineteenth century. The author, who has always been most at home in the Restoration and July Monarchy periods, is to add two further volumes : *Le Peuple des villes et des bourgs,** and *Les Cadres de la nation.* The present volume, while perhaps underestimating the intense variety of French rural life, is a valuable introduction to the history of rural poverty. It is a compliment to M. Vidalenc that, after stumping with him up hill and down dale, after glancing into hundreds of rural hovels, one is still ready for more. This is a valuable and ingenious piece of historical

* Volume Two was published in Paris in 1973.

16

Captain Swing

The two names on the cover of this book* are a guarantee of sound scholarship, imaginative insight, skilful investigation and intensive, ingenious research. The book itself is a tribute to the wise initiative of their publishers. It promises to be a marvellous tandem; and the promise is maintained. The reader will not be disappointed by this closely-written book, so well constructed that, were it not for the indications provided by the authors, it would appear to have had a single creator. The two authors have shown a remarkable understanding of each other's particular gifts, in the division of the toil; George Rudé is, as always, admirable in the description of riot and its spread, while Eric Hobsbawm displays his usual acuteness of perception, his flair for the striking metaphor and his abundant historical imagination. Such a pooling of skills is of great advantage to the reader, as well as providing a double stimulus for further research.

The introduction and the first three chapters (on agricultural England, the rural poor, the village world) are particularly well written, giving a sensitive and perceptive account of the conditions of the rural poor in the fifteen or twenty years before the "Swing" riots of 1830, with special reference to the counties of the south-east, the south, the Home Counties, and East Anglia. There are brilliant descriptions of the collective life of the village, of the decline of paternalism once the farmer has his parlour in which he sits alone with his family, the changing pattern of work and leisure, the conditions of hiring, the increasing gulf between the in-servants, who live and eat in the farm and who are employed on an annual basis, and those who are hired by the day, the importance of the newly established beerhouse as a meeting place for the rural poor, in distinction to the country public house, where the poor would find themselves in the presence of their "betters", the consequent emergence of village radicals among these beerhouse keepers, as well as among artisans and itinerants, as the effects of the Poor Law tended to tie the seasonal labourer or the totally unemployed labourer more and more to the confines of his parish, depriving him of mobility and of the safety valve

* E. J. Hobsbawm and George Rudé, *Captain Swing*, London 1969.

of emigration to London, the importance of Saturday and Sunday in the genesis of rural riot.

The book opens with a movingly evocative reference to the almost total isolation of the English agricultural labourer of the southern counties within a society that either rejected him or totally ignored him :

> If they could write—and in 1830 most could not—they would have little occasion to, except, perhaps laboriously, to some daughter or sister "in service" in a town too remote to be visited, some brother or son in the army. Except for their gravestones and their children, they left nothing identifiable behind them, for the marvellous surface of the British landscape, the work of their ploughs, spades and shears and the beasts they looked after, bears no signature or mark such as the masons left on cathedrals.

And in a very different vein, one can appreciate the pointedness of Dr Hobsbawm's sharp comment on the subject of the rural clergy : "The vicars of Victorian England found mediaeval documents a less recalcitrant source than their parishioners." Others like Gilbert White a century earlier, devoted their attentions to the local wild life, to botany, the early primrose and fifteenth-century reredoses. "Hodge" (the peasant) scarcely came into their spectrum at all, save in respect of the tithe.

The chapter on the rural poor is one of the best in the book, as good, in fact, as that on Australia. It is an important and compassionate contribution to the still largely unmapped history of poverty at its most dramatic, most shamefaced, least publicised level. There is an abundant literature on the subject of the "dark satanic mills"; but there has been little to recall—perhaps not even a gravestone—the fate of poor men, found dead in ditches, their stomachs full of dandelion leaves, or the bitter humiliation of the upstanding, strong young labourer—a married man and a father—driven to live off the parish, mobilised into road gangs, like a common criminal, and forced to display all the accoutrements of a cruel, derisive, uncharitable charity, with bells and collars, as though he were a performing monkey on an organ-grinder's box. It is an unrelieved picture of utter demoralisation, insensitiveness and mental and moral cruelty.

Dr Hobsbawm, aptly, compares the condition of "Hodge", in early nineteenth-century England, to that of the inhabitant of the black ghettoes of American cities at the present day. An American visitor to England in the 1840s, ten years or so after "Swing", was to contrast the broken, "forelock-pulling", degraded English labourer to the neat, well-organised, independent and self-respecting French peasant of the same period. This was a little more than fifty years after Arthur Young had contrasted the wretched position of the French rural poor, on the eve of the Revolution, with that of the Suffolk farmhand.

The reader is thus well prepared to place in its proper context what represents the core of the book, the closely written, day-by-day, some-times hour-by-hour, narrative account of the spread of the "Swing" riots, from East Kent, where they were principally directed against threshing-machines, recently introduced to the Weald, the mysterious Den Country, the Marsh, thence to the Medway Valley, the Tunbridge Wells area, East Sussex, West Sussex, Hampshire, Wiltshire and Dorset, and from Wiltshire and Hampshire to Berkshire, Oxfordshire, Bucking-hamshire and Bedfordshire, with a largely independent outbreak in East Anglia (the third of its kind in Suffolk since 1816), in areas that were not contiguous to the rest of the "Swing" territory, but overlapping into Huntingdonshire, Northamptonshire and Cambridgeshire.

While the riots thus spread, with great rapidity—less than a week from Sussex to Hampshire and Wiltshire—acquiring, in the process, particularly alarming proportions in Wiltshire and in Berkshire, dis-turbances continued endemically in East Kent, in which the movement had originated, and in parts of Sussex to the end of 1830. In most places, it was all over in a matter of a day or two; but in some villages between Canterbury, Ashford and the Marsh, or on the Kent and Sussex border in the Tunbridge Wells area, there were repeated disturbances, taking a variety of forms, from the late summer until the middle of winter. Detailed analysis of this kind, much of it based on county records, brings out all George Rudé's flair for research and dogged persistence; the historian of the "Flour War" of May 1775, is once more on the road, and it is fascinating to follow him as the disturbances spread, on an erratic course, westwards, not along the highroads and Roman ways —Watling, Stene—but through semi-secret footpaths or tracks cutting through the greenery, nearly always giving the towns a wide berth, that is, along lines of communication known only to the local man, to the poacher and smuggler, to the ploughman as he plods his weary way back to his airless cottage.

This might account for the peculiar way "Swing" moved in its western course, disappearing from sight, avoiding a dozen or more villages, to re-emerge in a place twenty or thirty miles away. It might also help to explain the disproportionate fears inspired, among property-owners and parsons, by the activities of very small bands of men—in East Kent twenty or thirty, never more than fifty, and nowhere, even in areas of spectacular sorties, such as Wiltshire, more than 300. The rioters, of course, had other very good reasons for avoiding the highroads, and in East Kent, especially in the Marsh, they were no doubt able to use the green tunnels of the smugglers' routes from the coast inland.

It was not surprising that bodies of cavalry, once they had been sent into the "Swing" areas, had such difficulty in meeting the bands of labourers on the move, even when they went by day, in their best clothes, and carrying flags and emblems; it was only when they entered towns, called parish meetings, or camped on the rector's lawn, that they were liable to be identified by the authorities. The incendiarists in particular, the men who blackened their faces so effectively, it seems, that hardly any of them were ever identified—and they are indeed the greatest unknown factor in the present book, so that we cannot even conclude whether they were private persons carrying out vengeance against specified individuals, or participants in a mass movement—would have been likely, on the contrary, to have progressed under cover of night through the deep runnels of half-abandoned tracks.

Riot is much more fearful when it moves mysteriously, and it was not surprising that "Swing", like rural movements in France in 1796, 1812 and 1848, should have been accompanied by the usual outriders of rumour and panic. In East Anglia, much was made of "gentlemen"— rather seedy gentlemen, it seems, of shabby elegance—"in green gigs", reported in a dozen places at once. There was the usual crop of foreigners and exotics; it was a tribute to the importance of "Swing", at least in terms of rumour, that it mobilised once again all the Englishman's favourite bogy figures: dark Frenchmen and Flemings, men in black travelling in green, sallow men with blazing eyes, the brutal, violent Irish, the emissaries of the Pope, "ranters" of strange cults, people who kept mistresses, men who travelled with large sums in Bank of England stock, "Jew-looking fellows", gypsy pedlars.

On the extent, then, of the "Swing" riots as well as on their persistence in certain areas, *Captain Swing* would appear to be exhaustive. It is unlikely that any village in which there was any activity at all that could be even vaguely associated with "Swing" has been omitted. Indeed —and this is a tentative criticism—one sometimes has the feeling that some have been let in on rather slender evidence: one rick burnt, or an assault on an overseer of the poor, or the destruction of a single machine, or a parish meeting to demand an increase in the weekly wage. This is not to suggest that the authors have deliberately inflated their evidence in order to make the "movement" more impressive in terms of spread and impact; but at times they do appear over-eager to attribute to "Swing" what may have been habitual forms of rural pressure and protest.

The reader and the future researcher are especially in the debt of the authors for the minute care that they have taken in calculating the extent of the repression—in itself a counter-proof of the extent of the "movement"—in terms of personal unhappiness, the break-up of families, imprisonment, deportation and, in nineteen cases, execution. George Rudé is an old hand with prison registers; he has also made admirable use of the Tasmanian penal records, and his account of the subsequent fate of many of these poor ploughmen and village artisans in Tasmania and New South Wales is deeply moving, as well as illustrative of his devotion, both to his subject and to the human beings that took the leading part in it. Indeed, whatever doubts one might entertain about the total spread of the riots in terms of localities, one would hesitate to write off as historically unimportant a "movement" that resulted in nearly 500 poor countrymen being deported to the Antipodes—and most of them no doubt were people who had never gone farther from their village than the nearest market town or the nearest fair (no wonder some of these rural deportees should have been afflicted, almost physically, with the nagging anguish of home-sickness)—more than 600 condemned to long terms of imprisonment, and nineteen executed. It is the fault, no doubt, of the material that one can thus learn much more about their life in exile than about that in England before their brief and tragic excursion into history. Since, like most of the rioters, the deportees were generally young men, there would be much more to know about their new existence, some of them living on to the 1880s and 1890s. This is a serious weakness but it is difficult to see how it could have been remedied.

Repression, as it generally is, was quite disproportionately severe, in view of the general mildness—one would be tempted to say deference—of this strangely orderly movement of protest. But this is in itself important, indicating as it does the extent to which the Government had been frightened by a form of protest which, in extent at least, appeared to it as quite unprecedented. The Government was probably wrong—many local authorities thought so, a number of magistrates played down the whole affair, giving rioters in East Kent, at the time of the first outbreak, sentences of three or four days' imprisonment—but the sheer severity of its reaction adds a further dimension to disturbances that were never consciously seditious. The Government, on this occasion, over-reacted as it had done in 1795. It might have turned a deferential and traditionalist movement into a revolutionary one, but as it was, repression was totally effective. Whether one calls "Swing" a "movement" or a "rising", or both, or merely a repetition on an unprecedented scale of various traditional forms of rural protest, it was the last thing of its kind.

The authors have taken similar care to calculate the full extent of the damage caused by "Swing" activities in the twenty-odd counties that were affected. It is unlikely that there is a single threshing-machine missing in their list (their total is 387); the burning ricks and barns have been counted with similar care, and, with considerable ingenuity, they have drawn on the records of the insurance companies to assess the financial losses incurred by the victims of incendiarism. (It is a further compliment to the gravity of "Swing" that the Norwich Union and other companies, after August 1830, refused policies to farmers in Kent and Surrey!) They have likewise established definite statistics on the subject of compensation. The one thing that has largely eluded them statistically—and not for lack of trying—is the total number of "Swing" letters actually sent; they have had to make do with those produced by the recipients—certainly a tiny proportion of the total, for people are generally, and understandably, reluctant to admit that they have been in receipt of anonymous threats, as though the fact itself was something shameful.

Captain Swing is perhaps even more valuable as an indication of the intense "localism" both of a "movement" whose form varied from county to county, even from village to village, and which can only be described at a national level in terms of spread, and of a repression that varied so much as to constitute a sinister sort of lottery It is apparent from the narrative chapters that the riots could sometimes jump as far as twenty or thirty miles a day, but that the rioters themselves seldom went so far, recruiting as they went their way, and returning to their beds each night, for as long as the disturbances lasted. The mass of rioters were clearly unwilling to go far from their homes, and the actual spread of the movement seems to have taken the form of a sort of relay race rather than of a marathon. In this respect, the authors insist on the importance of localities on the borders of two counties (West Kent and East Sussex: for instance, Frant, Wadhurst, Mayfield, Rotherfield, Goudhurst, Crowborough; West Sussex and Hampshire, in the Selsey area; Hampshire and Wiltshire, Wiltshire and Dorset, Hampshire and Berkshire, South Suffolk and North Essex) for the extension of the riots beyond the county boundary.

Here then is the complete map of "Swing", its cost, its form and its variety. Here too are the names of many of the leaders, or at least of those who were accused as such and punished accordingly, in Kent and Sussex, lightly; in Wiltshire, Hampshire and Berkshire, very severely. And here are the occupations of those deported and sent to prison. First, craftsmen (carpenters, blacksmiths, wheelwrights, tailors, thatchers, sawyers, bricklayers, beerhouse keepers, shoemakers, cobblers, glovers) amounting variously to a quarter, a sixth or a seventh of those convicted—a very high proportion. Secondly, inevitably, a majority of labourers, with ploughmen, herdsmen, shepherds in the lead, with not quite so many in-servants. Many of the rioters who were labourers operated, in the disturbances, on the basis of the family unit, or on the extended one of the village (especially in Kent). We have, too, some interesting instances of double or triple employment (labourer, beerhouse keeper and shoemaker, etc.). There are assorted *varia*: an ex-army officer, a pedlar, a horsedealer (a trade often on the edge of crime and violence), a naval deserter, an ex-policeman—some involved no doubt for motives of private vengeance, for a movement of this kind is bound to draw in a small proportion of misfits and malcontents.

The average age of those deported is between twenty-seven and thirty, most are married (the bachelor would be likely either to become an in-servant, or get out of the village altogether and try his luck, if he came from Kent, in London). From the Tasmanian penal records George Rudé has established the names, professions and places of origin of thirty-eight deportees—not much, no doubt, out of nearly 500, but still indicative of the likeliest types of composition. Only one has been identified for East Anglia—a movement which thus remains almost completely anonymous; only four for Kent.

For Hampshire, one is far better informed (nine individuals); there are eight identified for Wiltshire, and five for Berkshire, several from Kintbury. This uneven representation—so thin for some of the most important counties that it is very difficult to make anything more than intelligent guesses about the nature and the composition of "Swing" there—reflects above all the very unequal weight of repression from county to county; the Commissions sitting in Salisbury and Winchester were far more severe than the assizes anywhere else.

So much for the known facts, so carefully enumerated (there is a wealth of research behind each sentence in these apparently straightforward narrative chapters). One feels, however, that the authors are on more uncertain ground when dealing with general causes, organisation, motivation, effects, and when attempting to place "Swing" in the wider context both of traditional rural protest and of nineteenth-century social history. Concerned with a "movement" of infinite variety, unsophisticated, and often quite mysterious in its methods, springing from assumptions unstated because they were probably unstatable—nothing could be more difficult for us than to get into the mind of a Kentish hop-picker or of a Sussex cowman of the early years of the last century—and responding to ancient habits of collective pressure, they try to prove too much, too neatly, on evidence that is often merely tentative and too narrowly statistical. They propose a series of tests, not lacking in ingenuity but somehow too mechanistic. And the answers, too, often come out too pat.

In the section on the distribution of riots and in Part Three (on the "Anatomy of Swing") the authors are rather too ready with their pointers. And when any of their particular "Swing" theses comes out right, as they so often do, then the lights go on, the letters flash, the buzzers jangle, as when someone has hit the jackpot in a Reno gambling saloon. These two are not hidden persuaders. And something of this is reflected in their style: "as we shall see", "it is no accident that"—a revealing remark, for one feels that nothing ever is an accident for them.

Numbers, too, are often not allowed to tell their own story in their own words; both are out with their pointers again, underlining *"no less than"* thirty-five, 300, or whatever, even if the total would appear rather unimpressive. They are reluctant to let the reader make up his own mind; and sometimes they show a tendency to self-evidence, especially when attempting to explain negative factors: the absence of riot, the quiescence of a certain county. They ask, for instance, why, apart from Cornwall, there were so few food riots of the traditional eighteenth-century pattern in 1830. Might the answer not be that there was no food crisis in 1830? They make the point that the people most likely to suffer from incendiarism would be farmers. But ricks do, after all, burn rather better than most things. A similar concern to point the moral, to lead the reader by the hand, and to have an answer to every particularity leads to the repetitive use of the word "tend".

If "Swing" was so multiform—and there is no doubt about that—can it then be described, as the authors insistently do, as a "General Rising"? One often has the impression that, unconsciously, they are trying to get it both ways and that they have stacked the cards in such a manner that they must win on any count. At one time they are concerned to demonstrate that we are dealing with a "movement" that responds to certain general forms; and these forms are said to be unique, at least in combination. At another, they insist on the diversity of the "movement", a diversity which distinguishes it, like its spread, from previous disorders. If it is multiform, this is "significant"; but if it is confined to a single form of protest (arson, or breaking), this too is "significant". Incendiarism, we are told at one stage, is a traditional expression of private vengeance, but, in the 1830 context, it is at times given a political significance, at others it is attributed to the initiative of isolated cranks.

The connection between arson and the other "Swing" activities is never clearly established. But, in the period from 1832 to 1835, when the anger of the defeated labourers had changed to desperation, arson once more acquires a political and social significance as the only effective form of protest remaining to the unhappy labourers of the former "Swing" areas. And since arson is a semi-permanent feature of the English—and indeed of the French or the Irish—countryside throughout the first half of the nineteenth century, one can never make out how much it is characteristic of the specific "Swing" movement.

The same point could be made for another feature of the "movement": the demand by rioters to be paid for machine-breaking and to be given food and drink in the course of their expeditions, the latter a very ancient form of rural protest, at least in France. So much, in fact, of what is said to be characteristic of "Swing" can be associated with other examples of wide-scale rural disorder in the course of the previous thirty-five years, both sides of the Channel, that one is left wondering what was unique about the 1830 riots: undoubtedly, their spread; secondly, the emergence of the word "Swing" which personalised a traditional form of collective bargaining; thirdly, the primacy of "the men out of Kent", whose example was cited in the whole "Swing" area, including the south-west and East Anglia.

Perhaps the main trouble is this determination to seek a "pattern" at all, whether one in diversity, like a New England quilt, or whether an all-weave affair. The authors are aiming at "total history" : but they have not enough evidence, at the village or the human level, to make it "total". Facts have first to be established, then accounted for, though quite often they are forced to admit that, "in the present state of research", there can only be the most tentative answers. What never seems to occur to them is that quite possibly, in the village context, there is no clear answer at all. There is no attempt to "anatomise" à la Stone or Brinton (on the subject of a Revolution) a peasants' revolt, because, as they demonstrate in their brilliant opening chapters, the English labourer of the early years of the last century was unique—he had no European counterpart nor indeed any in Wales or Ireland. (This is perhaps why they do not mention David Williams's book *The Rebecca Riots,* though it deserved at least a reference, if only as an example of how to exploit personal and family case histories.) Both authors know too much about the European peasantry to make a mistake of this kind.

They never deal with their subjects clinically, because they are compassionate. But often they do try to bully them, to regiment them. Worse, they often seem to be out to bully and regiment events. They are constantly endeavouring to establish rules, albeit county ones. The Kentish game is played this way : arson first, smashing afterwards. In Wiltshire, the game is different. There seems to have been a fairly general, though remarkably vague, appeal back to a Kentish precedent, there are threats about "men coming out of Kent"; but one hears them, be it noted, in Berkshire, in Buckinghamshire, in Wiltshire, in Oxfordshire, in Dorset, in Gloucestershire, in Suffolk, not in Sussex and Surrey and Hampshire. In the latter counties, people would know that men did *not* come out of Kent; such references are the empty threats and the characteristic mythology of primitive rural unrest, and perhaps also a folk memory of 1381. The "men of Kent" are the "strangers" of the French eighteenth-century provincial disturbance, and "strangers" become more distinctively "strange" the farther away they come from.

The authors, too, as we have noticed, make much of the importance of border places, though, in the minute patchwork of England's "coloured counties", these certainly do not have enormous significance. The Thames and the Severn do not divide a world, a way of life and a mentality. And one is never far from any county border, once rioting has spread east to Goudhurst, Cranbrook and the Tunbridge Wells area, so that news, example and the resultant action are at all times likely to spill over. For the "Swing" men were not voters, and it is hinted that in the larger villages many of them, especially the artisans, may have been newcomers (one would like to know more about this), and so they were not necessarily given to think either in village or in county terms. Some, no doubt, had been serving in the army, fifteen or twenty years previously.

They make allowance for the elements of accident, of personality, particularly with reference to the exceptional unpopularity of a certain named overseer of the poor and of some great noble landlord (though, on the whole, the great land-owning families got off very lightly; perhaps they were too elevated to come into the spectrum of the poor man's anger and despair). But the local leaders of "Swing" themselves hardly emerge at all as personalities, and we have only rare examples of their reported speech (there is an eloquent example from Wiltshire: "We don't want to do any mischief, but we want that poor children when they go to bed should have a belly full of tatoes instead of crying with half a belly full").

London hardly figures at all in this account, because the "movement" did not even lap its fringes; the authors suggest, as an explanation for this, that much of the population of Middlesex, Surrey and South Essex was employed in market gardening for the provisioning of the capital and that they did not thus belong to the type of seasonal labourer (harvest worker, hop-picker) that formed the base of "Swing". But is not the seasonal labourer the most likely to seek partial winter employment in the metropolis?

Kent above all does not get its due. For here it all began. Why Kent? There are tentative suggestions but some or all could be applied to other southern counties of wheat or hops. And why, in Kent, Lower Hardres? For the business in Orpington, Oxted, Ide Hill and Sevenoaks does not seem very important, apart from the date—it started first (but, then, does arson ever start, or ever finish?). There must be more to it than just saying that it all started in Kent. The authors do mention contacts with France, the July Revolution, smuggling, law-evasion, desertion, and so on. And soldiers, especially Irish ones, were presumably particularly unloved in a county that, over the centuries, had so often been subjected to their passage out and their passage in—the latter, no doubt, much worse. There were more than milestones on the Dover Road.

Even in the present account, with its insistence on "the General Rising", "the Last Labourers' Revolt", and so on, one is constantly amazed at the naturally deferential attitudes of most of the "Swing" men, when confronted with the authorities: magistrates, landowners, farmers, even the parson. They temporarily abandon their inbred deference only when meting out some conspicuous, but non-violent, humiliation on an unpopular overseer of the poor. These are not rural egalitarians, they accept the established order of village society and their expectations are fantastically minimal: a very slightly better wage, the destruction of the machines, the opportunity to work while preserving their dignity. They go about their task of riot politely, dressed according to many eyewitnesses' accounts in their best clothes, seldom using threatening language. Nothing could be more unlike an Irish rising; it is the revolt of the proud, conscious of their own rights and aware that they are not doing anything that their fathers would not have done. It is a strange sort of rising that goes to the tune of "May it please you, Sir", and that strictly avoids any form of physical violence against persons (only one person was killed in the whole affair, and he a rioter, by the yeomanry).

This again is not to lessen its importance, at least in the contemporary and local framework. Perhaps this was the English way of rioting; it certainly caused an enormous shock to the higher authorities, no doubt long confident in the ox-like subservience of the dumb, semi-literate "Hodge". It was not the tone of the disorders that alarmed, so much as the awareness that the labourers appeared to be able to organise protest far beyond the limits of the parish, on something like a national scale.

The authors tend, in another way too, to give a somewhat inflated view of the impact and, above all, of the diversity and of the multiplicity of the disorders—this applies particularly to the statistical tables with which they so liberally sprinkle both their text and their footnotes—by laying down distinctions that are over-sophisticated between the various forms of "Swing" action. In this, they have let the lawyers and the police dictate to them their cue. A Kentish labourer, on setting fire to a rick at Oxted, is unlikely to say to himself: "I am now about to commit a felony, an act of incendiarism, a trespass, an offence against the 1827 Act." No more will a Suffolk ploughman, when he lights a barn, accompany his gesture with the rigmarole: "I am now committing a capital offence, am infringing the 1828 Act, am committing a pillage and a breaking-in." This is the way the forces of repression counted, not the poor rioters, who, as they are quoted on a number of occasions, believed that "we mean no mischief", knew nothing of the infinite variety of legal definitions, and thought in any case that they were acting in their own rights, at least when they held village meetings, or walked out of church, smoking their pipes in the church-yard, until their wage demands had been met (there was something symbolic, too, about this pipe-smoking, like the emblems, the flags, and the smart appearance).

The immediate cause of the protest—the threshing-machine—seems, at the end, almost irrelevant, for, as far as one can gather from this account, no one wanted the wretched things; the farmers were unenthusiastic about a device whose main effect was to drive a large proportion of the seasonal labourers on to the parish, many justices openly favoured their withdrawal and were not unsympathetic to their destruction. Only the manufacturers—the Ipswich firm of Ransome's above all —cannot have been very happy about a "movement" which put the threshing-machine out of use for a generation at least. In so far as

"Swing" was about the introduction of the machines—recent in East Kent—then it was indeed a victory, but a victory so many others were quite prepared to concede to the wretched, half-starved, morally humiliated rural labourer, while denying him everything else.

Perhaps the greatest merit in thus choosing "Swing" as the subject of a monograph is that it reveals, at least through the distorting lens of repression, a whole layer of English society that had previously been hidden from historical awareness. This is the advantage of defeated protest movements, at least to the historian. But, as is the case with all such movements that go wrong—and most do—our historians must be the police, the magistrates, the parsons, the people in high places. And therefore, knowing so little about the men—even about the leaders—one cannot expect to discover much about the inner motivations of the "movement". It is not even sure that those who were deported and who thus acquired a historical identity, *were* the leaders; all we know is that they were singled out from the general mass of several thousand brought to trial, for reasons best known to the repressive authorities.

Is this then *all* that one can go on? Is there no way of discovering what they said to the examining magistrates? And is there no trace of what the magistrates, the rectors, the Government informers, the squires, said about *them*? For if these had been truly, if momentarily, frightened, one would expect them—especially the parsons—to put names and faces to their fright. Vengeance, especially class vengeance, is verbose, thick with adjectives and abundant in moral judgments: that such a one was a drunkard, a ne'er-do-well, such another insolent, beat his wife, neglected his children, putting them out naked while he stood in the beerhouse, did not know his place, was a deserter, a criminal, a poacher, a smuggler, a horse thief, was rootless, had come but recently God knows from where, had no ancestral bones in the village graveyard, practised strange, egalitarian, undeferential religions, had his head befuddled with apocalyptic nonsense, used bad words and dreamed, as well as spoke, of blood. For this is the usual stock-in-trade of the repressive vocabulary, when addressed to the lower orders, at any time in the early nineteenth century. The literature of repression, one feels, is far from having been exhausted by the present authors. And one is often driven almost desperate by the blank faces of these desperate men, by their anonymity, by the mystery of their sudden involvement in unprecedented action. There is already a little—but so little—to go on in their strange spelling, in their few, crude, slogans.

The answers—some of them at least—are surely to be found in Kent. Let the historian follow Dickens to the Medway Towns, to the Thames Estuary, to the hulks, to the house on the cliff, and to those communities in London, south of the river, where Kentish villages were re-created, all the more self-conscious for having been transplanted. Let him seek, too, the other side of the Estuary, the area where the Essex labourer runs into the Essex porter or artisan, where London and East Anglia overlap. Let him seek in the letters of fashionable people, taking the waters in a developing Tunbridge Wells—Holy Trinity had been built about ten years before "Swing"—for an event that brought the cavalry to the Pantiles would not easily pass unnoticed in letters and memoirs. Even Jane Austen was aware, a decade or so before, of the dragoon and hussar officers, because they came to hunt balls. And some of the sisters of "Hodge" must have gone into service in Folkstone, Tunbridge Wells, Ramsgate and Deal (sea-bathing had begun).

What, too, of village memory? Would the men of Deptford have any historical awareness? How did "Hodge", young "Hodge", in conversation with his father, or his grandfather, envisage the Kentish past? And if "Hodge", as it appears in the present study, tended to be an *enfant du siècle*, born about the turn of the century, might not his father or his uncle have served in the army or, in the Chatham area, been pressed into the navy?

There are frequent references throughout *Captain Swing* to the radicalism of rural shoemakers, the authors even suggesting that a village that possessed more than one artisan in that trade would be likely to be that much more radical. Beerhouse keepers—the poor man's publican —are likewise seen as radical forces, a reasonable assumption, for a publican will generally take on the political colouring of the majority of his clientèle, as can be well observed in eighteenth-century France; on occasions, he may also create it. But, while one is ready to accept the radicalism of village shoemakers, one would like to know more about its causes. There are also remarks, almost *en passant*, about certain localities, both towns and large villages, as "well-known radical centres" (Lewes, Rye, Maidstone, Battle, Horsham, Robertsbridge, as well as Banbury and Ipswich are included in this category). Perhaps they were, as the authors say so; but one would like to know more.

Yet the people who would matter most in rural riot and protest—not so much in its preparation, for here we may accept the importance of the shoemaker and the beerhouse keeper as political educationists of the labourers and as links with the towns—would be the people in the know, above all the blacksmith, so much in the secret of concealed rural wealth and well aware of the size and content of the farmer's establishment : how many hands living in, where they slept, how many dogs, how much cash kept behind the fireplace, how many bushels stored away, how much food and drink in the larder and cellar—information valuable to any form of collective protest and bargaining that would consist in payments, in money and in kind, to the participants.

Dr Hobsbawm and Professor Rudé have done what they set out to do : to investigate the total spread of "Swing", to apply to their investigation the techniques and experience of recent work on primitive forms of protest and of rural disorders (both are admirably qualified in this respect), to place "Swing" in its historical context and to discover why a movement of rural protest, unprecedented at least in its scale and its rapidity, should have occurred in the second half of 1830, and, finally, to examine the composition of the movement and to suggest the motives that sent its participants on the road that, for some, was to end in the prison hulks and Australia. They are more concerned with the various forms that the movement took than with individual commitment to riot and with the exploration of a lost mentality. Their rioters—a few of them—have names, trades, villages, but that is all.

Likewise, in a general study that includes some 500 place names, it was not possible to explore any single village community in depth—and how to know which to choose before thus mapping out the general picture of the movement?—and they had to make do with such general distinctions as that between large and small villages, and such general indications as corn, hops or pasture, the presence of paper or clothing mills, the proximity of markets, the state of communications, the basic division of England between the higher agricultural wages of the North and the areas of relatively low wages south of Nottingham. Within these terms—precisely stated at the outset—they have produced a work of considerable importance, stimulating and exciting to read.

One may not be entirely convinced by all their claims for "the General Rising", the "Last Labourers' Revolt", the "movement". How historians, and not only popular ones, and examiners, *love* this word "movement", and how unaware of their participation in such a conveniently well-organised, well-defined team are most of those contemporaries, thus mobilised at the time. Historians should beware of the word; or they might emulate the anonymous author of a counter-revolutionary pamphlet of 1790. The pamphlet takes the form of an imaginary conversation between an unnamed questioner and a Palais-Royal prostitute given the evocative name of Rose Cutendre. "Depuis quand," he asks her, "êtes-vous citoyenne *active*?" To which she replies, from the age of fourteen. The next question is "Aimez-vous le *mouvement*?" "Oui, citoyen, j'aime *beaucoup* le mouvement." Rose at least, unlike many historians, knew what movement she was talking about. And one remains unconvinced by the way in which so many of the authors' tests, both positive and negative, come out right. These are minor faults of over-exposition; they may have tried to prove too much. What is even more impressive is that, unlike some recent American work on French rural revolt, they have succeeded in completely avoiding the hideous and meaningless jargon of sociology. This is a literate book, about barely literate people, for literate readers.

It is, in fact, a tribute to the stimulus offered by *Captain Swing* and to the fascinating glimpses afforded, through doors pushed ajar, of the dreadful realities of rural life, that, on putting it down, the reader wants to know *more*, his curiosity awakened by its intelligent and imaginative speculations. The greatest compliment that could be paid to the authors is that others should take up where they have left off; and there is every reason to expect that they will, now that the ground has been so carefully surveyed and so minutely mapped out. The facts, the frame, the statistics and many possible lines of closer approach are to be found in this important pioneering book. And now to the study of Lower Hardres. The many excellent historians of Kent cannot fail to respond to such an inviting challenge.

17

The festival of the Commune*

There are two possible approaches to the history of the Commune. The one would involve a detailed study—and the material exists at Vincennes —of the social origins, occupations, ages and places of birth of the Communards who were tried by courts martial, as well as of the much more difficult problem of the relations between the Paris Commune and the provinces and of the efforts of certain provincial authorities to form a *tiers-parti* with the intention of acting as an intermediary between Paris and Versailles and of preventing the irreparable : a military confrontation between Fédérés and Versaillais. The historian would then seek to proceed further, possibly with the use of literary material, memoirs and cross-examinations, so as to investigate the motivations that induced commitment to the Communard side, and he should likewise attempt to view the worsening situation as it may have appeared from Versailles, as well as from Paris. In short, apart from composition and personnel, there are three angles from which to approach the conflict: Paris, the provinces and Versailles.

Most of the work undertaken by historians up to the present has been concerned primarily with Paris. This is understandable in view of the fact that Paris was to be the principal loser, but it is none the less an incomplete and distorted view of a situation involving more than two groups, and, even in Paris, the *maires* of the twenty *arrondissements*, as well as the Masonic Lodges, attempted to act as intermediaries in order to bring to an end a civil war situation. Finally, in a negative

* The books reviewed are Edith Thomas, *Louise Michel*, Paris 1971; Stewart Edwards, *The Paris Commune 1871*, London 1971; Jeanne Gaillard, *Communes de Province, Commune de Paris 1870–1871*, Paris 1971; Henri Guillemin, *L'Avènement de M. Thiers et réfléxions sur la Commune*, Paris 1971; Susan Lambert, *The Franco-Prussian War and the Commune in Caricature 1870–71*, London (Victoria and Albert Museum) 1971; Alistair Horne, *The Terrible Year*, London 1971; Royden Harrison (ed.), *The English Defence of the Commune*, London 1971; Karl Marx, *The Paris Commune 1871*, edited by Christopher Hitchens, London 1971; Karl Marx and Frederick Engels, *On the Paris Commune*, London 1971; *Leon Trotsky on the Paris Commune*, London 1971; Maxime Vuillaume, *Mes Cahiers rouges au temps de la Commune*, Paris 1971; and Michael Bakunin, *The Paris Commune and the Idea of the State*, translated by Geoff Charlton and edited by Nicolas Walter, London 1971.

sense, there would be little profit in examining further the actual legislation carried out by the Commune, once it began acting, albeit unwillingly,
as a sovereign government, for this has already been done time and again.

The other approach might be described as invocative rather than
historical. The Commune is invoked to illustrate the development—and
the rightness—of a certain form of political and theoretical commitment,
generally to the exclusion of all others. It is a religious exercise as much
as one of self-justification; and, in most cases, it takes no account of the
Communards themselves—they are in any case all dead, so that they
can be made to witness for whatever one likes. The emphasis is now on
the Commune, rather than on individual Communards, on orthodoxy
and unanimity rather than on incoherence and confusion. Most forms
of left-wing, or so-called left-wing, thought in the course of the past
eighty years have claimed the Commune as their point of departure.
La Commune est à nous has been a slogan to be heard, yearly, at the
Murs des Fédérés, in the mouths of adherents of various political parties
and groups all claiming to belong to the left. All this has nothing whatever to do with history.

Centenaries, like international conferences of historians, rarely afford
a stimulus to serious historical research. Both are, by the nature of
things, rush jobs. There is little time for preparation, and even less for
serious discussion; and a fixed time schedule takes no account of the
problems created, for the researcher, by an over-abundance of entirely
unexplored material. So the congressists and the participants in centenary
celebrations are likely to fall back on old, well-worn themes.

The centenary of the Paris Commune has been no exception in this
respect. A colloquium held at the University of Sussex dealt, at some
length, with the Myth of the Commune, with its intellectual origins,
with Babeuf, *babouvisme*, Buonarroti, Marx, Bakunin, the June Days
of 1848, the present-day relevance of the Commune; but the Communards scarcely got a look in. On the last day of the colloquium, it was
suggested that the participants should go into perpetual session, so as
to produce an Instant Revolution. The advantage of this was pointed
out to the cleaners and staff, but the Sussex proletariat opted for Sunday
lunch : a great opportunity was no doubt missed as a result of this lack
of revolutionary awareness. There were exhibitions in Doriot's stronghold, Saint-Denis, in Brussels, at the Victoria and Albert Museum : a
conference held in Paris was dominated by a Soviet delegation who
arrived with the ashes of a Communard, an argument of greater weight,
in the prevailing atmosphere of *pietas*, than any amount of patient
historical analysis of new material.

The French Government was severely criticised, in some circles, for
not having organised an official commemoration of an event that resulted
in the destruction of large areas of its capital, in the deaths of some

30,000 Parisians, in the deportation of as many more, and in bitter memories dividing Paris from the provinces, and especially from the west. Silence would, in fact, seem to have been the most sensible course. No one to the right appeared to wish to organise an official commemoration of M. Thiers. It was easy enough for other countries to organise something; they were, after all, evoking someone else's civil war and were celebrating other people's dead. There was something Hemingway-esque in these rather ghoulish proceedings.

Of the spate of published works, three are worth mentioning in some detail. The late Edith Thomas, who died in 1970, had completed her biography of Louise Michel, her third book related to the history of the Commune, following *Les Pétroleuses* and her biography of Louis Rossel. The present work adds nothing to what she had previously written, so far as the Commune is concerned, save further to confirm the impression that Louise was an impossible creature, totally devoid of literary talent, bloodthirsty, provocative, hysterical, boring, repetitive, a *marchande de cadavres* who exulted in the invocation of her dead companions (she never gave a thought to dead gendarmes, sailors or soldiers), and who spent the last fifteen years of her life parading her mourning from one end of France to another—a sort of revolutionary Chaix (she must have known every branch line then in existence)—like an ageing actress running desperately against the tide of forgetfulness and forgiveness. She was no doubt, as Mlle Thomas so often reminds her readers, a generous and saintly person, ever ready to come to the rescue of the poor and the humiliated and to fill her flat with stray animals. And there can be no doubt about her courage. But what, in the end, did all this febrile activity amount to, other than, poor thing, to make her appear increasingly ridiculous and *dépassée*?

One cannot escape the impression that Louise had completely identified with the Commune and that her necrophiliac peregrinations through a remarkably tolerant bourgeois Republic—she was only arrested twice; perhaps the moderation of the repressive authorities in the face of her daily and strident provocations to revolt represents the true measure of her lack of relevance—were a desperate attempt to assert her own self-importance. She had taken a spectacular part in the Commune and she had been deported to New Caledonia. But that was all she had ever done. She was not going to let anyone forget it. She was a hopeless novelist, a dreadful poet, an unsuccessful schoolteacher, and an utterly confused politician (for instance, she refused to come out in favour of Dreyfus). She was no doubt attached to her completely apolitical mother, but, at the same time, she did everything possible to distress and alarm her and later exploited her mother's prolonged ill-health as a form of blackmail on the police and judicial authorities: "le coup de la vieille maman." The authorities who, even Mlle Thomas admits, were quite remarkably patient with her, allowed her out of prison to visit her mother regularly, and eventually let her out on parole during her mother's last illness.

More than half the book is given up to the sad and dreary chronicle of her endless public appearances. One's general impression is that, apart from being a bore, she was half mad—especially to judge from the indecent hullabaloo she kicked up at the time of her mother's death—and that the right place for her would have been in Charenton. In fact she seems to have been a *dévote manquée*; in her childhood she had been ardently mystic—a nineteenth-century Joan of Arc Mark II (the subject of another of Mlle Thomas's biographies). She died in a hotel in Marseille in January 1905 on the day the Tsar's police shot down the demonstrators led by Gapon—and not, as Alistair Horne states in his picture book, in London after the 1905 Revolution, which she thus just missed. Perhaps the best comment on Louise is one that can only be flattering to English good sense. In January 1883, on one of her frequent visits to London, where she spent a great deal of time in the 1880s, she is billed to give a lecture at the Steinway Hall, on the subject of the imprisoned Lyon anarchists. "Elle n'a soulevé finalement ni indignation, ni enthousiasme, ni curiosité et elle reprend le bateau plus tôt qu'il n'était prévu." Good for us!

Apart from Louise herself—and we are heartily sick of her before we are even halfway through this long book—there are occasional points of interest brought out from Mlle Thomas's considerable research in military records. Thus, at the time of the *canaque* revolt in New Caledonia, in 1878, when Louise took the part of that oppressed race (one must allow her credit where it is due), most of her fellow deportees reacted like Poor Whites and some of them were given arms by the colonial authorities.

Stewart Edwards has written a workmanlike and very readable account of events from September 1870 to May Week 1871. He is particularly interesting, in his introductory chapters, on the long tradition of "communalism" both in Paris and in other large towns, though he might have given even greater depth to his argument by taking it back to the period of the autumn and winter of 1793, when "municipalism", especially in the Midi, was allowed, for a time, in the absence of any positive policies from Paris, a comparatively free reign. Both the de-Christianisation movement of 1793 and the Counter-Terror of 1795–1802 were manifestations of extreme forms of decentralisation; and, so far as Paris was concerned, the sense of lost liberties would go back to the Ligue, perhaps even further.

During the First Revolution, there were a few brief exercises in direct popular government, but these were soon checked, and the so-called *sans-culotte* movement, while intensely "communalist", was never entirely autonomous. Any attempt by Paris to assert itself, in 1814 and 1815, was checked by the wisdom of the provisional government in calling in the Allies and renouncing military resistance. (A foreign occupation is a small price to pay for the avoidance of a civil war.) The June Days were the most recent assertion of Parisian autonomy. Under the Second Empire, the reality of government consisted of the gendarmes, the Prefect of Police, and informers. It was characteristic that Parisians were given no say at all in the plans carried out for—or rather against—their city by Haussmann. The main effect of the latter's demolitions was greatly to increase the over-crowding in the East-Central *arrondissements*, while in the course of the twenty years between the coup d'état and 1870, the population increased from 1,053,262 to 1,851,792. Of this last figure, 1,072,873 were not Paris-born. Twelve per cent of the population was totally illiterate, more than 50 per cent were only nominally literate, while casual labourers represented 15 per cent of the total population, the building trade accounting for a further 16 per cent. Twenty-one per cent of those arrested after the Commune had had previous convictions. Here, surely, are all the elements of Louis Chevalier's "classes dangereuses"; and it is difficult to follow Dr Edwards when he prefers the interpretation put forward by the statistical sociologist, Charles Tilly. But it would be imprudent to analyse the composition of the Commune primarily in terms of class; as Dr Edwards states, there was a considerable *petit-bourgeois* element, especially in the National Guard, that is, where it mattered; and, as he also states, most of the work on the subject of composition is still to be completed.

Dr Edwards is sometimes over-anxious to attribute to the Communards revolutionary aims and measures. This is perhaps the only time when he himself falls victim to the Myth that has always prevented a clear assessment of the achievements of the Commune. The measures carried out by the various ephemeral bodies that claimed to exercise authority, successively or even concurrently, were only those attributable to any wartime siege economy. As Dr Edwards himself remarks it was not what the Commune *did* that mattered—and in fact it did remarkably little save talk—the amazing thing was the mere fact of its existence.

Reading his book, one is struck above all by the mediocrity of the Communards. With the possible exception of Delescluze, there was not an able man among them; and Delescluze had been involved in 1848, in the ludicrous invasion of Belgium. Pyat was a cheap blusterer, Vallès an embittered *pion*. A number of others were restless *déclassés*—there was a surprising number of sons of wealthy men—while, among the rank and file, alcoholism seems to have taken the place of any more coherent motivation. If a medical analysis of composition were possible—which clearly it is not— it is likely that among these *enragés*, these *grands exaspérés*, there would be revealed a high percentage of people in the last stages of tuberculosis, especially from the East-Central *arrondissements*.

They were, above all, *des candides*. Never can leadership of a political movement have been so naive, so incoherent, and so incompetent. From the start, they seem to have had no control over events, they did not know where they were going, stumbling into one situation after another, including a civil war that they had not expected. What they had apparently expected was that urban France would eventually follow, while Versailles sat back and gave them time to decide upon a form of government (which they never did, though power was probably more effectively exercised by the Central Committee of the National Guard than by any of the other ephemeral authorities that coexisted with it). It was a curiously confused situation, for, while preaching and practising "communalism" and all the most extreme forms of decentralisation (even, and disastrously, in military organisation and in the conduct, after April, of the war), many of the leaders were sufficiently set in Parisian arrogance to believe that a Paris revolution would be rapidly emulated in the other large cities.

What makes the whole conflict so intensely tragic is this disparity of aims and intentions between the two principal contestants (for, as we shall see, there was, at all times, a *tiers-parti*, important especially in the provinces). For Thiers knew all the time what *he* wanted and how he would obtain it. It seems almost outrageous that such confused and woolly dolts, such generous and compulsive chatterboxes should have met with such terrible retribution. The *semaine de mai* is quite out of proportion with anything that preceded it; it is on a different plane altogether, like some appalling level-crossing accident that occurs at the end of a school outing to the seaside. Most of the leaders, the horrible Rigault excepted, were innocents who were not built to the scale of such tragic events. Perhaps this is generally the case with revolutionary martyrs who only achieve something by their death. Unfortunately, the enormity of their fate means that they are still with us, no doubt to mislead another generation into the meaningless paths of violence. At least the Communards had not gone out to seek violence. The barricades were purely defensive and represented a gesture of despair.

Francis Ambrière, in an autobiographical novel, has described the Occupation years as *Les Grandes Vacances*. They were indeed both long and unexpected ones, placing many Parisians, for instance, perhaps for the first time, in Lyon, in Toulouse or in Marseille—no bad thing in itself, since, for a time, it partly broke down the rigid cultural centralisation of the French intellectual. Dr Edwards, on a number of occasions, describes the Commune as a permanent *fête*, a people's festival, a long-drawn-out fair. Perhaps this is his greatest contribution to the debate about the nature, aims and achievements of the Paris Commune. For it was above all a collective holiday—even serving in the National Guard, especially in a wine-shop or café, was a holiday—a break in the normal course of time (which would habitually be marked, for the poor, by the desperate calendar of the rent, of bills overdue, of the Mont-de-Piété—a clockwork to which the Commune brought a temporary stoppage—this too would bring an air of holiday to most Parisians).

We hear that, in 1830, some of the revolutionaries shot at all the public clocks that came into sight, as if to emphasise this point. In 1871, they reverted, for quite different reasons—it was hardly as Dr Edwards describes it, "a leap forward"—to the Year 79, as if to catch up with an insistent past. The Commune certainly lived on a new and packed time scale, even more rapid than that of the First Revolution, in which every hour counted and in which the night would be devoted to guard duties, drinking, discussion, random love-making, walking in the warm, spring-like streets. (It might be said that, in the Commune, the inhabitants of north-eastern Paris rediscovered their own city, from which many of them had been expelled by Haussmann, returning with a proprietary air, to the ancient city centre of the Ier, the IIIe and the IVe.) It was, too, the sort of unbelievable period in which strangers speak to one another, in the street or in public places, in which all doors are opened—including those of the Tuileries—and in which fraternity, from being a concept, becomes a physical, palpable reality. In much of its course, the Commune represented a collective explosion of joy—giving, for instance, to that tiresome feminist, Louise Michel, an intense sense of purpose, participation and love—as well as a sudden awareness of a group identity. Such occasions are so rare that they are remembered and cherished by those who have experienced them to the end of a lifetime. The Commune was never more beautiful, more formidable, than in retrospect. "La Commune n'est pas morte" is a tender, as well as a proud, song, nor would it ever be dead in the hearts of those who had participated and had survived. For had they not stumbled, during those crowded weeks, however unwittingly, into a naive, secular Garden of Eden from which all evil and cruelty would be expelled, had not their vision been lit by a sort of tuppenny-coloured imagery, that of *la Sociale* of the 1848 prints?

The ambience of the Commune is more important, more revealing, than its confused narrative and its disputable message. It was, on the whole, a manifestation of collective generosity and hope. Later, as a result of pressure from outside, it blighted, hope died, the awful reality of middle-class retribution began to impinge on a startled candour, while the sky, hitherto so clear and spring-like, rained down fire and ash. That was the end of the holiday—and of so much else. Those who had taken part in the carnival, who had marched behind the bright red flags, were, in a matter of hours, staring with their dead eyes from open coffins, in crumpled clothing rumpled up towards the shoulders, clinging to round wreaths like the tyres on M. Hulot's car. This is not to sentimentalise about either the Commune or the Communards—there has been far too much of that—but the contrast between the ambience of the Commune, during its existence, and its manner of ending is so great as to be almost unbearable.

A *fête*, a festival, perhaps, but certainly *not* a revolution. For a fair cannot last indefinitely; it is as much an illusion as the antics of a clown at the circus, and there can indeed be no "sudden leap forward" into the stage sets of a New Jerusalem, merely by willing it. At some stage the normal pattern of work and leisure must be resumed, the *poinçon-neur* will be back making his little round holes in Métro tickets, while, perhaps, the lavatory attendant will never have left her underground post. Let us then not read too much into what Dr Edwards describes, over-optimistically, as "the active conquest of urban time and space; a restructuring of the city". There was indeed, after May, a great deal more of "urban space". For once, the historian has allowed himself to be influenced by the stupid jargon of May 1968. A more mundane, but more accurate description comes from the correspondent of *The Times*, on the first day of the Commune: it all had, he said; "a most strange and incomprehensible aspect to one not brought up to make barricades". The best that one can say of the Commune is that it was a tragic irrelevance, hopeless from the start, yet basically well-intentioned, the brief spring of a Paris attempting to break away from the continuity of administrative subjection.

So much for Dr Edwards's intelligent and valuable book. It is a pity, however, that he has taken so little care with place-names as to produce "Sainte-Roche" (for Saint-Roch), "La Gaillotière" (for La Guillotière), "Buttes de Chaumont" (for Buttes-Chaumont), "rue Tournon" (for rue de Tournon). He uses "depose" in the sense of "déposer" and translates "sage" as "wise" when, in the context, it means "well-behaved". When he refers to "the language of the Year III", he means that of the Year II.

Of the haemorrhage of books and collections induced by the centenary —and by the expectations of publishers and editors—the little study by Jeanne Gaillard, *Communes de province, Commune de Paris 1870–1*, in the series "Questions d'histoire", is much the most original, and certainly the most valuable for anyone wishing to undertake the immense amount of archival research still needed if we are to acquire a clear understanding either of the Commune or, above all, of the Communards (it is a surprising fact, that, despite the incentive given to Commune studies by the centenary, only Dr Edwards and Mlle Thomas, of all the authors listed above, have actually set foot in the French War Records).

Mlle Gaillard destroys a number of previously accepted generalisa-tions: the isolation of Paris (in fact, save during May Week, the trains continued to run between the capital and the provinces, people came and went without much difficulty, and even the outgoing mail was posted from Saint-Denis); urbanisation as a phenomenon strictly Parisian (Marseille, Lyon, Toulouse, Lille and Rouen had had even more dramatic population increases in the previous twenty years); the priority of the Parisian example both in chronology and in inspiration (the provincial "communalist" movement had got under way, in the south-east, during the winter of 1870 and had already lost its momentum by the beginning of 1871); the importance of the Breton *mobiles* in the forces of repression (a number of Breton peasants had in fact deserted), the conflict seen purely in terms of Town versus Country; and, finally, an interpretation in terms of the direct confrontation between two sides (one of the main purposes of her very suggestive little book is to illustrate the importance of the *tiers-parti*, both in Paris and, above all, in the provinces).

Mlle Gaillard also reveals, certainly for the first time, the extent, the originality and the importance in national terms—even if, ultimately, Thiers, having played along with it, could afford to neglect it—of the "communalism" of Lyon and the south-east, as well as the moderation both of the National Guards and of the municipal leaders in this part of the world. Apart from insistence on their municipal liberties, their main concern was to avoid civil war and, when it broke out between Paris and Versailles, to limit its spread and to act as intermediaries between the combatants, in an effort to preserve regionalism and to check royalism and a centralising reaction. This was, in other words, a radical, rather than a revolutionary, movement, aimed at attainable achievements, and not at the creation of a perpetual fair. And, with the formation, in Paris, of the Committee of Public Safety, in May, it became increasingly divorced from the capital. Its moderation could often be explained in terms of the social composition of the National Guard; but it owed most to regional loyalties and to an acute concern for local interests.

Mlle Gaillard quotes, in particular, two documents, both of them sharply indicative of the contemporary attitudes—indeed, not only of contemporary attitudes, for one could quote similar chapter and verse for the period of the First Revolution—of two leading towns, Lyon and Rouen. Of the former, M. Bérenger, *député du Rhône*, when examined by the Commission d'Enquête, has this to say—and it might well be written in marble on the Place des Terreaux :

J'ai toujours eu la pensée qu'il y avait à Lyon un esprit spécial, récalcitrant aux influences extérieures, et qui suffisait à lui seul pour expliquer tous les désordres qui s'y sont commis. Ainsi, il est très certain que, dans une très notable partie de cette population lyonnaise, la pensée souvent s'est produite, après l'investissement de Paris, qu'on n'avait pas besoin de Paris et du gouvernement et qu'on pouvait se suffire.

There is something that any historian of France should know and inwardly digest! Aubry, the representative of the Rouen section of the International, merely has this to say : "Rouen est indécis". An indecision, we may be sure, due to sound native prudence and *attentisme*.

The main areas of active "communalism" are those that had been the most active in protesting against the coup d'état : the south-east, to a lesser degree, the south-west, but, this time, without the Yonne, the Nièvre and the Allier—important centres of Republican opposition in 1851. She suggests that their absence in the "communalist" agitation may be explained by the fact that a considerable part of the more active population of these Departments—among the principal providers of Parisian man and womanpower since the eighteenth century—had emigrated to the capital in the course of the intervening twenty years. This is in fact very much the area of the "nouveau fédéralisme populaire" denounced by Saint-Just in December 1793. There had been a Ligue du Midi in 1850; but there had also been a general assembly of seventy-seven Sociétés Populaires du Midi, first in Valence, then in Avignon, then in Marseille, in the autumn of 1793. This tradition of self-help and "municipalism' was thus even older than she suggests. Even so, it is essential for our understanding of this confused period to take our eyes off the bitter conflict between Paris and Versailles and to be reminded that there were three, not just two, sides to the barricade, that, far from being a conflict in black and white, there were very wide areas of grey.

Mlle Gaillard's tentative suggestions will then not appeal to those who remain determined to see the struggle in terms of Paris versus Reaction; and it is not surprising to learn that she has been severely criticised by Marxist historians, determined to assert, at all times, the priority of Paris in revolutionary initiatives and programmes. What she effectively demonstrates is that even the ephemeral Communes that were formed briefly in such places as Lyon, Marseille, Narbonne were quite different from that of Paris, responding to different needs. Here was an original movement, seeking to escape from both the confined and centralist limits of the Department, to embrace the more living unit of the region. Thus she emphasises the proselytising role of both Lyon and Marseille in spreading the "communalist" movement to the smaller towns within their natural political and economic orbit. "Pour le Creusot et Saint-Etienne, l'exemple de Lyon est déterminant. Quant aux insurgés marseillais, ils comptent sur le concours des départements alpins et du Bas-Languedoc." Hence brief "communes" in Forcalquier and Sisteron.

It is reassuring thus to be reminded that, between the twin follies of Commune intransigence, at least from the beginning of May, and the calculated vindictiveness of Versailles, there existed a very wide zone of moderation and common sense, concerned with realisable priorities and with the preservation of a Republic, however moderate, the

existence of which appeared to be threatened by the prolongation of civil
war. This was in fact a radical, parliamentary movement, owing much
to surviving personalities of the Second Republic, as well as one of
"municipalism".

This is, of course, a less exalting picture than that of the elderly
Delescluze standing on the barricades. But it did at least have something
to offer France. What it does not have is the tragic horror of the last
week of the Paris Commune. In all the provincial movements, only about
300 people were killed—still too many—as opposed to a possible 30,000
in Paris. So perhaps it is not surprising that the movement in the south-
east, and in rare places in the south-west, has attracted very little
attention from historians, obsessed with the terrible drama of Paris or with
disgust or delight in the forceful policies of Versailles. It would also be
much more difficult to work on, owing to the diversity of each "muni-
cipalist" experience and to the lack of the court martial records that are
so terrifyingly abundant for Paris.

Even so, one is surprised to learn from this modest and perceptive
book how little is known about the provincial history of France between
September 1870 and May–June 1871, and what enormous areas of
research still remain to be undertaken. Nearly everything up till now has
been written in terms of the influence either of Paris or of Versailles on
the provinces. Mlle Gaillard has chosen a different, more profitable,
angle of vision, and the result is a study that has much more to offer
than any of the other books under review, including that by Dr Edwards.

When the Third Republic was finally stabilised, its political centres
of gravity were to be as much Toulouse, Lyon, Toulon, Marseille and
the diminutive market towns of the south-east and south-west, as the
industrial areas and Paris itself, from 1900 largely a stronghold of the
right. The Third Republic, in its heyday, was no doubt very far from
satisfying the regional aspirations of the "communalist" programme of
1870 and 1871. But, with the emergence of the Radical-Socialists, the
heirs in fact of Mlle Gaillard's radicals of the Second Republic, the
impetus in favour of a socially conservative pacific and secular regime,
closely identified with the defence of local interests, came primarily from
the Midi. In those happy, far-off days, the Deputy mattered; and he
could get things done for his constituents. "La politique du bureau de
tabac " is perhaps a far cry from the "communalism" that thrived on
the difficulties of the Provisional Government; but it went a long way
to meet local interests.

There must have been a great many *maires*, a great many municipal
authorities who, when confronted with the appalling spectacle of the
tribal war between Parisians and soldiers and sailors from the provinces,
after attempting unsuccessfully to act as conciliators—and it is much to
the credit of the Paris Communards that they were prepared to grant

them such a role, in an effort to get themselves out of an impossible situation (they had never wanted to get themselves into the position of constituting a sort of Counter-Government; sovereignty had been increasingly thrust upon them *par la force des choses*)—decided that henceforward they would devote all their energies to the welfare of their electors. One is agreeably surprised at the moderation and good sense of the Toulousains, for instance, both during the First Revolution and in the crisis of 1870–1. Ultimately, Tartarin is a more reassuring person than Raoul Rigault; after all, he had never killed anything, even the animals about which he boasted, and he had, above all the unspectacular merit of surviving and of living to a ripe old age, for the enjoyment of his friends and listeners. It was singularly fortunate for the Midi—or perhaps the Midi deserved it—that, following the appalling experiences of 1871, it did not possess an insistent martyrology to invoke, on suitable occasions, to look back to and to claim as its own. The Midi thus avoided much of the sterile necrophilia that accentuated the divisions of the left at the Paris level.

"Lecteur, sois dûment averti : tu ne trouveras pas, sous ma plume, de l'Histoire, mais du 'pamphlet'." The reader, thus familiarly warned by Henri Guillemin, need go no farther. His book is an arrogant and carping chronicle of abuse, much in the style of *Le Canard* or in that of General de Gaulle's famous trinity, "la rogne, la hargne et la grogne", with the emphasis on the second. He bandies about patriotism, in order to exonerate the Communards and blacken Thiers.

The catalogue put out by the Victoria and Albert is very well produced, with an excellent commentary. Alistair Horne has produced an illustrated history that has the merit of bringing home to those who look at it the full horrors of winter war and civil war. The corpses lie about in the snowy fields, east of Paris, or stare from their open coffins. This is the reality.

The other books under review concern the Myth. They are mostly reprints; their purpose is invocative rather than historical. Royden Harrison has been able to round up a few English defenders of the Commune; they were no doubt worthy people, but so was the correspondent of *The Times*, who condemned so severely the horrors of the repression. Christopher Hitchens has invented a Paris prison with the name of "La Moquette". We should be thankful at least to Dr Edwards and, above all, to Mlle Gaillard, for relief from the old, old, bloody, quarrelsome post-mortem, the corpse-snatching and rival invocations. The poor Communards are dead and gone, and it would have been more charitable, in this year 1971, to have left them in peace, rather than attempt to resurrect them in the defence of present or future violence, killing and intolerance. For, whatever they were—and they were often very silly—they were not revolutionaries.

18

A child's history of Vichy

There have been many histories of Vichy, as many memoirs, *plaidoiries*, indictments, nearly all of them suspect. The one exception, perhaps, is the candid, but no doubt inaccurate, account by Du Moulin de Labarthète, the Marshal's first *chef de cabinet*. Here however, we have an entirely different, original approach to that bizarre period that, like a closed garden seen from a prison window, must always have the added fascination of mystery to most Englishmen. For most of us, save for that prestigious minority who were dropped in France and who survived, the history of the Occupation can never be related to personal experience.

It is a gap we can never fill. Nor is there anything in our own historical past or in our personal experience that will help us in this respect. We do not know what it was like to live in France between 1940 and 1943. A tattered poster, still up in a few Normandy *écoles communales* in the summer of 1944: LE CHEF D'ETAT, MARECHAL DE FRANCE, AUX ENFANTS DES ECOLES, his New Year message, headed by the *francisque*, was the only tantalising and rather pathetic link between what had only recently ended and what we ourselves were witnessing. The poster, and such objects as a letter written in green ink, in a sloping hand, in a language identified as Slovak, found in a Normandy lane and brought in by a zealous child in sabots. It was only a love letter, addressed to a member of one of the German Divisions so recently there. One hoped that the recipient lived to see the girl again, even if he lost the letter. Or perhaps he had thrown it away? No wonder so many English historians have felt the urge to write the history of France during those Years Between, and have then given up the idea.

This time, at least, we are well served. For here is something of Vichy* —its leaders, its personalities, its enemies, its neutrals, its *fastes* and its *ridicules*, its occasional joys, its frequently almost comical juxtapositions, closely observed through the eyes of a child aged six in 1940, aged nine in 1943. They are sharp eyes, and sharp ears too. And, as one might expect from such an exceptionally endowed and well-placed witness, what is best in his short chronicle are the visual impacts. There is an unforgettable description of the arrival of Pierre Laval, in an enormous

* Pascal Jardin, *La Guerre à neuf ans*, Paris 1972.

black, armour-plated car, built for the Queen of England and only used once by her, when she visited Versailles, heralded first by *motards*, then by two black Citroëns, full of armed police, looking like killers (which is no doubt what they were).

Once these have taken up positions on the porch and in the bushes of the garden, the chauffeur opens the door of the "monstre noir de plus de quatre tonnes". Laval and his daughter get out. "Cet Auvergnat de 60 ans a une tête de péon métissé d'asiate, d'où son surnom de don Pedro. Ses yeux légèrement bridés, sa peau jaune attestent que l'invasion mongole est bien venue jusqu'au coeur de la France." There is no mention of the white tie, but the child noticed that Laval was dressed in a well-cut light suit and was wearing black suede boots—it is the sort of thing he would notice, as he is a child of wealthy parents.

There is plenty more for the portrait gallery. Here is the Spanish Ambassador to Vichy France, previously to France—he made a very considerable contribution to the transformation of the one to the other: "Son Excellence Lequerica, gigantesque dindon doré, ventru comme un galion de Charles quint . . . se pâme aux trois quarts d'aise. . . ." The metaphor is pleasing, though it is not that of a child of nine, but of a man of about thirty-six: the visual memory, however, is what gives it body. Then there is the encounter—fortunately, for all concerned, brief —with Abel Bonnard, the Vichy Minister of Education:

> Abel Bonnard était petit, précis et pouvu d'une chevelure blanche et mousseuse. Académicien français, poète du jeudi, ministre par malentendu, il appartenait à cette catégorie d'homosexuels tourmentés qui adorent les femmes et se détestent d'être homme.

Elsewhere, he appears at a reception with his eyes swimming in rimmel. This was the Minister who was entrusted with the reform of the history textbooks, who ordered the destruction of all existing copies of Lefebvre's *89* and the withdrawal of Malet and Isaac.

But undoubtedly the most incisive vignette is that of Mgr. Valerio Valeri, the Papal Nuncio, and a very important personage of the Vichy Court (he was replaced, shortly after the Liberation, by Mgr. Roncalli). "Vers minuit, le nonce apostolique débarqua à son tour. C'était une sorte de prélat à la Fellini, sanglé dans une soutane de soie taillée par Jeanne Lanvin. Il était dans tous ses états à l'idée d'être témoin au mariage de Danielle Darrieux et de Rubirosa." Then there is the scene, on the occasion of the reception given by Pascal Jardin's mother for the première of *L'Eternel Retour*, when Pascal, having called Coco Chanel "vieux poulet déplumé", is given a monumental slap on the face.

The Marshal is briefly displayed, walking in the woods, while he tells a cavalry story; "[il] était en civil et faisait des moulinets très brillants avec sa canne". There is a visit from Emmanuel Berl and his wife Mireille.

M. Jardin tells them of the dismissal by the Vichy Government of two
schoolteachers, Jean-Paul Sartre and Simone de Beauvoir, accused of
having, in their *internat*, allowed boys and girls to sleep together. M.
Berl's comment is : "Il est pourtant dans l'ordre des choses que les garçons
aillent avec les filles. A moins que votre gouvernement ne préfère que les
garçons dorment entre eux et les filles aussi?" Pascal may be in shorts—
and he is displayed on the dust-jacket in an Eton collar—but he really
does write like Saint-Simon.

Pascal Jardin was born in May 1934. His father's family were wealthy
printers from Evreux. His father, at the beginning of the war, was one
of the Directors of the SNCF. It was his task to evacuate the papers of
the railway administration from the rue Saint-Lazare to Deauville. In
January 1941, Jean Jardin was appointed *chef de cabinet* to the Vichy
Finance Minister, Yves Bouthillier; on 1 April 1942, he was transferred
to Robert Gibrat, Minister of Transport, a position he retained for only
three weeks, for on 20 April he became *chef de cabinet* of Pierre Laval,
a position that he held till the end of 1943, when, in order to put him
out of reach of the Gestapo, he was appointed French Minister in Berne.
He was dismissed at the time of the Liberation, and has apparently since
lived mainly in Switzerland.

Through his eyes as a nine-year-old, Pascal describes his father driving
at 150 kilometres an hour, on the empty roads of occupied France,
between Vichy and Paris, or, in the end, from Vichy to the Swiss frontier.
His father is always armed; and, one morning in 1943, Pascal is woken
up by the sound of gunfire. His father is shooting it out, with two
revolvers, from Pascal's bedroom, with a group of *maquisards*. Later,
when Pascal goes to the lycée at Evreux, after the Liberation, his school-
mates taunt him, as the son of a *collabo*; and his in-laws oppose his first
marriage, on similar grounds. During the Occupation, Pascal received
very little formal education, and clearly the period for him was one of
great excitement and enjoyment. Once in Switzerland, he was sent to
an extremely expensive boarding school; in the course of a fight, he
knocked off the glasses of a boy nicknamed "Bobo le Biglard", the future
King of the Belgians. Pascal himself eventually made a career as a film
producer.

La Guerre à neuf ans is not, of course, a work of history. But it has
something to offer that no history book could provide : it is a
témoignage of the intimate *mores* of Vichy, seen from within, through
the eyes of a child. He does not understand the look of horror on his
father's face on seeing Robert Aron, a Jew, temporarily in hiding,
coming down the main staircase, in the presence of Krug von Nidda,
the German Ambassador to Vichy. But he captures the atmosphere of
the parties and the receptions. Whatever happens to France, nothing
can be allowed to disturb the enjoyments and the social calendar of the

Tout-Paris, and the *Tout-Paris* is very much in evidence in his father's house. 1943, as Pascal comments was a splendid year for the French cinema and theatre. One is struck above all by the selfishness and the lack of imagination of these people. They were mostly not so much wicked as amoral. Whatever happened, they had to remain at the centre of things. There is even a certain social exchange between the *Tout-Paris* of the Resistance and that of semi-Collaboration. Some of the leading Vichy personalities are not only amoral, but intensely cruel. Paul Marion tells young Pascal that he should both enjoy and subject women; he himself is a cruel, predatory libertine.

The book ends on a scene of apocalypse. There are disastrous floods in the autumn of 1943. The Allier sweeps all away before its torrential course : "Près de moi, un paysan entasse dans une brouette des livres rares, des billets de banque, des pneus de voiture, un téléphone. La convoitise de tous ces gens est sans borne, sans choix, sans mesure. . . ." A month later, the family, in Jean's black Citroën, are heading like mad for Switzerland, with another black car on their tail. Their pursuers, the Gestapo, are blown up by a Resistance group, on a mountain road in the Jura.

Pascal is an observer. He never judges, makes no comment even on the cowardice of those who were to taunt him at school. He does not find it easy to form an opinion of Laval. His father, whom he admires and sees as a sort of buccaneer, is, however, a stranger to him. He thinks the Hôtel Matignon, when he is told that he is going there with his father, *is* in fact an hotel. He is puzzled by the *huissier*, but plucks up the courage to ask him to take him to the lavatory.

He gets lost in endless corridors, but eventually finds his father in a magnificent office, with six telephones on the Louis XV table. There is a similar dreamlike quality, a sort of innocence, about the whole book. It is as if Alain-Fournier had stumbled into another fairy castle, this one called l'Hôtel du Parc.

M. Jardin had a most unusual childhood. It does not seem to have done him any harm. He is never bitter, but, at thirty-six, still amazed, and very, very alert. Particularly attractive is his little play, acted by himself and his brother, in the family drawing-room, in the presence, among others, of Georges Bonnet. Napoleon wakes up in the Invalides, walks to the Deux-Magots, a friend shows him the telephone, he has a talk with *la dame-pipi*. Bonnet starts talking about Munich, objecting that Napoleon would not have known how to use a telephone. Pascal thinks Bonnet boring and unimaginative.

19

May 1968

This is a very modish book.* The author, who writes in Basic Marxisto-American ("When History Quickens its Pace", "A riot? No sir, it's an insurrection", "They either entered the mainstream or were thrown out, at least temporarily, onto the banks", "The returning man's gamble was the logical sequel to the utter failure of the previous martingale", "It was not all so corny"), with renderings from *Varoomshka* (thump, thump ... "Arise ye damned of the earth" ... bang, bang ... "De Gaulle, murderer" ... whamm, whamm ... "C'est la lutte finale"), is as determined as Jean-Paul Sartre to earn his place in the new monopoly structure of revolutionary youth. He is forty-two, so he may not make it; but he does everything possible to render himself acceptable, even desirable, to the young, self-styled revolutionaries of May 1968. Perhaps he did not even have to try very hard, because, as anyone who ploughs through this turgid, expletive book will soon discover, humourlessness, uncouthness, the rejection of all non-political cultural values, the repeated statement of ponderous self-evidences, total intolerance and the rejection of academic standards of scholarship all come to him without any apparent effort.

It is also rather an unpleasant book. For the author seems genuinely distressed that the student revolt of May 1968 did not degenerate into a blood bath. His main indictment, predictably, is directed against the leadership of the French Communist party, who, out of cowardice, or self-interest, or "reformism", failed to exploit to the full what the author considers to have been a potential "revolutionary situation"—comparable only to the one existing in France in 1944—and led the factory-workers and wage-earners back to work, after negotiating with a government no longer frightened by the prospect of a continuing general strike. They were, it appears, too old, too out of touch with the young (healthy) elements in the factories, who were anxious to see it through, if necessary, to a civil war. As he appears to be totally unaware of any French history prior to 1945, he is not surprisingly unable to understand the reluctance of the French Communist party to jeopardise the CGT and its own

* Daniel Singer, *Prelude to Revolution: France in May 1968*, London 1970.

magnificent organisational, electoral and municipal strength as a parliamentary force on the uncertainties and obvious dangers of "barricade politics".

But at least the reader will be able to draw his own conclusions, despite the author, as to the Party's fundamental good sense and pragmatism, when faced with the prospect of political adventurism, as well as to the utter irresponsibility of most of the smaller groups to the Left—the PSU, always desperate to prove its "revolutionary" aims, the CFDT, apparently prepared for a show-down with the government forces of repression and willing to embark both students and workers on a collision course with the army.

The rest of the book is devoted to an exercise in revolutionary optimism. As the title suggests, May was but a "Prelude to Revolution"; Mr Singer still sees plenty of hope of violence, civil war, subversion, street fighting, university-burning, parliament-burning (though, like those on the extreme right, he feels that the *Assemblée Nationale* is hardly worth even a match), and so on, either in France—his analysis of the vulgarity, mediocrity and pushfulness of Gaullist society is the best thing in the book—or, perhaps, in Italy. (He holds little hope for us or for the Dutch, and not very much for the West Germans.)

This is, then, a statement of hope. The barricades have been merely put off; and asphalting the boulevard Saint-Michel and the rue Gay-Lussac—he makes much of this symbolism—will not keep them down. There will be a replay, perhaps quite soon, and with better results. What exactly these will be is not clear. The author is a revolutionary theorist; and he appears to ignore certain realities of any revolutionary situation that develops into a revolutionary outbreak; the corpses of the victims on both sides. In this respect, May was both remarkably and happily mild. Two policemen were killed, two or three students and two young workers appear to have been victims of random fire; and many students were horribly beaten up by the police, after being taken to detention centres. Mr Singer is on easy ground in insisting on the extreme brutality of the CRS—the French Special Security Forces have few friends, and they are indeed exceedingly unpleasant—but he might have made more of the fact that, in all the gallant struggles with them and with the police—he dwells lovingly on the rapidity and cleverness of the student guerrillas ("revolutionary university commandos", a revealing phrase as to the author's estimate of the purpose of higher education, etc.)—the greatest danger was probably from various toxic gases. A soldier in the British Army—hardly, one feels, a candidate for the author's exclusive club of revolutionary elitists and engaged only in keeping the peace—would be in much greater danger, any night in Belfast, than the well-connected students who went into action shouting, *"CRS SS"*.

There is scarcely a hint, in this book, that universities are in fact about scholarship. For the author, they are merely promising cells for the disruption of civil society. So we are told little of what was wrong with French universities before 1968 : excessive absenteeism on the part of professors (many of whom lived in Paris or the suburbs, wherever they, briefly, taught), pluralism, a total lack of communication between teacher and pupil, *mandarinisme*, overcrowding, the absence of any form of pre-selection (perhaps the greatest evil of all), over-centralisation, bureaucratism, the fossilisation of the syllabus, the tyranny of endless examinations. Nor are we told very much about what happened to French universities *after* May.

There are however some useful hints in a confused narrative. We learn, for instance, that the most militant students, those who knew what a university was for, were those who studied sociology, psychology and politics. Naturally enough, they wanted to destroy their universities, at least as centres of free discussion and academic research. Even more revealing—and ominous—is the role, both as demagogues and as appeasers, of junior members of university staffs, *nontitulaires, chargés de cours, maîtres-assistants* (the CNRS was much to the fore in this respect, composed as it was very largely of those who never had to do any teaching in any case), who used the events of May to destroy or to discredit the old university hierarchy—one could hardly blame them for that—and to get themselves appointed to posts on the permanent staff, without completing their doctorates.

The Revolution might misfire; but at least many unqualified *assistants* were able to acquire permanent places in the universities which they had sought to destroy. One is, too, familiar, with the timidity of some holders of chairs; but there were others who risked physical assault to prevent the burning of libraries or the shouting down of unpopular minorities. In a work of this kind, it would in fact have been useful to be reminded of some of the effects of these much-vaunted "democratic procedures", often with votes taken in open assemblies, in an atmosphere of intimidation. Professor Vidalenc of the University of Rouen, on having his study invaded by "militants", had a heart attack; Professor Chaunu was manhandled by students in Caen. Professor Soboul was regularly interrupted and insulted in the course of the lectures that he was trying to give (about, it is true, an old, real Revolution, an antiquarian subject of no possible relevance).

These are, of course, all of them old, discardable, academic historians. But one must not be too gloomy. French historical scholarship has declined neither in output nor in quality. The Archives are still crowded with *chartistes* and with young, as well as with old, researchers; they even speak to one another. The Sorbonne is not entirely lost, though it is still in chaos. The militants have to some extent been funnelled away into their own anti-universities—an expensive solution—along with their master-servants. The Collège de France and the ENS have probably been able to retain their standards, and many provincial universities seem to have survived as centres of learning. Prospects for history, medicine and law are not too bleak, even if they are for mathematics, philosophy and sociology. Mr Singer has written a cautionary tale that should be read by all who are genuinely interested in higher education, if they have the patience to push on through a style about as elegant as that attributed to Mr Khrushchev.

The author acknowledges his debt both to his father and to Isaac Deutscher. One should always commend filial piety; but it does seem rather hard on Deutscher, who, among his many other accomplishments, could write English. The best account of the student revolt still remains that written by Raymond Aron.

20

Pre-revolutionary Paris

Although his family was of provincial origin—on the paternal side, they came from the *basoche* and the small nobility of Nemours—*l'abbé* Germain Brice could claim to have been Parisian born and bred. He was baptised in the capital about 1653, lived most of his life in the parish of Saint-Sulpice, and, in the context of the *Description**, he might be described as a "sulpico-imperialist", so convinced was he that this was the only quarter of Paris utterly worthy of careful development, strict legislation and the attention of gentlemen; and he died there in 1727, aged seventy-four.

There were nine editions of the *Description*, eight in Brice's lifetime; the ninth was published long after his death, in 1752, by *l'abbé* Pérau and Mariette, who completed the work and brought it up to date, as well as correcting a number of the original author's factual errors. The editor of the latest edition was thus well advised to have chosen this last version. It also has the important advantage of illustrating, almost house by house, street by street and quarter by quarter, the extensive building of town houses undertaken in the first half of the eighteenth century—that is, in the most hopeful and properous period of the *ancien régime* : that which followed the peace of Utrecht and the death of Louis XIV. In this respect, as in so many others, the great divide is the year 1715. In the five years of intense speculation that followed, the building of town houses, both on the part of the nobility, the *gens des finances* and the *parlementaires*, was given an intensive stimulus, while the Regent, by moving the seat of government from Versailles to the Palais-Royal, placed a further premium on the development of the rue Saint-Honoré, of the parish of Saint-Roch, of the faubourg Saint-Honoré and of the rue d'Antin. This set the trend of development westward, on both banks of the Seine, for the rest of the century. But the period of most rapid development was that covered in the ninth edition of the *Description*, between 1715 and 1752 (and the four following years, up to the outbreak of the Seven Years War, in 1756). As in so many other aspects of eighteenth-century life, the Seven Years War represented the other great

* Germain Brice, *Description de la ville de Paris et de tout ce qu'elle contient de plus remarquable*, edited by Pierre Codet, Geneva and Paris 1972.

divide. As Michel Gallet insists, it is from the 1760s rather than the actual accession of the young king, that the *style Louis XVI*, both in domestic architecture and furniture, can be dated. The war slowed up urban development in Paris for perhaps a decade, but there was a new spurt in the 1780s and this was maintained right up to the Revolution.

Apart from the rapid increase in the building of prestige town houses in the first half of the century, what emerges most forcefully from Brice's own account and that of his successors is the truly dramatic extent of the construction of religious houses: monasteries and convents, as well as of a few churches in the same period. Between 1716 and 1752, 22,000 new private houses had been built, 4,000 of them provided with a *porte cochère*, a clear indication of luxury growth. In the single parish of Saint-Germain-des-Près, by 1752 there were thirty-six monasteries and convents, most of them built since 1715. Both these developments filled the good *abbé* and his successors with considerable alarm. The former, on the subject of the luxury growth of the rue d'Antin, was to evoke the fate of Thebes, Memphis and Babylon; "un luxe immodéré" could, he thought, only lead to moral turpitude and to the eventual destruction of the Metropolis. Mariette and Pérau were likewise moral physiocrats; and they further emphasised that the enormous extent of unproductive monastic buildings, all of them surrounded by huge gardens could only increase the misery of the poor and contribute to the development of slum conditions in the surviving older quarters.

Brice, who owed much of his success to his position, from the 1680s, of Guide, Philosopher and Friend to the young Catholic princes of the Rhineland and of the other German states and to his profitable connections with the House of Saxony, wrote his *Description* with a very practical aim in view. It was his task not only to *décrasser*, to smarten up these young noblemen—and his clientele extended to the Lubomirski and the Radziwil families in the East—to teach them the rules of deportment, but also to provide them with competent riding masters; at the time of the Peace of Utrecht, there were seven riding schools in the faubourg Saint-Germain alone; by 1752, there were only three, a contraction perhaps due to the relative decline of the diplomatic position of France in Europe. Brice himself took them on in Divinity and Latin, as well as giving them a smattering of history (very much a smattering, for the earlier editions of the *Description* reveal the *abbé*'s own uncertain knowledge of pre-Valois France).

But his principal concern was to provide his pupils with a walking guide of Paris. It was perhaps the care with which this guide was arranged that accounted for its enormous success throughout the century; there was nothing to rival it till the publication of Mercier's *Le Tableau de Paris*, between 1782 and 1788, and Mercier was in any case more concerned with social observation than topography and the description of buildings and monuments. Brice gave his young German clientele the sort of minute, detailed, rather ponderous guide that the great Baedeker was to provide for their Wilhelminian compatriots in the nineteenth century.

For this purpose, he divided his guide into three main divisions : "la Ville", "l'Université", "la Cité". Within these broad categories, he established a series of walks, in logical sequence, street leading into street, and designed to take half a day each, with a pause for lunch, a meal well earned, if the itinerary had been strictly adhered to, for they were pretty hefty walks. Brice's young princelings must have been in tip-top physical condition : though, in the early eighteenth century, even the fat princes of the House of Hanover could no doubt be expected to cover plenty of ground on foot.

The walks start, logically, with the Louvre, the Tuileries, the quarters of Saint-Germain-l'Auxerrois, Saint-Honoré, the Butte Saint-Roch, already quite a heavy programme. Thence to the Halles, the rues Saint-Denis and Saint-Martin, Saint-Avoie, the rues du Grand-Chantier, Vieille du Temple, Saint-Louis, place Royale and neighbourhood, rue and faubourg Saint-Antoine, l'Arc de Triomphe (later the place du Trône), the château de Vincennes, and back by Reuilly, the Célestins, Quartier Saint-Paul, île Notre-Dame, to the Left Bank, porte Saint-Bernard, Saint-Victor, Jardin Royal, the Gobelins and the faubourg Saint-Marceau, a truly massive loop, the equivalent of a couple of present-day Métro lines. The other walks take in the rest of the Left Bank.

Brice provided a completely comprehensive tour of the city; and he was not afraid of exposing his more delicate princelings to some of the filthiest, most stinking and most over-crowded quarters of Paris; it was not just a *Tournée des Grands Ducs* of the high spots, of the new centres of luxury. Perhaps his walks were also to have a moral purpose.

Brice and his successors are much given to general statistical information which, one can reasonably assume, was highly inaccurate and was based on inspired guesswork on the part of the physiocratic *abbé*, who had no doubt drawn some of his inspiration from Vauban. Thus, in the 1752 edition, the authors, while taking into account the effects both of war and dearth, especially in the first three decades of the century— Brice in particular was well aware, as a churchman and as a specialist of ecclesiastical painting, of the weight of the 1709 famine on Parisian popular memory—come out with the amazing statement that the total population of the city at the time of publication was in the range of 800,000, including 150,000 servants. We do know, with some accuracy, that on the eve of the Revolution Paris counted between 600,000 to 750,000 inhabitants, domestic servants forming about 13 per cent of the total; and we can also surmise that the population of the city had been steadily increasing in the previous twenty years, so that we can place the 1752 figure in the same category of hit-or-miss fantasy which lay behind a great many of Mercier's statements in the 1780s. Mercier, for instance, was never at a loss to quote a figure; 232 middle-class girls a year, he confidently affirms, had abortions in discreet *maisons de santé* in the early 1780s. Of course he has no means of knowing. But he, like the 1752 authors, is writing for a public that likes to be offered firm totals. Equally suspect is the estimation of the horse population of Paris at 100,000 (one horse for eight inhabitants, according to their own reckoning), though they may be nearer the truth when they add that, of this total, 10,000 horses died or were killed each year. Perhaps the relative accuracy of such statistics is unimportant, for what matters is that they should have been accepted by contemporaries, just as it was widely believed by people like Brice that the population was declining in the first half of the century.

Brice is certainly on safer ground when enumerating the number of houses built since the Peace. These were, after all, visible, and we do know that he took a great deal of trouble to see for himself what was going on, just as he displayed a grimly ecclesiastical persistence in attempting to force open recalcitrant doors, in order to scout out the pictures and works of art in the possession of named patrons and connoisseurs. He was not easily turned away, and, when he was, the owner received a vengeful reference in the book, as if he had sinned personally against the *abbé*'s princely cares. We can then accept his successors' figures for the number of street lamps, quarter by quarter. *La lanterne*, at this time, had not acquired its sinister significance of 1789. The record goes to the prosperous rue Saint-Martin, the very quintessence of Paris civility, of "l'esprit parisien", with a total of 415 : next come Saint-Germain-des-Près (396), the Marais (361), the Palais-Royal (341), Saint-Antoine (333). At the other end of the scale, we find Sainte-Opportune (152), Saint-Jacques-de-la-Boucherie (183) and les Halles (142).

Generally speaking, the more recently built quarters, those containing the greatest number of *hôtels*, are better lit. In other words, street lighting was directed primarily towards the defence of property and the safety of the upper classes, while quarters like Sainte-Avoie and the Gravilliers could be left to the twilight of poverty, disease and stench. (The *abbé* and his successors classify both parishes and churches in terms of smell; before 1714, Brice states, the faubourg Saint-Honoré had been neglected for building purposes, owing to the stink of the great sewer and the prevalence of disease, while he displays the enthusiasm of an estate agent in vaunting the fine air of Saint-Germain-des-Près; Saint-Merri, along with some of the other finest Gothic churches still surviving, is dismissed as "dirty, ill-lit and stinking", Brice adding that the Paris churches as a whole are the dirtiest in Europe—but he had never been to Poland or the

Russian Empire.) The figures for street lighting in 1752 are confirmed, for the revolutionary period, in the late General Herlaut's famous thesis, written while on the General Staff during the First World War, on *L'éclairage à Paris pendant la Révolution.*

In his industrious enumeration of pictures, works of art, buildings worthy of attention, church architecture and charitable institutions, Brice comes in the way of a great deal of information which must be of the greatest value to the social historian, even though the *Description* has been used the most extensively by art historians and specialists of the history of architecture. Urban history is a whole and Brice is an integral part of it. Writing both during the terrible crises of the late seventeenth century and, again, shortly after the famine of 1709 and, in his eighth edition, just after the disastrous rains of the spring and summer of 1725, this tutor to the sons of the German nobility proves himself to be acutely aware of the calendar of popular fears as well as of that of disease and recurrent epidemics. The extension of the Hôpital Saint-Louis, he informs us, was provoked by an unprecedented outbreak of scurvy, following the 1709 crisis, and he mentions the two votive pictures of the two de Troys, father and son, kept in the church of Sainte-Geneviève, the one depicting the blessed fall of rain, following a long period of drought in 1709, the other the equally blessed break in the rain clouds in 1725, both attributed to the direct intervention of Sainte-Geneviève. Both pictures were brought out in the annual procession for that specifically Paris saint. However irreligious the eighteenth century may have been at its higher levels, the merciful changes of the season are still the object of popular thanksgiving.

Equally, he notes, on the second Saturday of each month, the cult of the Virgin will bring a record congregation to the image of Notre-Dame-du-Mont-Carmel, in the church of the Carmes. Elsewhere he comments on the subject of the church of le Petit-Saint-Antoine ("obscure et malpropre"), on the disappearance of some of the most feared diseases of the poor. "Cet hôpital" (attached to the church of the same name)

> étoit destiné pour une espèce de maladie épidémique, nommée *le mal de Saint-Antoine,* laquelle a duré en France l'espace de 4 ou 5 siècles, mais qui a cessé comme plusieurs autres incommodités populaires: entre autres *les Ardens, la Ladrerie, le Pic Saint-Fiacre, le mal de Saint Marcon & de Saint-Main,* & plusieurs autres, les quelles ne sont plus connues, que par la lecture des vieux auteurs. . . .

He repeatedly insists on the difficulty of supplying such an immense population with an adequate water supply—a problem of which present-day planners of "le Grand Paris" are only too well aware—and refers to the poor quality of the water at the disposal of the inhabitants of Saint-Antoine. A convinced urbanist himself, he frequently complains of the lack of light and the recurrence of accidents caused by such massive obstructions as the Grand Châtelet and the Bastille ("cette masse énorme de bâtiments gothiques enfermée d'un fossé profond gâte étrangement tout ce quartier, en coupant l'alignement de la rue Saint-Antoine, du côté de la Ville & du côté du Faubourg"). The *abbé* would have been the first to applaud 14 July 1789.

He provides further information on the subject of fairs, popular morality, circulation and retribution. As from 1705, the Foire Saint-Laurent would open on 24 July, going on to Michaelmas. The Foire de Saint-Germain ran from 3 February to Holy Week, much too long in the opinion of Brice, who lived in the area, as it provided a magnet to gambling, fisticuffs, drunkenness and turbulence, especially at dusk. A crime very common among building labourers was the theft of lead off the roofs of buildings in construction, one "roofer" throwing the stolen lead down to his accomplice, waiting in a neighbouring courtyard (*la cour* thus offered advantages other than those of prestige).

Of all the streets in Paris, that of Saint-Jacques and its prolongation in the Faubourg witnessed the heaviest circulation of people, horses and goods, with forty wine-carts a day penetrating Paris from the south. The rue Saint-Antoine, on the other hand, had above all a representational role, in the calendar of the monarchy; it was the route of all state entries, while ambassadors, about to present their credentials, were given a sovereign's escort at its eastern end. The execution of counterfeiters and forgers, the sometimes learned *abbé* notes, often took place near a place called la Croix du Tiroir, rue Saint-Honoré, because it was near the old Mint (the beautiful *monnaie* on the quays was built long after Brice's death).

There was a time and a place for everyone and for everything in this traditionalist world, a world always best described by churchmen. There was a place even for repentant prostitutes with the "communauté de Saint-Valère", rue de Grenelle, founded in 1706; while unemployed female servants were looked after, for periods of three days, at the hôpital Sainte-Catherine; in return, they had to wash and bury the city's daily supply of unclaimed dead. There was a time for singing, and the place was the chapel of the Filles de l'Assomption, renowned for the quality of their voices, who would draw vast congregations during Holy Week.

As a churchman, and with his intimate knowledge of the calendar of saints popular with Parisians, Brice can often reach down to a level of popular *mores* denied to a middle-class observer like Mercier. Indeed, his book offers a striking contrast between the fixity, the immutability of popular habit and fears, and the immense and painful changes being wrought by the ruthless expansion of the city westwards and by the equally heartless demolition of whole quarters in the interests of alignment and to display the newly acquired wealth in "la grande parade" of the *gens des finances* and war speculators. Perhaps nowhere is incipient class conflict more apparent and more bitter than in the beautiful, but ostentatious architecture of the new town houses. Brice himself felt this, when he mused uneasily on the fate of Babylon and Palmyra. It is even more apparent in M. Gallet's book.*

Only an art historian or an architectural expert could form an opinion of Brice's ability as a scholar and a connoisseur. Certainly he had the modesty to accept the criticisms of his contemporaries when he made factual errors. He had a genuine admiration for early church Gothic, though he complained that most of the Paris churches were dark and gloomy. But he had little taste for the later stages of Gothic and regarded Saint-Etienne-du-Mont as an architectural monstrosity. His taste tells us more about his attitudes as a moderate Gallican than as a critic. He much disapproved, for instance, of the ostentation of Jesuit churches, which he contrasted with the primitive simplicity of pure Gallican tradition, and it is quite apparent that his poor opinion of Jesuit architecture would have been extended to the Society itself. He was in this respect very much of an eighteenth-century *abbé,* as he was also in his dislike of monastic extensions and his belief that the contemplative orders served no useful social functions; he did, however, have plenty to say in praise of the nuns who were in hospital orders.

Perhaps the main impression one retains from his book is one of sadness at so much wanton destruction, at the loss of so many masterpieces. From his account, it is apparent that the dreadful Haussmann was not the only culprit. Brice mentions a number of churches that had been pulled down in the early years of the eighteenth century, and, if he had been Lieutenant de Police, and not just a comfortable and easy-going tutor to well-born, if not well-bred, young Rhinelanders, Poles and Saxons, it is clear that he would have used his powers to remove several public buildings, either because he thought that they were ugly, or because they blocked the road, caused accidents, cast shadows over the neighbourhood, or, crime of crimes, broke the alignment of a recently planned street.

M. Gallet is at present Deputy Keeper of the Musée Carnavalet. No one could have been better qualified to write a study of Paris domestic architecture in the course of the eighteenth century, and his knowledge both of the new town houses and palaces, of the architects, engravers, carpenters, painters, jewellers, goldsmiths and craftsmen who embellished them is prodigious. His book, as well as containing a very large number of very beautiful plates, plans and drawings (some of which are now at Waddesdon), offers a list of leading architects, with their biographical details. The study (very well translated), which has never

* Michel Gallet, *Paris Domestic Architecture of the Eighteenth Century*, London 1972.

been published in French, is an indispensable guide to anyone interested in this fascinating and, often, saddening subject.

But it is much more than a chronicle of changing tastes and styles. Like Brice, M. Gallet has a great deal to say which will be of value to the social historian, on such subjects as the architecture of libertinage, the architecture of class and the physical environment of masters and servants. He quotes a little-known novel of Bastide, *La Petite Maison,* which illustrates better even than *Les Liaisons dangereuses* an architectural fantasy favoured by late-eighteenth-century society; the hero, the Marquis de Trémicour, seeking to impress "La belle Mélite", takes her to a small *pavillon* that he has had constructed in a park, not far from Paris. Preceded by a Negro page, who lights the chandeliers and clusters of candles in their path—the Marquis has arranged for the visit to take place after nightfall—the girl's wonderment increases with the discovery of each new marvel: *trompe-d'oeil* on the wall of the dining-room, a hunting scene that climbs up with the grand staircase, ingenious mechanical devices at each storey, hangings in blue, woodwork in pale yellow, the larger rooms in white and gold, a profusion of monkeys, nymphs, dolphins, cenotaphs, pagodas, cherubs, waterfalls and grottoes among the decorative motifs, the visit increasing in inventiveness with each room, to culminate in the sheer amazement of the exquisite bedroom, its walls painted, according to the recommendations of *l'abbé* Le Camus, the recognised authority in the matter, in blue (as conducive to rest and sleep).

The Negro, after withdrawing the candles, disappears through a hidden door that responds to the pressure of a secret spring, taking the back staircase to his quarters, either on the ground floor (which is cold) or over the stables. Left alone with the Marquis, Mélite, overcome with gratitude, admiration and wonderment, succumbs in his arms. Architecture in the service of Seduction. Is not the whole theme of abduction, the *enlèvement,* in fact an architectural exploration? Is not the division between *côté cour* and *côté jardin* not merely a search for privacy, an affirmation of prestige and a stage convention? Is it not also an aid to abduction? *La belle* waits with a candle at one in the morning, *côté jardin,* a Picard servant produces a ladder, while liveried servants light the way with flaming torches, a closed carriage is waiting at the corner of the street, driven by a coachman with his face covered. The next morning, *la belle* wakes up in some "pavillon de Hanovre", finds herself facing on to a walled park, with sphinxes vaguely seen in the morning mist. Watteau was perhaps more of a social realist than has generally been imagined.

One is surprised at the absence of architectural metaphors in the seduction scenes in *Les Liaisons.* But Sophie knew the advantages to be derived from lunges in the direction of the bell-pull. Laclos was an

artillery officer not an architect, and he conducted seduction, as he might
have done a siege, in military terms. The second staircase might be used
to keep the servants away from their masters; but it could also come in
useful, as in the case of *Manon*. The increasingly elaborate mechanical
devices adopted in the course of the century were not only designed to
keep the servants at a distance; they too could be instruments of seduction. M. Gallet has hit upon an interesting theme.

He also helps us to understand the intense resentments of the enormous
armies of servants. "The ground floors were cold in winter. In the
Palais-Royal and the Hôtel de Noailles, we find them almost entirely
reserved for pages, gentlemen in waiting and servants." Liveried servants,
secretaries, and so on, were generally lodged in rooms of six to eight beds
above a stable of thirty horses; it is doubtful whether even resident chap-
lains would have been much better housed. Equally, the cruel meanness
of the mezzanine, as opposed to the splendour of the Ier, in any ordinary
eighteenth-century town house, further emphasised class divisions in
terms of location. The mezzanine, like the servants' room over the
stables, was no doubt a school for revolutionary militancy. And, as
mechanical devices became more and more ingenious, personal contacts
between master and servant became rarer. The servant's work might thus
be lessened, but his resentment correspondingly increased.

In another sense, too, late-eighteenth-century architectural styles might
be said to have contributed to class antagonisms. "The detached block
of the Italian villa", writes M. Gallet of the 1780s,

> succeeded the secluded precinct of the hôtel court. It was a supreme irony that,
> at this moment when aristocratic society stood at the edge of the abyss
> applauding *Figaro,* it exposed itself to the full glare of the Third Estate...

A very good point. The aristocratic connoisseur was furthermore beginning to live in a late-eighteenth-century fantasy world; "Cottages,
dungeons, pagodas, cenotaphs aroused in him a longing for distant
lands and recollections of times past. In forlorn caverns echoed the
lugubrious murmur of falling water. . . ." Dickens would, rightly, have
made much of this sort of thing. Alongside this bizarre fantasy, we may
note the funereal mood of the engravers Delafosse and Desprez, around
1785.

The Revolution did not bring to a halt all building. "La maison
Batave", an exercise in community building, near the Halles, was completed in 1792, while the amazing Le Doux, a revolutionary before the
Revolution, built a few of the houses that had been commissioned by the
American, Hosten. But the Revolution itself constructed its monuments
only in cardboard and plaster. They were indeed little more than stage
properties, just as David was little more than a stage designer. The
beauty of French domestic architecture, which reached its most perfect

expression in the "pavillon de Hanovre", in Le Doux's stupendous Hôtel Thélusson and in the exquisite Hôtel d'Orrouer early in the period (1733), was never fully recovered, save for a few exceptions under the Empire. For the revolutionaries, beauty was a trifle, a luxury, a form of social arrogance, an assertion of inequality. They were of course right, but at what a cost! The degradation of so many of the *hôtels* described and depicted in *Paris Domestic Architecture of the Eighteenth Century* began in 1792 or 1793, when they fell into the hands of speculators or, worse still, of Ministries.

Haussmann did his best to complete the process, and conservation, when it came, generally came too late, though Paris has still got more to offer, in terms of eighteenth-century domestic architecture, than any other city in Europe. M. Gallet's book can thus be used as a guide, as Brice's was, as well as an architectural dictionary.

Architecture, it is true, was again to be placed in the service of Seduction, but hardly in the style of "la petite maison". Nothing could have been more hideous than the stuffy, overcrowded town houses of mid-nineteenth-century *cocottes* and *poules de luxe*. Fantasy was lavishly employed, especially in the mechanical devices and in the local colour of the celebrated 122, of Third Republic fame; but it was not a fantasy of a sort to dazzle "la belle Mélite". Most Paris brothels tended to look like public lavatories—English ones, not French ones—the Sphinx, like a swimming bath in the Egyptian style. Their disappearance cannot be accounted an architectural loss, though it is undoubtedly a cultural one.

Central Paris

This* is a very important book, a pioneering work in urban history. It might be objected by some that it is a study of Paris in the absence of the Parisians: and it is true that Anthony Sutcliffe is a very far cry from Professor Louis Chevalier, especially as the latter is seen in his recent work *Les Parisiens,* which attempts with great effectiveness to relate the Parisian to the particular environment of his quarter or his suburb, as well as of his place of work, and to locate both in time as well as in space. Louis Chevalier is indeed far more aware of the continuity of Paris history than Dr Sutcliffe, whose principal point of departure—and it is a very important one—is a royal edict of 1783 limiting the maximum height of buildings. Dr Sutcliffe is more exclusively concerned with the physical environment and its evolution than with the people who are subjected to that environment. His approach is purely factual and is massively statistical. So this is no romantic study of *vieilles pierres*, in the manner of Georges Lenôtre. But that is one of the book's many merits: the author is not out to expatiate on the picturesque aspects of Saint-Merri, Saint-Gervais or Sainte-Avoie, because he knows that the "picturesqueness" so often hides, both from the passing tourist and the middle-class preservationist living well away to the west, the permanent realities like tuberculosis, as well as the mounting discomfort of overcrowding and dilapidation. He knows what historical interest, and the fascinating jumble of ancient, narrow-fronted plaster houses, may mean in terms of human misery to their inhabitants, often crowded a whole family to a room. The people who live in the rue Volta, the only street in Paris with fifteenth-century half-timbered houses, would not feel themselves particularly privileged.

Indeed, as a result above all of the demolitions carried out by Haussmann, and of the rare demolitions that have followed 1870, slum conditions in the central areas of Paris have steadily worsened. Haussmann thought in terms of prestige and accessibility: he was concerned to show off certain public buildings—both old and new—to advantage, by isolating them. But he gave little thought to the human consequences of his demolitions and failed to provide any cheap adequate accommo-

* Anthony Sutcliffe, *The Autumn of Central Paris,* London 1971.

dation for those who were driven out. When new accommodation was provided, under the Second Empire and the Third Republic, it generally satisfied the needs of a different clientèle, the blocks being divided into apartments and the rents generally being beyond the reach of the former inhabitants. Furthermore, the limit on height meant that the new buildings would actually take a smaller number of householders than those that had been destroyed. The result was that the surviving areas were further invaded by refugees from neighbouring quarters. The victims of the demolitions in the rue de Rivoli moved east, from the Ier, to crowd into the IIIe and the IVe.

This has been the general pattern—at least in the IIIe and IVe— over the last hundred years, though as far as the Marais is concerned there is at present a likelihood of increasing middle-class investment and residential settlement in what appears to be in the process of becoming as much a Museumville as the Vieux-Montmartre, the Place de l'Estrapade, or the Quartier Saint-Paul in Lyon. In all such instances there are three possible choices : complete demolition, with the destruction of all traces of a historical past unique not so much in terms of individual buildings as of a whole quarter; the degeneration of a quarter into a total slum; or massive preservation, in the form of a Malraux-type *frigorification*, accompanied by the usual face-lifting, cleaning of façades and so on, with the retention at least of the outward aspects of the quarter—minus its normal inhabitants, driven elsewhere, into suburban *bidonvilles,* or into the Buffet-like spikey horrors of Arcueil and *la grande banlieue.* Saint-Paul, La Croix-Rousse, Le Vieux-Genève, Carouge have become *quartiers d'agrément,* inhabited by well-to-do intellectuals and professional people, who, having moved into some of the quarters of nineteenth-century revolutionary ferment, can sometimes enjoy the sensation of being revolutionaries themselves.

It is an extraordinary story that Dr Sutcliffe has to tell. Paris, unique among capitals, has succeeded in preserving in its centre—or in what was its centre up to the 1840s and 1850s—something like 70 per cent of buildings dating back to the reign of Louis XVI or even earlier. The author is concerned only with the four central *arrondissements* : had he extended his survey to the Left Bank, the picture would not have been very different. The east centre on the Right Bank—the IIIe and IVe— was largely overlooked by Haussmann, as already underprivileged and slightly peripheral. Apart from that, its survival was a result of neglect, lack of municipal funds, medical advances, the fractionalisation of properties (most landlords would own only one or two houses, and the properties themselves tended to be on a very narrow frontage, but extended back in depth—both factors that would make large-scale expropriation or purchase or area-planning extremely difficult), low rents or controlled rents in the period between the wars and, in the ten years following the Liberation, the persistence of artisan forms of trade and industry, and the accidents of two wars, both ruinous to the finances of the Hôtel-de-Ville, without being in any way destructive of its buildings. The active intervention of the preservationists came very late and counted in fact for very little. The Commission du Vieux-Paris was, one suspects, a good alibi for Hôtel-de-Ville negligence: few of its members appear ever to have resided in the quarters that they wished to preserve. In any case, under constant pressure from the elected representatives of the outer *arrondissements*, especially under the Third Republic, there was very little that the Hôtel-de-Ville could do about the IIIe and IVe even if it had wanted to. The author makes the useful point that authoritarian regimes like the Second Empire and the Fifth Republic are better equipped to undertake large-scale town-planning than a democratic regime in which the representatives of the four inner *arrondissements* had to compete with those of the other sixteen for the allocation of such limited funds as were available. Under the Third Republic, the VIIIe, the XVIe, the XVIIe and, to some extent, the VIIe were always likely to get more than their fair share for public works, improvement and construction.

By the 1930s, it had become apparent that tuberculosis could be held in check by purely medical means, without the massive clearance of the areas over which it had had the most persistent hold in the course of the previous century; at this time it was, in any case, a much greater threat in the suburbs. So, apart from the partial demolition of Sainte-Avoie, the IIIe and IVe were left almost entirely alone. Saint-Merri, which had the highest death rate from tuberculosis in 1923 (and which had been the principal centre of the cholera epidemic of 1832) is still with us; and so are Saint-Gervais, Saint-Nicolas-des-Champs and the Blancs-Manteaux. It was a victory for preservation achieved by default in the absence of any other plan. The fate of the Ier is still in the balance, though it now seems likely that the rue Saint-Denis will be preserved along most of its length. Some *hôtels de passe* in which the very lowest grades of Paris prostitution plied for so long (right round the clock, night and day) are in the process of becoming *hôtels de tourisme*; many more have been sold to speculators, concerned to convert them into middle-class apartments; and the Halles district, emptied of those directly employed in the provisioning trade, is destined to be redeveloped as a middle-class residential zone or as some grandiose *cité des arts*, set aside to lodge eminent intellectuals from abroad, while the original inhabitants are driven eastwards, or into the suburbs, near the new Halles. The attraction of a central location near the river and of a quarter with such strong historical associations—Mercier, in the 1780s, described the rue Saint-Denis as "la plus commerçante de Paris"; Louis Chevalier claims that, up till the Revolution, *l'esprit de la rue*

Saint-Denis constituted the quintessence of Paris wit and irreverence —seems likely to guarantee its physical survival, though under entirely new management.

In the IIIe at least, a certain number of skilled artisans and small tradesmen in *articles de Paris* have been able to hang on, and both the IIIe and the IVe still have their contingents of Polish Jewish immigrants, of Algerians and Portuguese, though in declining numbers. Jewish immigration from the East has almost dried up, and the mass of Algerian and Portuguese labour has moved to the appalling *bidonvilles* of the periphery.

In short, though the outward aspects of the Right Bank centre have been preserved almost intact, in human terms this eminently Parisian complex is in the process of complete destruction. This is especially true of the Ier, the population of which has been steadily declining over the last hundred years. A social evolution so complete cannot fail to alter the character of Paris as a whole, by destroying the neighbourliness of the *quartier*, the village mentality of those who live above their place of work, depriving the city of much of the wit, the individualism and the independence of the small artisan and of the violence and joyful sexuality of the old population of the Halles.

The Right Bank centre has, over the last eighty years, lost much of the importance which it previously derived from its central position within the city, and which was further underlined by the construction of the Samaritaine, the Belle Jardinière and the Bazar de l'Hôtel-de-Ville. The Cité itself was entirely destroyed by Haussmann, the worst of many acts of vandalism committed by the authoritarian and insensitive Alsatian (he tore down the Church of Sainte-Marine, knocked down the choir of Saint-Leu and was about to set to on the Arènes de Lutèce, in the Ve, when the fall of the Empire saved, in *extremis*, that monument of Roman Paris). The Palais-Royal began its long agony in the 1840s; what had been the centre of the world in the 1780s, under the Directory, and even in 1815, has now become an arcade of seedy shops—medals, ribbons and postage stamps—and a playground for children. Even Colette was unable to give lustre to that sad relic.

One of the most interesting sections of this valuable book is in fact the discussion concerning the gradual displacement of the centre of Paris, over a period of 170 years. In the late eighteenth century, there could be no doubt as to the preponderance of what now constitutes the Ier. The Palais-Royal was the social centre of the city, with the rue Saint-Honoré firmly established as the most fashionable shopping area. The decline of the rue Saint-Honoré parallels that of the Palais-Royal : in the 1840s and 1850s, the luxury trade began to move westwards, to the rue du faubourg Saint-Honoré. After the Revolution, there was also a residential move to the north-west, to the Chaussée-d'Antin, as bankers and moneyed people tended to clear out of the violent areas of the centre and the east centre, where they had found *sans-culottes* and worse living, literally, on top of them. Even Réveillon went west. But the most important displacement came under Haussmann : with the Gare Saint-Lazare early established as the most important station for the suburban traffic, and with the cutting of the avenue de l'Opéra (it was not, however, completed till 1876, in time for the Exposition) the development of trade, banking and every form of economic activity became emphatically centred on the VIIIe, in the area between the new Opéra, Saint-Lazare, the Chaussée-d'Antin and the boulevard des Italiens. This transformation was deliberately accelerated by the construction of the rues Halévy and Auber, to facilitate access from Saint-Lazare to the Opéra and beyond. Saint-Lazare is probably still the main point of entry of the armies of the *banlieusards,* though Louis Chevalier, writing of the early 1960s, makes similar claims for the bus and Métro stations of Vincennes; but most of those who arrive from the east likewise work in the VIIIe.

The growing predominance of the Opéra and the Grands Boulevards was further favoured, and has since been perpetuated, by the construction, in the 1890s, of the Paris Métro. The lines, constructed just below the surface—the Paris subsoil, with its honeycomb of quarries and the prevalence of sandstone that easily crumbled, was felt, by the early Métro engineers, to be unsuitable for the construction of a deep, tubular system, on the London model—followed the rectangle of Haussmann's wide new thoroughfares and of the older boulevards. The Châtelet station, it is true, was a focal point for north-south and east-west traffic, but it did not have the importance of the Opéra, the meeting-place of four lines. The Métro system continued to favour the IIe (one line followed the course of the rue Réaumur, serving the Bourse and the Sentier quarters) and, to some extent, the Ier (Vincennes-Étoile, the first line to be constructed, was a recognition of its still important geographical location, though it was probably more designed to favour the development of the Concorde, Madeleine and Rond-Point areas) and further contributed to the isolation of the IIe and the IVe. The area between the rue des Archives and the Bastille is served by no stations, except for Arts-et-Métiers at the northern end, and Saint-Paul at the southern.

While well-to-do residents continued to move, under the impetus of Haussmann, first to the Plaine Monceau, then to the Champs-Elysées and beyond, towards the Bois, establishing the VIIIe, XVIe and XVIIe (in parts) as the most desirable areas for middle-class residence, the Champs-Elysées was never a serious contestant to the IIe and VIIIe as the true centres of Paris. As Chevalier has suggested, the Champs-Elysées enjoyed only a brief preponderance, in the 1920s, as the centre of fashion and of the developing film industry. Only one newspaper ever moved there; and since the 1930s, it has steadily declined as a centre of taste. Only emperors, kings and *chefs d'état* ever reach Paris by the Gare du Bois de Boulogne, taken out of its dust-covers every decade or so for such occasions. The Quartier De Gaulle is too peripheral to attract to it the principal activities of Paris, though it is discreet enough to serve as a rendezvous—rue d'Argentine, rue des Acacias—for the *deussaquatrier*, the successor to the *cinqaseptier* (*Je te trouverai, chérie, sous De Gaulle*). Nothing, it would seem, is likely to dislodge the VIIIe from its dominating position.

The decline of the east centre is, then, the main theme of this fascinating book. The author dates it from the Revolution; and in this he may be wrong, for the movement from the Marais had already begun with the development of the faubourg Saint-Germain. Certainly the violence of the Revolution hastened the move westward, but the ultimate condemnation of the area came with Haussmann.

As wealth, trade and industry moved out, an increasingly depressed proletariat moved in. At the best of times, the two *arrondissements* were bordered, to their east, by the alarming and envious armies of the *classes dangereuses*—it was a short step from the rue de Lappe to the Quartier Saint-Paul—and the area behind the Hôtel-de-Ville became, in the nineteenth century, the principal centre for lodging-houses, particularly for building workers who, although they were hired there, can never have found much employment in a part of Paris in which scarcely any building at all took place between the 1780s and the 1970s. It escaped the building boom of the 1900s. An original French proletariat from the Limousin and the Massif Central, entering by the Gare de Lyon or Austerlitz, just across the river, as well as refugees from the Cité, was later joined, at the time of the pogroms, by poor Jews from the Russian Empire—the Marché du Temple had in fact been a preserve of Jewish furriers since the eighteenth century—and later still by Algerians. With each new wave, overcrowding got worse, and the houses became more dilapidated. It was only due to the fact that they had been so well-built in the sixteenth to eighteenth centuries that so few actually collapsed into the street, though a number had to be propped up on wooden staves. The author gives the east centre a long respite—at least to the end of the century.

But it is a future without a function, save possibly as a magnet to tourism. The presence of the vast complex of the Archives Nationales is hardly likely to revitalise a quarter : rather does it accentuate its decrepitude. It also symbolises a phenomenon frequently commented on by the author : the steady increase in the average age of the inhabitants of the IIIe in the course of the last eighty years. The presence, too, of the Mont-de-Piété is perhaps even more symbolic of parasitism, decline and a run-down poverty. The "Spectacles du Marais", organised with great pomp, and to the sound of many trumpets, by André Malraux in the mid-1960s, brought the inhabitants of the XVIe and the XVIIe, the intellectuals of the XIVe, to the courtyards of the Palais Soubise, the Hôtel de Rohan, the Hôtel Lamoignan, the Hôtel de Beauvais, to listen to concerts or plays; but they did not linger. Nor did their affluence. *Son et Lumière* did nothing for the inhabitants, save to deprive them of sleep. It would take a greater magician even than Malraux to bring a new sense of identity to the once magnificent east centre. It is a sad story; but, if Sedan had not come so providentially when it did, it could possibly have been even sadder. The empty shell of what had constituted the more basic elements of the *sans-culotterie* has survived almost intact —Jacques Roux could find his way round his parish, almost house by house, even if most of his parishioners of recent years would turn out to be Muslims—while the Editions Spartacus, of Trotskyite inspiration, can propose to the middle-class revolutionary a complete tour of *le Paris révolutionnaire* almost entirely within the confines of the two *arrondissements*. The Marais has much to offer almost anyone save its inhabitants.

Dr Sutcliffe does not, as I say, sufficiently take into account the continuity of Paris history, quarter by quarter, save in respect of the survival of their buildings, nor indeed the continuity of that ancient theme : Paris versus France, the provinces versus Paris. He describes, for instance, the anti-Parisian federalism and the efforts at decentralisation undertaken in the post-Liberation years and expressed most eloquently in Jean-François Gravier's *Paris et le désert français*, published in 1947. But this kind of attack represents an ancient tradition of representative regimes, while authoritarian ones are always likely to redress the balance in favour of the seat of government.

Historians of the eighteenth and nineteenth centuries will be struck by other forms of continuity that emerge from his study, particularly, of the east centre. Eighty years after the Revolution, the average size of a workshop here was a master and eight or nine journeymen; many of these workshops were in huts encrusted on the side of former mansions and situated in courtyards of buildings, the delapidation of many of which had been accelerated by the Revolution, when, as a result of the sale of *biens nationaux*, most of them came up for auction, to be snatched up by speculators or fragmented by a score or more of independent artisans. Thus, in the 1850s and the 1880s, not only were the cadres of a *sans-culotte* way of life still standing : the *sans-culottes* themselves were still there, or at least their social equivalent. Saint-Merri had witnessed outbreaks of cholera in 1832, 1849, 1854 and 1865; it topped the list for deaths from tuberculosis throughout the 1920s; it had been under special surveillance, both from the Lieutenant de Police and the Bureau de Santé, in the last years of the *ancien régime*; and it figures as a plague spot in a number of *Traités de Police* published in the 1780s and the 1820s. More astounding, the author records an outbreak of the plague in the Clignancourt area in 1925.

Many of the features that he claims as characteristic of the two *arrondissements* of the east centre in the first half of the nineteenth century have been described, in detail, by Mercier, writing in the 1780s, and by Restif, in the 1790s. His neglect of both authors gives his book a certain lack of depth, while he certainly overestimates what he describes as "the industrial expansion" of the eighteenth century. For, one suspects, in the east centre, people have lived six or seven to a room for a number of centuries.

In the early years of this century, and, again in the 1920s, the Hôtel-de-Ville made desultory efforts to provide both cheap and hygienic housing for the lower income-groups, in the "Habitations à Bon Marché": but these were mostly built on the periphery or in Montrouge. Nothing of the sort was done for the inhabitants of the IIIe and the IVe. Many of them were foreigners, others recent arrivals from the provinces, others again had moved in from other areas recently demolished. Very few of them worked either for the state or for large enterprises. The only effort on their behalf was a massive clearance of the riverside section of the IVe, started under Vichy (a regime which, despite its many political turpitudes, seems to have had quite a good record in the matter of public health; the "Chantiers de la Jeunesse", whatever the intention of their creation in the form of character-breeding and the development of leadership instincts, probably saved many former slum children from tuberculosis) and completed under the Fourth Republic. The effect of this, as of all previous demolitions, was to make the conditions in the surviving areas even worse. The author concludes soberly, on the subject of the physical survival of the east centre: "Whether or not this can be regarded as a satisfactory state of affairs depends on whether one can reconcile the survival of one of the oldest and most fascinating city centres of Europe with the tribulations of many of those who have to live and work there."

22

Succès de vandale

Of the Western capitals in the past two world wars, Brussels and Paris were those that experienced the least destruction, either from artillery and aerial bombardment, or from rockets. On Good Friday, 1917, the church of Saint-Gervais, in the Marais, received a direct hit, during Mass, from a shell from Big Bertha; and in the Second World War, the northern quarter of la Chapelle was heavily bombarded in the course of an RAF attack on the marshalling yards of the Gare du Nord. There was also considerable damage, just outside Paris, as a result of the bombing of the Renault works in Boulogne-Billancourt. Brussels got away with even less damage, though it was attacked by the Luftwaffe a few days after its liberation, in September 1944.

The damage which has been inflictd on these two cities is not, then, the result of enemy—or Allied—action. It is the result, almost always, of vandalism from within. In Brussels, *la ville haute*, once a delightful combination of seventeenth and eighteenth-century domestic architecture, and also containing a few fine mediaeval churches, has largely been destroyed by the Common Market. The construction of the Gare Centrale and its link-up, by a central underground line, with the old stations of Nord and Midi has resulted in the disembowelment of the seventeenth-century quarter of the rue Haute and the rue Blaes, beyond the porte de Hal, on the rising ground leading to the rue Royale (among the buildings destroyed was the delightful Maison des Arquebusiers, an *haut-lieu* of Brussels municipal history); the pulling down of what had been left of le quartier des Marolles after the redoubtable Pollaert had gutted this heavily populated area, during the reign of Leopold II, when constructing the enormous Palais de Justice (no wonder that in Brussels patois "espèce d'architecte" is the most unforgivable insult!); the isolation of the church of Saint-Hubert and that of Saint-Gudule, standing in a forlorn wilderness; and the disappearance of the old Mont-des-Arts, including the shop in which Paul Colin was assassinated by a Resistance fighter in 1943.

Les Marolles, both a home of linguistic oddities—*espèce de tonnenlinker,* and other combinations of French, Flemish and Bruxellois—and a wonderful maze of tiny, steep streets, the pavements of which would be covered, in the spring and summer, by card-players, is now merely a memory of a lost folklore, the one-time home of the *smokeleers* and of the Belgian capital's brighter pickpockets, counterfeiters, and specialists in false papers. The only comparable attack on a city's popular culture was the blowing up of the Vieux-Port in Marseille; but at least that was carried out by the Germans. For the doubtful privilege of becoming the capital of Europe—or rather of "Europe"—Brussels, or at least *la ville haute,* has paid the enormous price of an almost total loss of identity. The lovely Saint-Gudule, once surrounded by the harmony of such seventeenth-century town houses as the Hôtel d'Oursel, is now incongruously exposed to a faceless Place de l'Europe. It would be interesting to hear the comments, in *la langue des marolles,* on the subject of such impudent vandalism.

Georges Pillement, a gallant old fighter, has a sadly similar story to tell on the subject of the wanton destruction of Paris over the past seventy-five years: similar, at least in the extent of the damage, and the persistence of short-sighted or deliberate vandalism. For, whereas in Brussels there has been a single culprit—"Europe"—in Paris there have, over the years, been any number. M. Pillement, in his justifiably angry book,* lists the worst of them. They include the Banque de France, a persistent offender, in its constant need to expand its premises above and below ground; M. Cognacq, the founder of la Samaritaine; the neighbouring la Belle Jardinière; les Galéries Lafayette, to which the lovely hôtel de la duchesse de Berry fell victim; l'Assistance Publique (victim: hôpital des Enfants Trouvés); Michel Debré, as Minister of Defence (the destroyer of the Temple de l'Amitié, 20 rue Jacob); the American beautician, Helena Rubinstein, who had a seventeenth-century town house on the Ile Saint-Louis pulled down, in order to erect an apartment block; a whole line of Prefects; the Mont-de-Piété; the Army; the *sapeurs-pompiers*; the *gendarmerie*; the Ville de Paris itself, which ordered the demolition of a charming folly in Bercy, to make way for the extension of the Halle-aux-vins; the main Paris branch of an English bank, boulevard des Capucines, responsible for uprooting the delightful Pavillon de Hanovre, and exiling it incongruously to the far end of the parc de Sceaux; insurance companies; building societies; hospitals; the old Compagnie Nord-Sud which, when constructing its own underground line, insisted that the streets immediately above it should follow its track, in order to assure its regular custom, so that a whole section of the rue du Cherche-Midi was swept away to make room for the prolongation of the boulevard Raspail; building speculators in alliance with the *conseil municipal*; and, of course, more recently, especially under the Fifth Republic, the sort of technocrats who, too grand themselves ever to use public transport, have failed to modernise the TCRP, to add

* Georges Pillement, *Paris poubelle,* Paris 1974.

to the Métro lines, to provide mini-buses, and have thought exclusively of increasing the speed of circulation of private cars within the city, thus, in most cases, adding to the chaos, while cutting huge swathes through the centre. The name of the terrible Delouvrier at once comes to mind.

Though President de Gaulle took the initiative of having the Grand Trianon done up and made into an official residence, and though he himself at one time contemplated moving from the Elysée to the Pavillon du Roi in the fort de Vincennes, no doubt in order to emulate Saint-Louis (his proposed move at least had the permanent advantage of giving the French war records extended premises), for a man so deeply concerned with the past, with the continuity of French history, he seems to have shown little interest in the efforts of such bodies as the Commission du Vieux-Paris to preserve as much as possible of that history on the ground. The period of his presidency was in fact one of extensive destruction. But if de Gaulle had allowed a lot to go because his angle of vision rarely reached down to the level of mere *buildings*, his successor, Georges Pompidou, was an active, indeed grandiose and visionary, vandal, who managed to achieve, in a quarter of the time, almost as much square-*kilométrage* of destruction as the Alsatian Attila, Baron Haussmann.

The foreign visitor, on seeing for the first time the vast area of destruction contained in the quadrilateral between the rue Beaubourg and the boulevard de Sébastopol, and extending down as far as the rue de la Verrerie, might assume that Paris, too, had experienced something on the scale of the Warsaw Rising. But he would be wrong, for this scene of devastation is what has been officially described as *le plateau Beaubourg*, and, unofficially, as *le trou Pompidou*, and a mighty *big* hole it is : the late President, an active patron of modern art in all its uglier forms, had set his eye on this area as a suitable place to erect a *centre des arts*, or a series of experimental theatres. There is nothing there at all at the moment; but the rue Quincampoix has been cut into three, the church of Saint-Merri stands almost alone, deprived of its natural *entourage* of old streets, and the old quartier Sainte-Avoie has almost entirely disappeared. Pompidou also had his plans for the quarter of les Halles and the rue Saint-Denis; he managed to get the markets down in his lifetime, with the result that the old market church of Saint-Eustache stands, like Saint-Merri, on the edge of a desert.

But at least the site is to be preserved, and the rue Saint-Denis has been saved. Had Pompidou lived even a little longer, there would probably have been little of historical Paris on either bank. As it is, apart from his *Grand Trou*, his principal monument will remain the gigantic buildings to be seen caught in the perspective of the Arc de Triomphe when viewed from the Carrousel. The election of M. Giscard d'Estaing has brought a welcome halt to the *zèle gaullo-destructeur* of the Hôtel-de-Ville and the Conseil de Paris. The new President has dropped the *voie-exprès Rive Gauche*, which would have ruined the little that has been left of the banks of the Seine and would have brought down, in a matter of years, Notre-Dame; and he has granted a reprieve to the Cité Fleurie.

As M. Pillement shows most convincingly, part of the trouble has always been that no single authority, at least since 9 Thermidor, has ever held responsibility for Paris as a whole, that the city, far from ever having had a single master, has always been saddled with a whole lot of them, most of them acting independently of one another.

In other French cities, a *maire* can do a power of good, or evil. Herriot in his very long reign in Lyon, Médecin in Nice, were active preservationists, whereas Mondon, the unspeakable *maire* of Metz, has managed to destroy most of the old city. In Paris, buildings are pulled down in a semi-secret manner, on the casual recommendation of a single authority, and even the eagle eye of a Georges Pillement or a Michel Fleury may miss some *ordonnance ministérielle* tucked away, and in small print, in the *Bulletin municipal.* In Paris, irreparable decisions are often taken in a furtive manner; *les démolisseurs*, like pickpockets, prefer to avoid publicity. To begin with, there are two Prefects, the territories of each of whom are not clearly defined. M. Pillement suggests that *hauts fonctionnaires*, at the summit of their careers, and for whom promotion to Paris will represent the ultimate reward, after many years sitting it out in Gap, or Mende—the Prefects have rarely been native-born Parisians (though the good Poubelle was); some have been Corsicans—are unlikely to feel strongly about a city in which they were not brought up. But the Prefects are far from enjoying a monopoly of destruction. Each Minister has been allowed his allocation of wreckage; and that of Environment, Alain Chalandon, managed to have pulled down 81–83 rue de la Verrerie, a *crime en longueur* to which we will return.

But the most persistent and joyful demolitionists have always been the official architects of the city—there would be a very strong case for introducing the Brussels insult to Paris—who, even in the days of horse traffic, thought less in terms of people, of beauty, of the past, than in those of the speed of circulation. Already, in the 1780s, the Lieutenant de Police is ordering the widening of this street or that, while limiting the height of houses, and a series of eighteenth century royal *ordonnances* required that all half-timbered houses should be plastered over, with the result that buildings that had previously been perfectly solid became damp and often eventually collapsed into the street. This sort of thing has gone on ever since; straightening, widening, chopping off corners, making winding streets stand at attention, cutting swathes of wide avenues through the centre—the Commission des Arts of 1795 had already planned most of the horrors that were to follow over the next two centuries—uprooting trees, narrowing pavements, removing statues, and, more recently, honeycombing the city with shallow *parkings souterrains*, into which will no doubt soon crash the few churches and historic mansions allowed to survive. One should not be too prone to blame the Gaullists, though they have been especially active *démolomanes*. They have a long tradition to look back to.

Indeed, one of the few consoling features of this sad chronicle is that things might have been even worse. M. Pillement lists, with fascinated horror, some of the plans of "improvement" that were not in fact carried out (the two world wars offered a welcome respite in this respect). From 1901 to 1914, a series of authorities examined lovingly an atrocious project to prolong the rue de Rennes—in its drab ugliness the joy of any town-planner—across the Boulevard Saint-Germain, right up to the Seine. The rues de Seine and Mazarine would have gone, the rue Jacob been cut, the new street would have eaten up the rear courtyard of the Institut. Fortunately, for once, MM. les Académiciens served a purpose other than their own mutual admiration : they protested, they wanted to keep their rear entrance. In 1912, *on croit rêver*, there was a proposal to drive a road through the middle of the Palais-Royal, to speed the flow of north-south traffic. In 1916, thanks to the war, the lovely rue François-Miron was given a temporary reprieve. And because of shortage of labour and material and high building costs, there was a lull in pulling down from 1916 to 1920.

Early in the 1920s, Le Corbusier presented *his* plan for the quartier des Halles : it was all to come down, to be replaced by eight huge tower blocks facing on to the Seine. By some miracle, it was not adopted. But, frustrated in his attempt on Paris, the Swiss *démolomane* and collectivist was able to give his full measure much later, in Marseille. One should be thankful for some small mercies, and Paris was at least spared a Perret or a Le Corbusier.

For *Paris poubelle* makes extremely depressing reading, despite these occasional, almost accidental, reprieves. The "improvers" regarded it as a great concession to the complaints of the preservationists if they allowed them, out of municipal funds, to take a photograph of some eighteenth century marvel lined up for destruction. *Mais prenez donc une photo*; and an awful lot of the illustrations of this book originated in this way. Save during the two wars, the process of destruction has been continuous : construction of the ugly rue Dante (1899); destruction of the maison de l'arbre de Jessé (1900); of the Abbaye aux Bois (1901); of the Enfants Trouvés (1902); hôtel de Chastellux (1903); the first assault on the rue Mouffetard (1904). 1906 was a bumper year for demolition, on both Banks. In 1907, the boulevard Raspail was extended. In 1908, the Tour Dagobert came down, in 1909, the couvent des Dames Anglaises. The year 1911 saw the end of Sue's *tapis francs*, rue de la Grande Truanderie. In 1913, the quay facing on to the southern end of the Pont-Neuf was "disengaged" (*dégager* is a favourite word with *les circulomanes*), the rue Dauphine and the rue de Nevers truncated, and a hideous circus in brick erected : if not the *worst* building in Paris, at least the most prominent bad one. The building boom started again in 1922. In the following year, Cognacq, the art collector, pulled down the lovely Hôtel de la Vieuville. The Hôtel Fersen went too in the 1920s. The last barracks of the Gardes Françaises, rue de Penthièvre, went in 1929.

Since the Liberation, the demolitionists have been busy mopping up the remains of the rue Mouffetard, tearing apart the whole quarter to make room for the rue Jean Calvin, suitably named, for it is a sad street. On the Right Bank, the area from the Seine to the level of the rue François-Miron has been razed.

The old headquarters of the *poste aux chevaux*, rue Pigalle, went in 1965. They have also had a go at the upper ends of the rue Saint-Jacques, and most of the rue de l'Ouest seems at present to be imminently threatened by the spread of the appalling Tour Maine-Montparnasse. Recently I called on a friend who lived, 83 rue de la Verrerie, in a wonderfully rambling *Cour des Miracles*, the remains of the old *hôtel des voyageurs de la ville de Reims*, which contained, among other treasures, an outside wooden staircase dating from François I, and eighteenth-century staircases and floors in wood and diamond-shaped red tiles. All that remained of the house, and its neighbour, No. 81, was a huge hole. Both houses had been placed on the protected list by the Commission des Sites. But the owners had allowed them to fall into such a state of disrepair that they had obtained a discreet order from M. Chalandon for their destruction. As M. Pillement remarks, this is a method of hastening demolition much favoured both by the public authorities and, sad to say, by the owners, including some who belong to very old families, anxious to obtain a maximum profit from the sale to property speculators of a terrain in central Paris.

M. Pillement himself, as an experienced observer of impending vandalism, has witnessed the progressive deterioration of many of the finest eighteenth-century *hôtels particuliers*, the removal of iron work, of *portes cochères*, and has, on many occasions, always unsuccessfully, attempted to warn the authorities responsible. The authorities have not wished to know. He even instances cases of buildings having not merely been neglected in this way, till they could reasonably be described as a public danger : he quotes cases of others that have been deliberately rendered unsafe by the removal of parts of the roof or of supporting props. His comments on the avidity of building speculators are in contrast to what he has seen happening in places like Prague or Warsaw, where every effort has been made to preserve as much as possible of the historic past of these ancient towns. Perhaps he is being too pessimistic, for, in Paris, there are a number of people as vigilant as himself :

Hillairet, Dauvergne, Fleury, de Saint-Rémy, historians, antiquarians, archivists, actively concerned to bring to a halt seventy-five years of thoughtless destruction.

There have been, also, in recent years, some serious efforts at preservation. The case of the Marais has been much quoted, and it is certainly true that a number of *hôtels particuliers* have in fact been saved, cleaned up, their courtyards cleared of all manner of encumbrances—wooden sheds, glass roofs, as well as of the many activities and the many artisans that they housed. But this has been preservation at a very great cost. The houses of the Marais, with their many ancillary activities dispersed, have been frozen into the lifelessness of museums. The shells have been preserved, but there is nothing much inside. There was much greater excitement in discovering, behind the chaos of workshops, *baraques*, tin roofs, the vague outline of the Hôtel de Venise, or the Hôtel des Ambassades de Hollande, or the Hôtel Lamoignan, than in thus being directed, by a series of maps attached to the street lamps, to the now dead town houses of a quarter that has been completely museumified. Even so, this is perhaps preferable to complete destruction. And, in any case, no one has worried about the smaller dwelling-houses and the less fashionable streets.

Of these last, so many long since gone, M. Pillement writes with the nostalgia of an urban poet, as well as with the necessarily suspicious alertness of a witness very much aware of the equally vigilant contrary concern of public authorities and speculators in search of profitable destruction. He refers to the extinct rue de Venise, once the principal centre of tuberculosis : "La nuit est venue; les pauvres maisons hydropiques ... reniflent une dernière fois les relents de pommes, de poires ou de fraises que les vents traînent selon les saisons, et ferment les paupières. ..." And he evokes the neighbouring rue de la Reynie, also gone : "Rue de la Reynie oncques voiture n'a jamais passé. Les corpulents marchent de biais, seuls les maigres vont à leur aise en collant leurs les bras au corps ..." (though, in this category, the thin can still get down the rue de Nevers and the rue Visconti, near where Oscar Wilde died : I have never made out how he could even get into it). He is even more eloquent on the subject of the poor rue Brantôme : "Nul passant ne s'y attarde pour déplorer sa trop régulière misère. ... Seul le vent y muse souvent, mais en vain, ce gros malin, essayant d'agiter les trois couleurs des drapeaux de zinc des lavoirs. ..." How right he is to compare these ancient, humble streets, to some poor old woman who has never had looks :

La rue du Maure n'a jamais eu de jeunesse. Elle est née triste entre de hautes maisons. Elle a un coude charmant entre deux vieux murs. Elle est silencieuse, mais elle ne pense à rien. C'est le royaume du sommeil. Revenues du fin fond des faubourgs lointains les voitures à bras s'y endorment le soir, accablées de fatigue et de misère, leurs bras levés vers le ciel et un rayon de lune dans leur ventre creux...

The tin flags of the *lavoirs*, so unseasonable, for they at least can never merrily crack to the gusty wind, the hand-carts of the *marchands de quatre saisons*, their arms raised in tired and hopeless protest—"we have come from Vanves, from Montreuil, from Montrouge"—the odour of rotting fruit, brought on a timid wind, the cats that compete with the multi-coloured posters to give a semblance of life and movement to these dark, damp cuttings: these are as evocative of a Paris that once was and is almost no more, as the hidden courtyards, the old hand pumps and fountains, or the mounting steps of Belleville. Alas, rue de Venise, *M. Pompidou est passé par là.*

M. Pillement has written a sad book, for it is the relentless inventory of so much beauty lost, and so often lost needlessly. He understands that a street, in its irregularity, is an entity that represents something, that contains a message hidden from the average *passant*, but perceptible to anyone with time, patience and imagination to spare. He talks primarily of what has gone. Fortunately, even after years of *gaullo-destructomanie*, there have subsisted plenty of obscure corners, deep courtyards, private *voies sans issue*, tiny shuttered *bicoques* almost entirely hidden in thick foliage, along an abandoned *ceinture*, green *volets* lit by hearts or diamonds, minuscule *vins charbons*, high front steps leading to street doors that have not been opened for a hundred years, blind windows, railings climbing beside an old winding staircase, the semi-secret, just visible, entry to an oddly rustic fairyland, the swing doors of a tiny hotel, rue de la Goutte-d'Or, full of menace, evocative of sordid violence, the artisanal architectural fantasies of the *facteur* Cheval: gothic crenellations, terracotta *châteaux-forts* picked out in sea shells. Cranes and storks cut out in wood with metal beaks, old *Abeille* tins filled with scallop shells, laid out in complicated patterns; messages of love or insult on oozing, leprous Utrillo-like walls, forlorn cemeteries approachable through thick undergrowth, the sound of someone practising on a French horn, the bright medley of a *marchand de couleurs*, the gaudy ceramic bricks covering the wall of a *pensionnat*, Villa Poissonnière (*Voie Privée*), the chains blocking one entry of *bains publics*, the 1920-style advertisements on glass, in one of the closed *galéries*, beloved of Aragon, the tangled, romantic ironwork of these *ponts des suicidés*, the discreet, unpretentious entry to the Morgue, the old-fashioned shop-front of the Maison Borniol, the leading entrepreneur in death, the many-headed golden horses of the *boucherie chevaline* opposite the horse slaughter-house, rue Brancion, the endless fantasy, excitement, naivety, inventiveness and individualism of *le Paris Insolite*, a Paris fortunately both too secret and too humble to attract the dangerous interest of a Pompidou or the avidity of a speculator.

7—TDF * *

23

The pissotière

The pissotière, a more permanent monument of the Paris scene than the pig-snouted bus, or the G7 taxi or the *agent à double barbe* of the porte Saint-Martin, and a tribute to the steady architectural conservatism of the ironwork poets of the Voierie, is likely soon to be a museum piece, *classé monument historique*, and no doubt disconnected from its base : an object of aesthetic satisfaction, but no longer the sought-after terminus of needed relief, a poor, tame edifice in cast-iron, deprived of its pungent smell which, for the specialist—the *renifleur*—constitutes more than just an *hors-d'oeuvre* to the wealth to come.

Yet what long and faithful service have these round, welcoming artistically perforated chapels of fraternity rendered to the Parisian male, from eight to eighty (most of those questioned in the present work* date their first visit to the temple to eight, ten or twelve), and to the foreign tourist ! From the 1890s no Paris landscape could be complete without the obtrusive *théière*, the old-fashioned, two-storeyed edifice, pushing to the front, like a sentinel—there is one bang outside Notre-Dame, one outside the Bourse, one outside the Morgue, one, often in the cruder, more basic, lean-to variety, at the entry and against the wall of each cemetery, one outside the Bibliothèque Nationale. The Panthéon, the mausoleum of *les Grands Hommes*, suitably gets two, twin guardians at the national shrine; each railway station is flanked by two or three, each little square is given unity by the *édicule* placed in its centre, so that the needs of religion, travel, tourism, scholarship, speculation and reverence are immediately satisfied with the rigorous impartiality of a secular, stony-eyed Marianne.

They form the central motif in the golden age of the postcard, standing out at the tram termini, porte de Montreuil, porte des Lilas, porte de Clignancourt, or under the shadow of the Sacré-Coeur or the Moulin de la Galette, or competing with the harmonious façade of the Monnaie, or merely breaking the fearful monotony of the boulevard Voltaire and of the *boulevards extérieurs*. Near their narrow, odorous entrance linger the usual over-dressed, hieratical postcard figures : the boy in the sailor outfit with outsize hoop, the bigger boy in knickerbockers, the nurse, the

* Claude Maillard, *Les Vespasiennes de Paris ou les précieux édicules*, Paris 1969.

gavroche in peaked cap, the *apache* in a loudly checked cloth one, the top-hatted *cocher*.

They stand out like scattered urban lighthouses, above the waters of the Venetian streets of the 1910 floods. And they are never far from the dread cross-flagged proclamations: *Mobilisation Générale* of August 1914; they must have been much in demand during those hot nights. Between 1914 and 1918, the *vespasienne* is the light that did not fail for so many poor *poilus*, the symbol of a longed-for leave and of a lost civilian paradise. They figure weirdly, palaces of mystery, temples in the night cults of Dada and surrealism.

This was the Imperial Period of the *vespasienne*, firmly rooted in the "pavé de Paris", tied to the sewers by a multitude of pipes, witnessing, on its outer walls, for apéritifs, medicines and for the varying brands of political extremism (their political message is never moderate, corresponding no doubt with the urgency of need of the user), and, in the secrecy of the inner temple, after relief, to the sad boastings or to the lonely, humble hopes of sexual deviation. Their round pale globes light up the velvet night for Utrillo or for Van Gogh. They have acquired *droit de cité* among the politicians of the Conseil Général and can be used as mute, but convincingly odoriferous apparati of sighing blackmail, outside a restaurant (preferably *avec terrasse*) or a theatre or a private residence (they are so easy to move).

For the hidden armies of pederasty—antique-dealers, dress-designers, sailors, waiters, grooms, jockeys, valets, coachmen, boots, actors—they are the free equivalent of the *gros numéro*, places of rapid pleasure, stimulated by the pungent smell of urine and put to music to the sound of waterfalls. And so they constitute too, with their narrow entrances and their three confined, stand-up cubicles, admirable murder traps; those placed on a treed square or at the end of a long dark road or amidst the Siberian silence of the wintry *boulevards extérieurs* are closely watched by *apaches*, themselves watched by Casque-d'Or. At a favourable moment these will spring, with the stealthy feline grace of the Désossé, and, then, instead of a pair of feet facing inwards, the passer-by might have the surprise of seeing a hatless head, at urine level, in the space between the bottom of the decorated ironwork and the pavement.

How many lives were thus terminated, after a copious banquet, like that of the bourgeois depicted in *L'Assiette au beurre*, in June 1901, his corpse splayed out at the entry to an *édicule*, a cloth-capped figure with a face like a skull and his girl stooping over him? As recently as Christmas Day, 1957, 4 September and 24 October 1959, commercial travellers were quietly knifed to death in *pissotières*, their bodies left standing in the act of relief, wedged forwards into the compartment, like those New York gangsters shot, with their stetsons pushed forward over their noses, in telephone boxes.

In the autumn, the season at which they become blocked with the falling leaves, one or two, particularly located on lonely streets, blackened Martian edifices, their slits dark with squinting, menacing eyes, seemed, before their destruction, to issue warnings of a violent, silent and smelly death, amidst green piping and blocked-up gurgling drainery. There was one such black Bastille, darker than the night, squatting expectantly at the end of a long straight road that cuts through the cimetière du Montparnasse and that, in the 1930s, was credited with half a dozen victims.

Since the turn of the century, the enemies of the *urinoirs* at the Hôtel-de-Ville have tended to be—or at least have proclaimed themselves as such, for realisation has dragged far behind promise—the partisans of underground lavatories and of *châlets d'aisance*, more banally *châlets de nécessité*, Switzerland's leading contribution to Paris topography, hidden in discreet foliage in the gardens off the Rond-Point. Of the former, there were ninety-three in 1920, ninety-seven in 1940, and ninety-six in 1963, hardly an effort to meet the expanding needs of a masculine population increasingly faced with the disappearance of familiar and well-liked points of relief above ground. For forty years, *les édiles* have talked much of grandiose underground establishments—they even sent over a commission to report, very eulogistically, on the facilities provided at Piccadilly Circus Underground Station—but, characteristically, only the Communist members have ever pressed hard for something to be done.

The Golden Age ended some time in the 1920s; the Decline set in during the early 1930s. In 1930, there were still 1,200 *urinoirs*, catering for every taste, with the armies of *la pédale* concentrating on certain favoured spots near les Halles (rather like the lady from the XVIe who explains: "je fais mon marché aux Halles, c'est tellement plus économe" —it has, for her, other advantages too), much to the indignation of *les forts*, as conservative sexually as they were politically. By 1939 the number had been almost halved, to 700. This was reduced to 561 in 1954, 347 in 1965, and 329 in 1966. Two more years of Gaullism have no doubt added further to the holocaust of these ancient symbols of anti-clericalism, *le pot de vin*, heavy drinking, the habits of the *boulevardier* and of the *apache*, of objects that have contributed so richly to popular slang, and that have been such consistent invitations to the inventiveness and candour of popular literature. There could—and should—have been a Prix Pissotière to cater for this sort of talent.

Each year a few more *vespasiennes* are removed to the chagrin and discomfort of the elderly—a group as much neglected by the Fifth Republic as by its two predecessors—while nothing is put in their place. Men are clearly to be reduced to the unhappy, furtive status so long experienced by women, very much the underprivileged in this important matter, and to be driven into an enforced *consommation* in order to benefit from the existence of some wretched contrivance among the telephones. It is, of course, understandable that banks, great corporations, embassies, theatres and cinemas should be anxious to remove the curved sentinels placed so often on their thresholds. But some other place must be found for them : the slaughter-houses, the markets, the cemeteries (the dead at least are not going to complain), the churches (with their long services), the hospitals, the railway stations have always cried out for need.

Just what does happen to these monuments of a considerate and artistic past? One can imagine some junkyard, to the north-east of Paris, full of uprooted and once useful edifices, in strange, jumbled companionship— the *théière* next to the lean-to, the rotund up against the rococo or the neo-classic—awaiting the hammer of the *ferrailleur* or the visit of the American collector (for we learn that they are already in the market), in Les Lilas or Montreuil, a lesser-known *puces*, near those secret places where the round, snout-nosed buses of the 1920s decay amidst rank grass.

So *Les Vespasiennes de Paris* is more a record of things past than a guide to the living geography of Parisian relief. Many favourite palacettes have disappeared : that on the corner of the pont Neuf, that at the entrance to the Luxembourg, rue Guynemer, that opposite the Thermes. And most of those with the best views have gone. Even the "Liste Noire" is largely of restrospective interest and those of a certain inclination would be sadly disappointed if they treated it as a guide; even the construction on the place Saint-Sulpice has been pulled down. The Liste is rather a reminder of the geographical distribution of the active public centres of les *amateurs* in the early 1960s : a heavy concentration in the XVIe and the XVIIe, as in the Ier (les Halles) and in the XVIIIe, representing the convergence of the highest and lowest classes in the democracy of deviation.

There is an interesting appendix, based on a series of questions put both to habitual users and to the underprivileged of the other sex. From this it emerges that feminine opinion is remarkably tolerant towards the existence of these noisy temples from which they are for ever excluded but the scent of which they have to share. There are some small gems of social observation : one questioned states he is "Pour", with the proviso : "A condition qu'on voie à travers. Le soulagement semble meilleur à voir les autres continuer à s'agiter." A taxi-driver is likewise in the "Pour" camp : "Nécessité publique, surtout pour nous chauffeurs de taxi." Another appendix contains a standard *procès-verbal* for "outrage à la pudeur". Perhaps the numbers are being reduced in order to release the police for more important duties.

The book is copiously and acutely illustrated, often by the author himself who, at some risk, has photographed the passing customer, both before and after. There is little trace of vulgarity, "la pompe à merde" is not quoted (but there is something for the *amateur* on page 119) and M. Maillard has on the whole succeeded in avoiding the earthy *poujadisme* of Gabriel Chevalier and Dubut and the cruel, unfunny humour of "le cocuage". This is not a funny book, but a melancholy one. It will be appreciated, nostalgically, by all those who have known what it was to experience relief in fraternal, cascading surroundings, with an outlook on chestnut and plane tree, on tiny, intimate squares, alongside one's fellow-men likewise engaged and with politics briefly forgotten. The politics are for outside, inside is for *soulagement*. The most endearing, most reassuring view of Paris is that seen, or rather surprised, through the starred or heartshaped slits, from inside. It is better to look out than to look in.

24

The mysteries of Paris

This* is not quite what one might have hoped for, despite the promise
of the initial itineraries, below ground, at street level, and above eye
level (in Paris interest is vertical and one must never lose sight of the
unexpected *pan de ciel,* caught between two leprous, grey buildings, the
sudden joy of the light of the Ile-de-France). For the opening pages
constitute a fascinating *invitation au voyage,* through rediscovered
Tunnels of Love, half-forgotten sewers, barely discoverable *ceintures,*
overgrown with weeds—and can there be anything more mysterious,
more evocative, than the still discernible tracks of an abandoned railway?
—along the oblong of the *Fermiers-Généraux* by Métro (Nation to
Porte-Dauphine, Porte-Dauphine to Denfert-Rochereau), the exploration
of 5,000 streets and *impasses,* the reconstruction of the old north-south
axes of communication: rue Saint-Denis, rue Saint-Martin, rue Saint-
Jacques, rue du faubourg Saint-Jacques, and of Louix XVI's slow progress to the place of execution, along another Métro line. There is
promise too of a covered journey, from the Grands Boulevards to the
rue de Rivoli, under the glass and ironwork of the galleries, the *passages,*
Louis-Philippe's contribution to Paris, and the most bizarre monuments
of the VIIIe, XIe, Xe, and Ier.

And yet it is a vain promise, for it is necessary, here and there, to
leave the protective cover of the galleries and to come out into the open,
while the authors omit altogether the *passages* of the Quartier Saint-
Lazare, those of the Cité Trévise, and those, even more bizarre, behind
the rue Mazagran. Nor do they walk in the path of Aragon, picking out
other relics, this time of the 1920s: Porto Flip in gold or brown marble.
They do not have the imagination and the devouring curiosity of *le
Paysan de Paris,* and are thus unable to do full justice to the extrava-
ganaza of the Buttes-Chaumont (though the *pont des suicidés* gets a
passing reference) and to the twisting ironmongery of Modern Style.
There is no excursion into the courtyards and small workshops of the rue
Saint-Charles, another relic of Louis-Philippe, the haven of the *bricoleur,*
hidden places where the first aeroplanes were hammered and strung
together, at weekends or on long summer evenings. Nor do we follow

* *Guide de Paris mystérieux,* Les Guides noirs, Paris 1968.

the 96 as it puffs and pants up the rue de Ménilmontant and the rue du Télégraphe. And the nearby rue des Amandiers, the heartland of the Ménilmontant workshop and the most eloquent monument to the independent artisan of the nineteenth century, is omitted altogether. One is thankful at least for the evocation of the literature of the Métro : *Dubo, Dubon, Dubonnet,* the litany of the 1930s.

But there is nothing here to compare with the underground journey of *Le 6 décembre,* Léopold van Swaavenhage's (the author's real name was Duprat) fantasy about the train, a Métro for those who have passed on, that hauls away the bones from the Père-Lachaise, Pantin, Thiais, Montparnasse, to make room for the more recently dead (*concession à perpétuité* is only a comparative term). Readers too will get better value for their money with *Le 6 octobre* and will enjoy a more imaginative exploration of the canal Saint-Martin with Dabit and Simenon, and a more coherent, less anecdotal, description of the "climate" of each quarter and of its inhabitants, in Louis Chevalier's *Les Parisiens.* On re-emerging, after so many guided tours (including that of the Paris of *Fantomas*), after the visit of the chapels and back rooms of so many peculiar cults, after climbing so many storeys and observing so many *plaques,* one comes away with a feeling of disappointment.

The Tunnel of Love was little better than a fairground shudder, in cardboard and painted wood, smelling of dust and old sweat. Paris, it is true, has no *traboules;* but it does possess its hidden, communicating courtyards and junkyards, its huge green *portes-cochères* behind which are shut away secluded gardens, ivy-covered fountains, a wilderness of marshalling yards, a maze of old coaching inns and horse markets, even a pair of blind, stucco lions, staring out on the suburban commuters of the old Montparnasse line. This is better than the yellow *Cyclorama* and the pseudo *bateau-mouche,* but it is still very conventional stuff. Restif and Mercier are never mentioned. And while so many bizarrely named streets are included, the rue Dieu and the impasse Jésus do not qualify even for a brief *coup de chapeau.*

There is, however, much to be grateful for. M. and Mme Pigeon are not forgotten, under their stone eiderdown, cimetière Montparnasse. The cults are nearly all there : the *père Antoine,* the French Orthodox, *le dieu Cheneau,* a *bottin* of commercially successful gods, weekend gods, crapulous gods, aristocratic and artisan holy men, postmen prophets, French *fakirs,* including that great figure of the 1930s, the *fakir* Birman. The *chapelle comtiste,* now the property of the Brazilian Embassy, is, however, missing. The sites of murders—brutal, inexplicable, savage, alcoholic or, as in the case of Petiot, grandiose (will the rue Le Sueur *ever* lose its Poe-like power of evocation?) are lovingly described; the old Morgue is accompanied by an apt piece of social observation from Charles Nodier : "Il y a des jours de l'année où la Morgue est beaucoup trop étroit : le lendemain d'une émeute, le lendemain du Mardi Gras, le lendemain d'une fête nationale." (Chevalier makes a similar comment on the subject of Victor Hugo's funeral, an occasion which culminated in an immense, delirious outbreak of collective sexuality, in the gardens and side-walks of the Champs-Elysées.) The rue Goujon and the terrible fire in which a substantial proportion of the feminine *Tout-Paris* was burnt or trampled to death are the occasion for a splendid quote from Leon Bloy : "Le trop petit nombre de victimes, il est vrai, limitait ma joie." Under the rue Caumartin there is an account of the murder, in 1886, of *la môme Crevette*, the original holder of that title, not the grandmother of the Princesse de Réthy, who sold shrimps on Ostend beach.

The Guide also has much information on some of the stranger byways of Paris social history. There is a reminder of the *marché aux mégots* of the Place Maubert, still at the end of the nineteenth century the area of the most abject poverty, and, as late as the 1950s, the principal rendez-vous of the Paris tramps (there is no mention of the famous Café Aux Cloches de Notre-Dame, now a furniture store, on the corner of the rue Dante and the rue Lagrange, another monument of Maubert-Mouffetard). The rue Champollion, we learn, was the site, in the 1880s, of women's brasseries, the best known of which, la Brasserie des Excen-triques Polonaises, drew most of its custom from prostitutes and emanci-pated working-class girls. The *roi du baratin*, Mengin, who, under the Second Empire, sold pencils, place de la Bastille, with his servant, Vert-de-Gris is given a well-deserved place, though one regrets the absence of more recent holders of that coveted title, such as Dédé les Bretelles or Mimile l'Andouille, the orators of the boulevard du Montparnasse in the 1950s.

The *pétomane,* now revealed to the English public, figures under the Place Blanche; his unusual musical gifts were discovered during his military service, so justly entitled, in the lush years of the Third Republic, *l'école du soldat.* Other celebrities appear briefly : the marquis d'Argent-court, a street-singer of the rue du faubourg Saint-Antoine, rumoured to have been a former *chauffeur,* who, under Louis-Philippe, dressed in the fashion of the regime, *habit à la française,* and who was even-tually murdered; Hautier le Breton, the "Hercules of the Boulevards" in the 1890s; and Maxime Lisbonne, the owner of La Taverne du Bagne, rue de Clichy, who made a fortune as a *restaurateur* by insulting his customers—a line of business that has since been followed with equal success by many in that trade.

The authors of the Guide do not err on the side of historical accuracy and often display an eager readiness to accept the most reactionary interpretation of events. They have relied more on Lenôtre than on Hillairet. Thus, on the subject of M. de Salm, the period from Germinal

Year II to 9 Thermidor Year II does *not* constitute a year; it is just under four months! The origin of Notre-Dame-de-Bonne-Nouvelle and of the boulevard of that name was not the expulsion of the inhabitants of the Cour des Miracles, it was the birth of the future Louis XIV. And Coffinhal, who is alleged to have smashed the statue of the headless woman, quai de Bourbon, was not a member of the Convention. If Cléo de Mérode had taken part in the *vachalcade* of 1877, she would have been a child of ten. We have the old myth about the masonic origins of the French Revolution, and the equally hoary legend that the fall of the Bastille was instigated by secret societies. Under the rue de Tournon, there is a reference to *L'Armée des dames nationales*; Restif called his book *L'Année des dames nationales*. And there are other instances of hasty research and prejudice.

This is a street guide. It contains no insights into the relationship between quarter, professional specialisation, provincial origin, violence and temperament. While, under "Maubert", there is a reference to the *marché aux mégots,* there is no means of finding out that the quartier Maubert-Mouffetard contains the oldest, often poorest, and predominantly feminine population of Paris. We hear of notorious inhabitants of the Place Blanche, but learn nothing about the predominance of *faux ménages* among the inhabitants of the faubourg Montmartre; nor is there anything to tell us that, up to the Revolution, *l'esprit parisien* flourished in the rue Saint-Denis and that, in the nineteenth century, it emigrated, up the hill, to Belleville and Ménilmontant. This is a gallery of eccentrics, an assemblage of curia, rather than an attempt to define the Parisian, in his own terms or in those of the provinces. There are, too, some startling omissions. But the Guide, which has some amusing illustrative material, is to be walked with rather than read; it has much for the *curieux,* if not for the *chercheur.* Grand Guignol gets its full due, so do the backways of religious bizarreries, blood flows abundantly, and there is a shudder on every page. The loud music of the fair ground is always perceptible.

25

Maigret's Paris

The best historian of Paris, if he ever set his mind to it, would be the *afficheur*, the man who climbs his ladder to stick up, with the indifference of the technician, billposters, advertisements for patent medicines, announcements of public sales by auction, decrees of general mobilisation, electoral declarations and political denunciations, on the considerable amount of space still left available after the passing of a much repeated law of July 1889: *Défense d'afficher*—Stick no bills. The damp, blistered sides of Paris houses have screamed with the strident history of the capital for at least two centuries: red on black, black on yellow, black on white, blue on white, in butterfly variations of anger, denunciation, self-justification, promise, threat, command, information or cajolery. The pursuit of the Parisian has to be spread as widely as that: it cannot be confined only to the Archives and the works of reference; he is to be followed, for example, in two centuries of novels, from Restif and Mercier, through Maupassant and Darien, to Charles-Louis Philippe, Dabit, Fallet, Guimard, Aragon, Albertine Sarrazin, Queneau and Simenon.

Le 6 octobre, the first volume of the immense *Les Hommes de bonne volonté* of Jules Romains, opens with an evocation of the approach to the capital, as an express train runs screamingly through the suburbs: the chaotic mass of disparate villas of Villiers-le-Sec, the damp, black tenements of Aubervilliers and Pantin, capitals of tuberculosis, a green bus seen on a small square, a 30-foot face a greenish grey, staring out of the murk, the huge advertisements painted on the cut-off sides of steep houses—*Suze, le jambon Olida, Porto Antonat*—the approach to the Gare de l'Est.

Simenon, too, is constantly and attractively reminding one that history should be walked, seen, smelt, eavesdropped, as well as read; he seems to say that the historian must go into the streets, into the crowded restaurant, to the central criminal courts, to the *correctionnelles* (the French equivalent of magistrates' courts), to the market, to the café beside the canal Saint-Martin, a favourite hunting ground, to the jumble of marshalling yards beyond the Batignolles, to the backyards of the semi-derelict workshops of the rue Saint-Charles, to the river ports of

Bercy and Charenton, as well as to the library. There is a real Maigret quadrilateral in Paris: it's bounded by the rue des Archives, rue de Turenne, place des Vosges, rue du Roi de Sicile, Quartier Saint-Paul, rue Vieille du Temple, making up the old faubourg Saint-Antoine and the Marais, on the Right Bank, beyond the Hôtel-de-Ville. This is where he likes to place his lonely, secret little people, because he knows it is, or was, a *quartier de petits gens* and of Jewish immigrants. He is as fond of it as of Maubert-Mouffetard, on the Left Bank, in the Ve *arrondissement*, the ancient centre of poverty and of the Paris tramp; as fond of it as he is of the XIIe, in the wastes of the avenue Voltaire, to the east of the Marais, or the lock at Conflans, the place where the Oise joins the Seine.

It is a geography savoured by Maigret, because he dislikes desk work and is endlessly excited by the prospect of smelling out the ambience of a quarter never previously visited, or neglected for many years. And it is pleasant for the reader, who is thus taken well off the routes of any guide, even those, underground and often invisible, of the recently published *Guide de Paris mystérieux*. Maigret is only grumblingly and briefly seen in the precincts of Saint-Germain. If it is to be night spots, he prefers Pigalle and the place Blanche. He's aware, very much aware, of Saint-Médard, the church at the bottom of the rue Mouffetard that has given its name to that crowded quarter, but he's not of most of the XIVe, on the southern fringe—he's not missing very much. Yet he's spotted the old carters' inns and the *restaurants des chauffeurs,* often with courtyards like country inns, that specialise in *boeuf gros sel,* with leeks and carrots, in or off the rue des Favorites, in the XVe. He has, on occasion, to penetrate the hostile steppes of the XVIe and the XVIIe, the citadels of the Parisian upper bourgeoisie, of bankers and industrialists and rising technocrats—the home, too, of young Maoists and of idolators of Che—and go up in voluminous but slow-moving lifts, climb up heavily carpeted stairs, even show his card to discreet, shocked concierges—boulevard Malesherbes—boulevard de Courcelles . . . But he isn't happy there—at least not until he can get away from the wide avenues into some side street, to find a small café opposite a *boulangerie.* The Ternes, the seamy side of the Étoile, is much more his style of things, and one can appreciate why: the rue des Acacias, with its individual houses, might be in provincial France. Maigret is admirably selective in his omissions. Pigalle, les Halles, the rue de Berri and the rue de Ponthieu, both off the Champs-Elysées—all these had to be in, but he manages very well without the Latin Quarter, and so can we.

The historian, at least, may well have been obliged to follow him to a place of work, the Archives de la Police, that he shares with the heavily-built, slow-moving *commissaire.* And if some of the regular subjects of the historian are stowed away, in green boxes, at the top of the Police Judiciaire, the French equivalent of Scotland Yard, 36 quai des Orfèvres, he should have an eye too for those who are there in the flesh, handcuffed between two rugger-built inspectors, or sitting nervously on the green plush benches, in the corridor, on the first four floors (there's been an improvement in the furnishings since Maigret's time). For history is not only at the top, on the fifth floor, among the bombs and pistols and guillotine blades, alongside the fingerprint people : it's vertical too, so that the historian climbs through a sort of inverted order of crime and delinquency, mounting from murder and homicide, through embezzlement, to blackmail and counterfeiting. Perhaps, in fact, the order is purely the accident of a building bursting at the seams. But it's just as much the job of the historian as it is Maigret's to observe, and to explain, at least the changing pattern of clientèle in the PJ's week, as seen from the corridors : Monday, *ces demoiselles,* a noisy, chattering, impudent, loud-mouthed, humorous, chain-smoking, garish throng; Monday, too, is reception day for the hangers-on of that ancient trade—*souteneurs,* hotel-keepers and so on, though, now that the Halles have been moved out, there will be less of both than in the more conventional times of Maigret. On Wednesday, it's the turn of the counterfeiters, Section Financière, while the summer season, which thins out the usual presences in the hazy corridors, multiplies that of small, well-dressed, lithe, professional-looking men, their dark hats on their knees : cat-burglars and housebreakers for whom the holidays of most represent the working season of the few. Murderers, male and female, in *crimes passionnels,* may be seen emerging from the inspectors' rooms, hiding their eyes against the flash bulbs of the press, very early in the morning or very late at night—they're not day birds. Elderly couples in black, dressed like provincial employees or in the ancient suits of peasants, in their Sunday best, are the parents of the assassins or the assassinated; they have come up by the night train.

Saturday's haul includes young men in leather jackets, the uniform of the suburbs, who have invaded the city, on their strident two-cylinder red motor-bikes, and who, plying hilariously in gangs drawn from the same factory and the same barrack-like block of cheap flats have been involved in punch-ups with middle-class students, in an effort to make pay night seem more memorable. Sunday is a quiet day in the PJ, but it isn't for the morgue: the hours between one and four on Sunday morning are favoured by participants in *crimes passionnels.* Infidelity is likeliest to be a weekend luxury, at least when found out, for there can be little check on the 2 to 4 p.m. variety—even murder takes time and has to be fitted into leisure. And for exactly opposite reasons, suicide will favour the same night hours of the beginning of the weekend when lonely people are loneliest.

Maigret's *enquêtes* have brought him awareness of another calendar—

intimate, and perhaps dangerous, because too intimate—a calendar that marks the hours rather than the days, like that of public transport. He has an eye—and we with him—for the *gros Auvergnat* standing behind the bar in his blouse, washing out glasses, as well as for his customers, as they succeed one another during the day and—near les Halles, porte de la Villette and rue Brancion—during the night, for cattle and horse-slaughtering observes no repose. An eye for the 7.45 employees, *pousse-café,* the nine o'clock painters, building workers, glaziers—in their white smocks and paper hats—*un petit blanc sec*; for the 11 o'clock *commis voyageurs, représentants, un petit blanc sec*; the midday-to-one rush of ricard, pernod, chablis, beaujolais, the afternoon solitary marc or calvados, the furtive *martini sec* offered by the customer, *après consommation* in a neighbouring hotel room, to the prostitute, who has time on her hands, 4 p.m.; the 6 o'clock rush, the apéritif regiment, the evening card-players (a dying race in Paris if not in Simenon's west of France), the solitary 3 a.m. on repeated marcs, the Sunday-morning queues at the PMU, the cafés that contain authorised municipal betting shops, the *gros rouge* of the all-night horse-slaughterers. It is a drinker's day, round the clock, as complete as that described, nearly 200 years earlier, by Mercier.

Maigret is a historian of habit, of the *déjà vu*, like any good policeman; he is a historian of the predictable; and even in the 1940s, 1950s and 1960s, one still feels that he is an observer of the 1930s, whether in Paris or in the provinces. He is also a historian of class. He is at once at home with the concierge (as befits a policeman) with whom he is so much in accordance: his own father was a gamekeeper and likewise a faithful retainer of the well-to-do and the high-born. He is basically loyal: he has much in common with the bank clerk, the shopkeeper, with the young provincial semi-failure in the Paris setting. He is not wholly a townsman himself, still something of a peasant. He can smell the impending rain—he is like the Breton greengrocer next to the Maine-Montparnasse conurbation, an elderly lady who states that it will be wet tomorrow, because the martins are flying high. Maigret, in fact, is very much the archetypal Parisian of the eighteenth, nineteenth and twentieth centuries, still half a countryman, with rural values, still carrying the native province with him in the Paris streets. We are stuck eternally in the Third Republic.

This is why Simenon is so reassuring to people of a certain generation. It's a cosy, slippered world. The *patron,* in his blue overalls, standing behind his aluminium bar, breathes heavily over the glasses as he wipes them with the corner of his apron; *truands*—people who would prefer to avoid social contacts with the police—head for discreet inns on the Marne, to plan operations or to lie low; boxers past their prime take to running bars in the neighbourhood of the Champs-Elysées, their wives, one-time strippers, have gone to fat, go in for blue rinses and are excellent cooks. Simenon, like Eugène Sue, has the secret of eternal youth; both are profoundly counter-revolutionary writers. Sue canalised popular violence into myth. Maigret explains away youthful revolt in pipe-puffing, paternalistic terms, an invisible tear in his eye, for he knows, while he waits for the inevitable eventual blubbering breakdown of the young man who, for hours, has been fighting so hard to keep it all back, that it has to come out in the end.

So Maigret is perhaps a bad social historian in so far as social history is the awareness of change as well as of continuity. But he is a very good popular historian in so far as popular history is the observation of habit, routine, assumption, banality, everydayness, seasonability, popular conservatism, especially in leisure, eating habits and clothing, the pattern of the week, that of the weekend, that of the *grandes vacances* (how he loves the empty Paris of mid-August, but how he curses, like any *aoûtien*, the fact that virtually every *crémerie*, every *boulangerie*, is shut!); he thinks nostalgically of a quiet, shady green spot down by the Loire, but he never goes; he is always about to retire.

The Parisian, both in Simenon and in real life, is an elusive being, hard to define in terms of place of birth. After the Second Empire, Paris might make fun of the Southern accent, mock the gawky Auvergnat or the unlicked Lyonnais who put on black sleeves to protect his jacket, generalise about the alleged greed of Normans, laugh at the way Belgians spoke French, and refer to the simplicity of Breton girls. Such attitudes would often conceal the fact that the mockers themselves were of Southern descent, had Auvergnat parents, had only recently arrived from Lyon, or, like Bel Ami, from Canteleu, on the heights above Rouen, had, on arrival, gone to the Hôtel des Nantais, reassured as they were meant to be. Even today there is no one more energetically Parisian than the young man who is making his way in the city, ensconced in those little tribal corners of *pays* that, time and again, Maigret succeeds in revealing: tiny ant-heaps hidden from the passing eye, the family relationships of which, a whole network between Paris and the native village, the attentive *commissaire* has managed to unravel. When Gaby or Marcelle or Dédée or Micheline is found murdered, in a maid's bedroom in the VIe, she is likely to have come from Narbonne or Pézenas, La Rochelle, Roubaix, Quimper, Douai or Moulins, rather than from Pantin or Vanves-Malakoff on the frayed fringes of the city. Simenon is right to have made so much of the girl with the fibre suitcase as she nervously feels her way through a Paris terminal. He is a novelist of loneliness and alienation, of the process of urbanisation in individual terms.

Few writers could be more aware of the family: he is a twentieth-century *Physiocrate* who implies that the country boy should have stayed at home and that the young girl, if only she had listened to her mother instead of doing a bolt up to Paris, would have come to no harm. His books are full of matriarchal figures, and most of those who come to a violent end, who are disgraced, abused, mocked or ruined, have stepped out of the family unit. The ties of family are so persistent that, after an absence of nearly thirty years, *la Tante* suddenly re-emerges, to take over what is left of a sinking ship. Perhaps what is most depressing, most petit-bourgeois, about Simenon is this insistent presence of aunts, cousins, sisters-in-law and grandparents.

Much of what he sees and writes is already an evocation of the past, but so long as Maigret is with us—and we cannot let him retire, much less die—there is still hope for the *pêcheur à la ligne*, for the Sunday painter, for those who like to drink standing up at the counter, for those who seek simple, modest, harmless enjoyments, for those who can smell spring in the air, for those who, like Maigret, are descendants of the proverbial Parisian *badaud* and who are inquisitive about small things. So ultimately our debt to Simenon is not only as an unconscious historian, but as a poet of a world of fraternity and simplicity already almost submerged, and remembered with nostalgic affection—the uncomplicated world of *le Grand Bob,* one of his most sympathetic characters, and of so many other weekenders on the Marne.

26

The geography of Simenon

The pallid girl in the Brussels-bought neat black dress, and wearing a shiny black mackintosh, steps out of the warm comfort of the ticket office of the small station, redolent of coffee and cheroots, into the icy wet of the Place, a dank November afternoon, somewhere in the misty wastes of the Campine—it could be Hasselt, but it does not matter. The rain dripping in rivulets down her hair and face, she heads straight for a large cream-coloured tram, heated by an enormous, old-fashioned cast-iron stove, which, at some invisible signal, clanks into motion, its bell clanging, passing first through the black streets, the *pavé* glistening under the yellow lights, passing the occasional café with men in peaked caps silhouetted at cards or dominoes, lurching past low, cream-coloured houses, to head for the open fields and the *pays plat*, at increasing speed.

It is raining again; but this time the rain is less implacable and no longer icy, rather a warm mist, *la bruine* of the west of France, through which the young doctor can vaguely see the station clock, like a pale moon hanging on its own without support. He has three minutes to cover the next 200 yards, has too many marcs inside him (he has been dining with a colleague). The little train is already in by the time he reaches the ticket hall; there is a girl just ahead of him in the queue, fumbling in her purse, a cheap affair spelling out Prisunic. As she reaches for change, he has plenty of time to list the jumbled contents: lipstick, eye-shadow, powder, an identity card, a crushed packet of Disque Bleu, some old PMU tickets, black-and-white photographs of an eight-year-old school-girl, a book of Paris bus tickets, hair clips and a cheap black comb with straggling wisps of hair in its teeth.

As mentally he establishes an inventory of the contents of the gaping bag, leaning over the girl's shoulder, so close that he can smell her wet hair, in an automatic, masculine effort thus to breach into an intimacy suddenly and so casually revealed (and the reader too is eagerly following his gaze), he takes in the girl's clothes, a damp, pathetic, rabbity coat, shoes with the leather coming off the stiletto heels, and, of course, a fibre suitcase, the clasps gone, done up with string. Not a local girl, he concludes, and one that has only just arrived from Paris, in a hurry and no doubt on a sudden impulse. All this is taken in in about thirty seconds.

By the time the girl has bought her ticket, which he is able to see is for la Roche, the train has pulled out and the couple are left in the empty station.

Cointrin airport, on the frontier, between Geneva and Ferney-Voltaire; the Swissair plane touches down. It is Belle arriving from America: a large village not far from the Lake, china rabbits and dwarfs in the garden, a background of terraced vineyards and the line of the Jura, the up-and-down, somewhat infantile, pseudo-innocent Swiss voices, the forty-year-old teacher at the Lycée Internationale, a Savoyard, not quite accepted, though a Protestant. All the ingredients, in fact, of an *affaire Jaccoud* in the making. And once more we are off to a flying start.

The odd couple, off the *micheline* from la Rochelle, heading up the long main street that leads from the station to the cathedral—and how proud the reader is to spot Fontenay-le-Comte—another shabby hotel, a long, long journey behind them, from Montpellier, via Niort and la Rochelle, the unpacking in a mirrored bedroom, and we are off once more, though this time it starts in reverse, with backs to the station, *à l'arrivée*.

The Gare de Lyon at 5 a.m. A girl in a thin mac, whitish under the station lights, carrying a battered brown suitcase in false leather, tied down with a strap. Through the barriers, she pauses, looking for the Métro, but it is not open yet, even the cafés far over the other side of the ramp are still dark. She heads for the waiting-room, pushing wisps of hair from her face, nervously clutching her case. Then the Métro (Vincennes-Neuilly), the search for a cheap hotel (she has one or two addresses, written in mauve ink on a torn piece of graph paper). This girl is from Moulins. Paris awaits her. It is the twentieth-century replay of that old eighteenth-century literary favourite, "les dangers de la ville". And we follow the progress of the *petite Moulinoise* with the same eager voyeur-like curiosity as that of Restif's *Ursule*.

A pretty girl (it is Michèle Morgan) in tight mackintosh and beret, her face intermittently lit up by the street lights, as she trips over the huge *pavés* of the quayside, down on the port, at le Havre, lugging an enormous, battered suitcase, tied together with rope. What is she up to, in the port area, miles from the station, at this time of night? A café near by, glowing in the surrounding dark like a lighthouse. Michel Simon is in there, behind a heavy brocaded curtain, and up to no good, judging by the shifty look on his face and by the way he shambles about the room. The fog hangs in wisps, every now and then the night is pierced by the lugubrious sound of a ship's fog-horn.

Or here is the burly figure of the *commissaire* who, after travelling all night, gets out at a *chef-lieu* of a western department; a pause for a morning calvados in the café opposite, inquiries about the *gare routière*, a jolting bus ride amidst squat peasant women dressed in black, to the village in the Marais-Poitevin. The *commissaire de police* tries to put him in the picture, but admits that, as a stranger himself, he cannot make head or tail of it; he decides to stay at the local café, orders a *pichet* of fresh white wine, a local product, and very good; the habitués look at him with blatant curiosity. They know, of course, who he is and why he has come. And we are off again.

The scene at Pointe-Noire as the broken-down boat loads up (the engineer has said there is something wrong with the pumps). It is the ship's doctor's umpteenth trip along the west coast, to Bordeaux. He watches the passengers as they come aboard, some he knows, others are strangers (but won't be for long). He retires to his cabin, to emerge at lunch, in the first-class dining-room. The scene is set.

In Simenon people are always just leaving or just arriving, his reader right behind them, keyed up by the same excitement, curiosity and uneasiness with which these battered travellers set off or arrive at destinations most of which they have not previously known. It is good stuff to read, especially on departure, as the train gathers speed and Villeneuve-Saint-Georges careers by in a racing jumble of white and pylons, lending to each journey the satisfaction of ambience so well observed, of intimacies gradually, but completely, penetrated (each feminine character in this *littérature de l'arrivée* does not have to wait long before being subjected to a sort of moral striptease—in one case, she does a physical one too, before ending up dead and naked on the beach—carried out with clinical precision but not devoid of compassion, for most indeed have so little to carry, and that so pitiable, so soiled).

For Simenon has worked on his Chaix, he knows where to change, he has taken the little *micheline* from la Rochelle to Fontenay-le-Comte, or that from Rouen to Saint-Valéry-en-Caux, he has travelled in the Courriers Normands from Port-en-Bessin to Bayeux, or from Caen, via Honfleur, to le Havre, he knows the little train that goes from the Gare Saint-Louis to Arcachon and Hourtin, he can enumerate the bus routes that lead out from the Cours de Vincennes to Fontenay-sous-Bois, Joinville-le-Pont and le Perreux, from the porte de Clignancourt to Saint-Denis, la Briche and Enghien. He is at home with the canal de Roubaix, with the multiple waterways of north-eastern France and with bargees in general, and knows the tram routes for Etterbeck, Anderlecht and Saint-Josse-ten-Noode.

Simenon territory extends over the meandering urban border, dividing *estaminets* and shops. He is perhaps his best on home ground, above all in his native, mysterious Liège, where it all began, before the usual *montée à Paris* and hack-work for right-wing papers. But he is good, too in the Borinage, in the tiled kitchens of Charleroi (one of his most brilliant scenes), in the desolate farms of the Campine, or behind the drawn pink curtains of the sort of Brussels *auberge* frequented by heavily powdered and *Innovation*-scented Luxembourgeoises of generous proportions and willing dispositions.

His empire extends to the Steen at Antwerp, to the rue du Pélican of the Jewish diamond workers, to the estuary of the foggy Schelde and the fortresses of the old Barrier. His characters walk in sight of the multiple pointed towers of the cathedral of Tournai; they wander within fortified Oudenarde. He is as much a *bénéluxien* as Nicolas Freeling. He is convincing about the Vendée, the Deux-Sèvres, the Charente-Maritime and the Calvados. The Côte-d'Azur he tackles, but he is clearly not quite at home with its bright sunlight and its unfamiliar herbal smells; away from the rain and the wisps of fog, he too has become a tourist, like his *strip-teaseuses*, girls from the West or the Centre, who have been swept into Nice night-clubs, into the heartless cruel, vindictive world on the Mediterranean.

He can also take in, though rather as an object of wonder and pity, the refugee from the East: Riga, Vilno, Kishinev, the sort of people that his mother had put up in her boarding-house in Liège, the sort too that ended up, until things improved, in the rue des Rosiers, very much Simenon stamping ground. He does, it is true, take in West Africa, Panama and North America. But there he does not have the touch of Georges Arnaud, nor the unfailing exoticism of Blaise Cendrars, Emmanuel Roblès or Georges Gonchon; the tropical scene is beyond his scope. He would have done better to have avoided altogether the United States and the "arpents de neige" of Canada. To have tackled so many localities, to have travelled so extensively, so diagonally, in second-class compartments has made him presume too much on his powers of observation and absorption.

The Anglo-Saxon, of all conditions, presents him with an intractable problem; one suspects that he does not like the breed as a whole, though he is clearly rather *snobé* by the titled gentleman who stays at the Georges V. The problem displays the limits of his ability as an observer when removed from an ambience both familiar and reassuring (reassuring because familiar). He has had the sense to keep Maigret away from London; it was unwise and unfair to have sent the poor *commissaire* to New York, so far from the Brasserie Dauphine, from Mme Maigret's *pot au feu*, and from the appreciated calvados.

Simenon's endless attraction is his sensitive rendering of atmosphere, of the feeling of a locality, and the acuity of his social observation. John Raymond in *Simenon in Court* is right to describe him as a "connoisseur of environment", for this is his greatest gift. But elsewhere he is perhaps unfair to his hero, in making too many, and often too irrelevant, claims for his talents. No one is going to doubt his industry; *Touriste de bananes* is excellent travelogue, but it is too much to describe it as "one of the fiercest indictments of colonial bureaucracy that has ever been written". Simenon is not out to indict, but to amuse and to entertain; he does not have a political message, and it is unfair to dress him up as a Gide or a Forster; the clothes do not fit. Nor is he a great psychological novelist; all his efforts to explore and to explain the more hidden motives of individual behaviour creak with banality and pretentiousness, on the level of the pseudo-medical, pseudo-philosophical conversations, over liqueurs, between Maigret and his friend Pardon. Simenon is an honest artisan in simple, fast-moving narrative. He writes as he sees and as he smells.

27

Simenon on Simenon

There are obvious dangers inherent in publishing a series of notebooks—of *carnets intimes*—written allegedly for oneself; the temptation to a false candour, to a note of self-deprecation that does not quite ring true and that is rather a thinly disguised form of self-glorification ("we all have our little weaknesses, even I have my little weaknesses"); the temptation to philosophise, to pontificate, to prophesy, to make generalisations about the past, the present and the future, about Life and about Man; the danger of embarrassing the reader with intimate revelations, or of boring him with the minutiae of a private family chronicle, or that of treating him to a daily chart of blood pressure, vertigo and the movement of the bowels. Then there is the question of motive: were these jottings *never* meant for publication? Why, then, publish them, if only ten years later?

Georges Simenon's most remarkable achievement, in this respect, is to have avoided all—or nearly all, for some will find his revelations of sexual appetite embarrassing—these dangers of the genre. He does, it is true, philosophise, but he is the first to catch himself out in the process of doing so, so that we are at once disarmed.

When I Was Old* is a very modest chronicle and, above all, a very worried one: between 1960 and 1962 Simenon became increasingly worried about the health of his French-Canadian wife, Denise (his worries on this count were to be only too tragically confirmed when she had a complete breakdown a few years later); already, here, there is a daily hint of mounting strain, followed by brief intermissions of reassurance and complete mutual happiness. He is worried too about his own health, about approaching sixty, and he takes to golf. Yet these insistent medical alarms are not boring. Even more surprising, in such a man, is his worry about his capacity to write. During the period of gestation before each novel, there are agonising doubts and, occasionally, when faced with the arsenal of sharpened pencils and notebooks on his desk, of real panic. Can he keep it up? Should he keep it up? Is he not repeating himself? (We learn that he never re-reads any of his own books.) Is he not losing

**Georges Simenon, When I Was Old, translated by Helen Eustis, London 1972.

his touch? Should he not retire (like Maigret) to Meung-sur-Loire? But, of course, he does not retire, just as Maigret has always to be kept at fifty-two, giving him three more years at the Quai des Orfèvres (though, presumably, he could be called out of retirement?).

All this was written ten years ago, primarily for his wife, but also for his children, and Simenon, at seventy, is writing as much and as freshly as ever. The notebooks indicate a momentary faltering, a period of hesitancy and questioning, of stock-taking for which we at least, his readers, can be grateful, for it has given us this revealing, unpretentious, terse chronicle.

Simenon is a truly modest man. He knows his own limitations and does not make for himself the claims that have sometimes been made for him by some of his more florid admirers. He describes himself as a craftsman, has a healthy distrust of intellectuals, of *bellelettriens*, of literary occasions and intellectual conversations, feels ill at ease at social functions, and is quite unambitious in conventional terms: recognition, decorations, and so on. He can, it is true, well afford to be. Characteristically, apart from the closed circle of his wife and family—especially the three youngest children who figure in this account of two years—he prefers the company of doctors. Maigret's friend Pardon is not entirely an invention.

He has little use for politicians or for politics; for de Gaulle in particular he displays an eloquent loathing. He is no hero and has an engagingly healthy distrust of heroics and of display. *La grandeur* is not for him, for he knows its cost in human suffering and easily penetrates the confidence-trick behind the posturing. He and his characters are the antithesis of André Malraux and of Saint-Exupéry; and he is not deceived by the conscious public image adopted by Anatole France and by Gide. He is a modest, limited man who has sought to write about humble, ordinary, unprestigious people. There is nothing patronising about his approach to any of his characters. He is also kind; he is even prepared to grant that politicians may sometimes believe in what they are doing. He does not subscribe to the thesis of total badness even in public figures. Unlike Marcel Jouhandeau, he is also discreet about his two wives and about his family. He is of reassuringly human proportions.

For there is something especially reassuring about Simenon's determination, both in 1939 and 1944–5, to exclude public events from his private rhythm, from the carefully controlled breathing that explains his immense stamina, by determinedly getting on with a novel. As he points out, only one of his novels, *Le Train,* refers to "l'Exode" and to the disasters of 1940; and it is the story of a humble man who, unwittingly, borne along by gigantic events, eventually finds himself in a position to put public catastrophe to private advantage. No theme could be more reassuring. It is of course the sort of determination that most enrages the *engagés*—and he makes the revealing statement that he considers total commitment to be totally inhuman (he does, however, admit to a genuine liking for Astier de la Vigerie)—for it disarms them. During the Occupation, in his home in the west, he was neither *vichyssois* nor *résistant*. He laid in provisions of food, petrol and fuel, made things as comfortable for himself and for his family as he could, and merely went on writing. He wrote in fact some of his best novels during those years. One is thankful for such people. And his horror of violence, of brutality is constantly apparent, especially in a chronicle written during the last stages of the Algerian crisis and at a time when his own country seemed threatened with civil strife.

Simenon is also a very wise man, especially in the way he plans his life, seeking in a routine and in the reassurance offered by material objects, as well as in the love of his wife and children, that second wind which enables him to maintain his prodigious momentum. There is a sunny, reassuring serenity about this attachment to routine rigorously adhered to, marking out the pattern of the week, of the seasons, of the years : buying the papers at Lausanne station on Sunday mornings, the beautiful Sunday emptiness of towns, especially Swiss ones, descending the rue de Bourg to an empty place Saint-François (followed, could it be with a meal *chez* Godiot?), visiting the market in the majestic, wide central street of Morges, observing his children's fetishes, with an eye, too, for the weather (he admits, somewhere else, to have little aesthetic judgment, especially so far as buildings are concerned, though often he can describe them as eloquently as a painting of Utrillo).

Simenon is a twentieth-century Restif de la Bretonne, adhering to a purely private calendar, using the house and the family as a fortress, excluding the hubbub of the public world, leaving that to his wife and his secretaries (for there is plenty of business to be done in that marvellously organised household). One can understand why, after so many wanderings, he should have opted for the canton de Vaud; Lausanne, he writes, was just about the right size for his purpose; he did not need to live in it, but near it. He is still a provincial and a Liègeois can have much in common with a Lausannois.

Is this then the wisdom of ageing, that which comes with "l'automne de la vie"? For, in this account one is constantly startled by Simenon's previous imperious mobility : so many moves, so many houses—he is always buying more of them—a restless geography of sudden, impulsive *déménagements*, like a travelling circus. Furniture removers, if no one else, must have made a fortune out of him. We find him, in his notebooks, musing on a further move, hesitating between Montpellier, Aix, the Loire Valley—Rouen is eliminated, Belgium is out of the question (there is nowhere, he states, where he would less like to live). Then he has doubts about setting up tent (a metaphor, for he likes to build for four centuries) in the Fifth Republic. We leave him about to move once more, this time to Epalinges. Perhaps he really has come to rest.

This would be a pity, for we learn much about Simenon's writing methods from these jottings. The canal novels, for instance, were written on canals. He bought a boat, went from Paris to the Rhône delta, then up the canal du Midi, as well as covering the immense Belgian and Dutch canal network. Old towns, he observes, do not face on to railway stations or roads, they turn their backs on them and face on to canals and rivers: and seen from them, they reveal some of their secrets. He has written about La Rochelle and Fontenay-le-Comte near the former and in the latter. He leaves nothing to chance, arming himself with the whole battery of Chaix and of other railway timetables. Here too he displays his unique ability to describe time, ambience and place. There is a memorable description of the rue de Lappe and *la Bastoche* in the 1920s, when it was still a very dangerous place indeed. (It was still so in the 1930s, when the reviewer was showered with plaster from a café ceiling brought down by a ricocheting bullet, in the course of a "discussion" between professional gentlemen.) Simenon is a big man; this must have helped.

Let us hope that he still sets out, every now and then from Epalinges and the security of the Confederation. It is clear that he must have done so, for, in a recent novel, he depicts the social vacuum of an "Alphaville". But Geneva and the canton de Vaud have not escaped him and it comes as no surprise to learn that in the 1960s he followed "l'affaire Jaccoud" with passionate interest. No wonder, for it has all the elements of a non-Maigret Simenon. Jaccoud was a comparative newcomer to the rue des Granges; he was not Genevan-born, but a Savoyard (the sin of sins in the city of Calvin), so that he never really made the HSPG (Haute Société Protestante de Genève) though he married into it. He was expendable. Simenon, too, when he first cut the cords and went to Paris, moved around in a group of painters and sculptors who were all Liègeois. How he would have loved the Jaccoud theme! Indeed, he used it later.

There is an engaging frankness too in his account of his childhood as a reporter in Liège. *Rouletabille* then was more his level; it was from *Rouletabille* that he graduated to Maigret. It is here that first occurs that insistent theme of the cutting of the cords. Is he then worried for himself in this obsession with what his children will think of him now, and after his death? Is it a desire for self-perpetuation? Is it his innate moralism? For he is a moralist, though a very gentle one. He refers, with fear, to his wife's Jansenism, states that he rejected the Christian Brothers, while retaining something of Jesuit teaching. He is a moralist who does not expect too much. Most of his novels are deeply pessimistic. One is not surprised that he took to Dostoevsky rather than to Turgenev. His pessimism is sometimes facile, like his psychology; but it is part of him. For an author so little inclined to flippancy and facetiousness, a declared enjoyment of Raymond Queneau comes rather as a surprise. Whatever Simenon is, he is *not* a humorist.

We can accept him on his own evaluation as a social anarchist. (He is by no means the first anarchist to be very, very rich; but at least, unlike some, he has worked for his wealth and, in doing so, has given only pleasure to a great many people.) His rejection of all collective ties other than that of the family is both defiant and, perhaps, reassuring. Or perhaps it is a further expression of ultimate pessimism.

At least we can be glad to hear that he no longer thinks of himself as old—or did not in 1969. He cannot be allowed to become so any more than Maigret can be permitted to take out his fishing rod (translated bizarrely as "fishing pole"; we also have "insane asylum", "presently" for "at present", and something called a "mackinaw"). Why, he muses, in moments of discouragement, must he go on? Why cannot he settle down to golf and holidays?

There are two answers : he cannot stop (how he *hates* formal holidays, the *attrape-nigaud* of the century!) and we cannot let him stop. One cord that has *not* been cut is between Simenon and his innumerable, almost obsessive readers. One cannot allow oneself to conceive of a situation when on going to a station book-store in the Gare de Lyon (the rainy, windswept Simenons are best read going South) there is nothing new on the stand from the Presses de la Cité. His books, like the man himself, belong to the railway age. A number of his titles even indicate the fact. So both can see us through, let us hope, for many more years, so far as Europe is concerned, at least. "A la bonne vôtre, Monsieur Simenon."

28

Maigret retired

So Maigret has at last retired, presumably to Meung-sur-Loire, to a medium-sized house—*maison de notaire*—with all the requirements: a cool cellar, a commodious and immaculate kitchen, kept spick and span with Alsatian thoroughness by Mme Maigret, a verandah covered by a trellis of vine, a large hall with a pipe-rack and plenty of room for fishing-rods and tackle, the *faux-Henri-III* Galérie Barbès furniture, brought from the wastes of the XIIe, the poorest, most anonymous *arrondissement* of Paris, and rather lost in the big, airy rooms, the strange, uneven river within easy walking distance, a hat-stand with a selection of straw hats; a very long weekend indeed.

But Maigret has not taken well to retirement, prowling about "comme un ours en cage"—a big, clumsy bear in a big, well-aired cage, bored out of his mind, not even bothering to lift the lids of the many brass pans, to savour the next round of Mme Maigret's cooking—and Mme Maigret can now cook all day, without all those succulent meals being lost with the evening telephone call. Mme Maigret is the most unliberated of females, her function is to cook meals that her husband will never eat, to wait for his return, to get up before him so that he may wake up to the smell of freshly ground coffee, to retire into a corner with Mme Pardon. As one of the most perceptive writers in the present compendium*, Evelyne Sullerot, points out, the relationship is sexless: "jamais il ne *couche* pas même avec Mme Maigret, auprès de qui il *dort*". And now they are together all the time, and bored to tears, which is not surprising. There is nowhere to go in Meung; to post a letter perhaps to Lucas or Janvier, or "un petit coup de blanc" at the café. But the wandering within Paris and the *flairage* are over, no more steps down into the little café below the level of the street, quai de Jemappes, the *patron* in blue overalls and watery-eyed, and the Brasserie Dauphine will have to get on without him. There is nothing to do, and Maigret dozes in a chair, tries to occupy himself with a line, potters about the orchard.

And Maigret's creator—and alter ego—Georges Simenon, has also retired, as he said he would, after completing the last books in 1972. The big house at Epalinges has been sold, and he has moved to a flat in

* Francis Lacassin and Gilbert Sigaux (eds.), *Simenon*, Paris 1975.

Lausanne. It must, presumably, be a big flat to contain all those thousands of volumes, the Collected Works, in every imaginable language, from Serbo-Croat to Chinese, for there is a world market for Maigret. There is no point any more in taking the train from Lausanne to Nyon or on to Geneva, to sit behind *La Feuille-d'Avis*, or better still, for it is much bigger and affords more cover, *La Gazette de Lausanne*, so as to observe the passengers, unsuspecting material for the next, or the next but three, the 300th book. Simenon, too, having subjected both himself and his entourage to a rigorous time-table, must be a little bored. It is true that there is plenty still to see. He can walk up to Saint-François, or travel up the funicular, he can admire the colours of the stalls on la Riponne, there are nearly always a couple of trains at the station, the *buffet de la gare* is always full, with a coming and going of soldiers, and, down at Ouchy, a white boat will be heading for the French side. But what is the point? When, up till now, everything observed has been observed to a programme, so that even a scudding cloud, a puff of smoke in the sky, a shaft of sunshine on a wall, or the rich odours coming up from the cellars of a restaurant, have been carefully noted, and enlisted as evocative material for the next book but four. For Simenon, if he is anything, is evocative. No *flâneur*, he wanders for a purpose. But what happens when the purpose has been removed?

So it is time to look at the balance sheet, and this is the purpose of *Simenon*. In terms of volume, the *bilan* is indeed prodigious, quite unequalled: 102 Maigrets between 1929 and 1972; 116 novels between 1931 and the same concluding year, not to mention the *nouvelles policières*, the interviews, the articles for *Paris-Soir, Le Jour, Je suis partout, Preuves* (Simenon may claim to be apolitical, but the papers to which he has contributed do not suggest a man of the Left), the lectures, the introductions to novels by others. The momentum, too, is unbelievably strenuous, though gradually it slows: for instance, six Maigrets in 1931, six again in 1932, five in 1939–40 (as if the author were writing against time, or were attempting to obliterate the sense of impending doom), six in 1946, partly as the result of the backlog of writing during the Occupation, then a steady yearly average of two or three, as if the author had caught his second wind. Much the same tempo with the novels: seven in 1932, six in 1933, five in 1936, seven in 1937, six in 1939, then again a yearly average of three or four.

Part no doubt of the fascination that he has continued to exercise over people of my generation is that, especially in his Maigrets, the 1930s go on well into the 1950s and 1960s. For Maigret is a man of the 1930s, who continues to move against a background of political scandal and ministerial intervention, twenty years after the disappearance of Stavisky. The flow continues unabated during the Occupation, years spent near La Rochelle or in Fontenay-le-Comte, so that the Liberation is marked by a spate of novels and Maigrets set in the Charentes or the Vendée. For a writer so consistently prolific, it is the non-prolific years that must be indicative of something about this normally mysterious, reticent man. Why nothing at all in 1934? Was Simenon entirely taken up by the Stavisky scandal, did the disappearance of the *Conseiller* Prince, his body discovered on the railway line at the evocative la Combe-aux-Fées, between Paris and Dijon, push Maigret for a time out of the picture, while his creator busied himself with *reportages* for *Paris-Soir*? And then, later, at the time of *l'Expo*, could it be that Weidmann, the German mass murderer, operating from his base in la Celle-Saint-Cloud—and Maigret very much favoured *la banlieue-ouest*—had temporarily put the *commissaire* out of business? All we can say is that there were no Maigrets from 1934 to 1937 and that in 1938, Simenon did a series of reports, reproduced in this compendium on the patterns of Paris crime, *arrondissement* by *arrondissement*. Certainly some of the energy was diverted into the novels, the flow of which continued during this unusual interim. We can only guess at the causes of such a break, for Simenon is unwilling to reveal anything of his working life.

If Simenon is to survive as an artist, it is as a writer evocative of place and ambience. It is interesting to note that he has lived, at one time or another, and sometimes only for a few days or a few weeks, in nearly all the localities about which he has written. Sometimes the connection is obvious: in order to write *La Marie du Port*, he spent a month in an inn at Port-en-Bessin in 1937, drawing on his experience of the Bessin further for *L'Aîné des Ferchaux*. A holiday spent at Etretat was later exploited, as was a brief visit to Dieppe. According to one of the authors of the compendium, Simenon was not always a very profound observer of the peasantry of the Charentes, but he constantly returned to the area of la Rochelle in the 1930s and 1940s; and he went specially to Bergerac in order to set a novel there. Before becoming a writer, he had been secretary to a member of the landed nobility from the Bourbonnais; and at various periods, he had lived in Paris and la Ferté-Alais. Many of the Maigrets of the canal world were actually written on a boat, and in his role as an anti-Loti, Simenon took the trouble to see Tahiti, West Africa and the Canal Zone for himself. He is not the sort of man ever actually to have stayed in a sleezy hotel, though one may suppose that he may have *monté* in the wake of a prostitute; and he can evoke with complete conviction small hotel-rooms along the Côte, in the back streets of Nice or Antibes.

But it is equally clear that evocation can wait. It does not need to be immediate, it can be stored away, even carried across the Atlantic, and then brought out, often years later. We find Simenon describing the activities of a group of Paris weekenders, in a fishermen's retreat in the Marne valley, or the bitter family disputes of a group of Flemish peasants in the Campine, from the unlikely location of a farm in Arizona. Some of Maigret's most characteristically Parisian *enquêtes*—right down to the smell of a *vin de Sancerre* or a *pastis*, of sawdust on the floor of a *vins-charbons*, quai de Valmy, the corner table in the Brasserie Dauphine, or the huge silent lifts of a rich building in the XVIe—were written up in Canada, Arizona or the canton de Vaud. This ability to allow ambience to distil, and then to evoke, at the moment of maximum fruition, and when it has acquired its full bouquet over the years, is perhaps the most striking example of Simenon's talent as an "impressionist", *l'homme sensuel*, in the fullest sense, relying as much on his nose and ears, as on his eyes. For, with him, smell and sound are as compelling factors of memory as vision.

For instance, both the Maigrets and the novels are full of the sound of church bells, the very evocation of provincial quiet and sadness, certainly no message of joy (though one of the contributors refers to it as a further example of Simenon's Catholicism—more likely a memory of childhood for, in Liège, he had grown up to the constant sound of bells); just as they are redolent of smells, pleasant and unpleasant—the mean, enclosed odour of petit-bourgeois poverty, the rich aroma coming from Mme Maigret's kitchen or from the basement of a restaurant and titillating the *commissaire*'s appetite as he walks by.

In other words, Simenon's movements often have no direct relationship with the work in progress. Indeed, it often seems that he can achieve the greatest evocative effect from a distance, and no doubt with the benefit of a certain nostalgia. Certainly the place where he wrote offers little indication of what he wrote. *Pedigree*, the autobiographical work devoted to his pre-1914 childhood in Liège, was written in the Vendée. All that we can advance with certainty, looking at his immense list of publications and the succession of addresses from which they were written, is that Maigret's creator was almost as much a wanderer as Maigret himself, as were the principal characters of the novels; and that the theme of flight, so central to all his work, and recurring in novel after novel (often even in the titles) was something with which he was personally familiar, often as a form of escape, but also as a source of inspiration and renewal.

Fortunately for us, Simenon can transport his own unique observation of France—or, for that matter, of Belgium—with him anywhere he goes, even if that observation, never static in space, often appears to have the same sort of timelessness that characterizes Maigret, and indeed Mme Maigret, and that makes both so eminently reassuring, at least to the reader who has been on the journey, in the wake of the slow-moving, tentative *commissaire*, as he takes in the feeling of a place, ever since the 1930s. Simenon himself is of course aware of la Défense and Maine-Montparnasse, as he is of the tower blocks of la Courneuve or Arcueil, but he has taken care to preserve Maigret from the realisation of such impersonal and looming horrors. For as long as he could, he determindedly maintained the *commissaire's* horizon on a familiar provincial scale of four or five storeys—the rue des Acacias, the rue Turenne, or the main street of Fontenay-le-Comte; and when it proved impossible to conceal from the inspector the new scale (and the new vocabulary: "le standing", "le life-style", "le take-off") he mercifully decided to suppress him.

A great deal has been written about the geography of Simenon, so that it is hardly necessary to go over that well-mapped course once again. But there is some interest in listing what has been left out. For instance, neither Maigret nor his creator has ever taken in Lyon, and Toulouse is also off their beat. More surprisingly, Brussels and Antwerp are only evoked peripherally (one suspects that he shares the Liègeois view of the Belgian capital). And, perhaps because of the former presence there of a genuine "populist", he has given LRT (Lille-Roubaix-Tourcoing) a wide berth, abandoning that fruitful terrain to Maxence van der Meersch. Nor is he always quite such an accomplished observer and traveller as all that. He can be painfully superficial, and, in her article, Evelyne Sullerot draws attention to the numerous *belgismes* that he places in the mouths of Charentais peasants, as well as to the fact that, though living for years in or near la Rochelle, he never seems to have captured either the appearance or the spirit of the members of the local HSP, "affables et mélancoliques, à la sortie des temples protestants blanchis à la chaux".

Simenon takes a great deal of trouble with his homework, and in this book there is an impressive *bilan* of Paris crime in 1935, based on a number of nights spent at the Prefecture. He is certainly no great stylist, though *L'Aîné des Ferchaux* is not far off achieving the dimensions of a work of art. Further than that it would be hard to go. I do not believe, for instance, that Simenon was a deeply motivated Catholic writer, on the evidence that M. Labbé killed or tried to kill seven old ladies. And certainly too much can be made of his "philosophy". He is often vulgar, such as in the frequent references to women and girls who wear no knickers. And he is deeply pessimistic. Gide was flattered by his interest, but the correspondence between the two is revealing only of the fatuity of the *pontife,* purring as he was stroked, and the anxiety of the pupil to do well at such a prize-giving. It is hardly a literary debate of deep significance; but at least it does suggest that if Gide had absolutely *nothing* to say, Simenon had something. Certainly we will all be the poorer for the absence of Simenon and the disappearance of Maigret, for both are sturdy individualists, unimpressed by passing conformisms and *snobismes,* deeply interested in human beings, and motivated above all by sympathy, compassion and the desire to understand.

29

French slang

Maître Rheims has for many years been an *amateur* in the best sense of the word. His curiosity, as well as his profession (*commissaire-priseur*) has stretched widely, to include carpets, chinoiseries, postage stamps, *tableaux de maître,* bedding and old clothes; just after the war, he was entrusted with the sale of the furniture and bizarrely priapic fittings—taps, light switches, door handles—of some of the better-known establishments: the 122, the Sphinx, the Chabanais, struck down by the "loi Marthe-Richard"—a hint of what was to come under the auctioneer's hammer, some eight years later, with the sale in Cairo, under the auspices of Sotheby's, of the ingenious clockwork contents of King Farouk's palaces.

The daily bric-à-brac of the *commissaire-priseur* ranges from chamber-pots to bedside tables, from jewellery to plumbing, from learned works to pornography, as the variegated ever-flowing detritus of the Puces, the debris of the humbler markets, and the secrets of the shuttered Faubourg are scooped up, displayed and noisily disposed of, with the help of the *aboyeurs* ("à qui mieux? deux mille, deux mille cinq . . .") in the joyful cacophony of the Hôtel des Ventes. Just as the *commissaire-priseur* is dependent on an army of *brocanteurs, fripiers* and other intermediaries, these last must remain in at least unofficial contact with receivers and their providers. The Hôtel-Drouot is the visible tip of a pyramid which reaches deep down into the jungle of *antiquaires* and *marchands de tableaux* and the dusty underwrold of humbler collectors.

Something of the variety of this semi-secret society may be perceived physically at any big sale, even better on the day before a sale, when the objects are exhibited to the public; old crones tied up in skins and moulting furs may be seen in whispered discussions with immaculate antique-dealers and monocled *amateurs.* The Hôtel-Drouot is the nineteenth and twentieth century equivalent of the old Palais-Royal—a place in which all classes and conditions mix in terms, if not of equality, at least of complicity. It is a society of habitués, employing their own language and their own signs. An experienced *commissaire* can read as much from a slight movement of the eyes—from a forefinger raised to the lips, from a minute inclination of the head—as he might learn from a whispered conversation overlooked by a stuffed bear, a one-eyed tiger and a moth-eaten and somewhat bored-looking Monarch of the Glen.

So M. Rheims, in turning from objects to words, has followed an inclination towards which many of his colleagues must often be tempted and for which most would be unusually qualified. The words, in this instance,* resemble a great many of the objects that are part of the stock-in-trade of the calling : not articles of great value, of astounding beauty, of immense elegance and distinction, of exquisite craftsmanship, but rather an infinite range of "du toc", inventors' pieces, composite bizarreries, complicated gadgets, pseudo-archaisms, mock-gothicisms, a simili-cosmopolitan mish-mash, the "sabir" of la Goutte-d'Or and the rue du Château des Rentiers, the language, compelling and strident, of Aubervilliers and Joinville-le-Pont, the visually expressive slang of the "petit peuple", the cynical, often brilliant humour of *l'argot*, the rhyming, piled sibilance of *le javanais*, the livid, screaming vituperation of a Céline. These are words that have not made it officially, that have not been admitted into the inner sanctum, even if, as in some cases, they have been in circulation, *sub rosa,* for four or five centuries. There is a lot of dross, a lot more silliness; but the Maître's haul includes a number of artificial pearls that are well worth rescuing and that are often far more expressive than those that they imitate.

The careful reader of this bizarre jumble-sale of a dictionary is likely to come away with several general impressions, some of them not unflattering to English assumptions. One is above all surprised at the apparent inability of French writers to create a language of Nonsense : Artaud's attempts to recreate *Alice* in French do not have any of the vigour of the original; they sound, and are, contrived. The play on words affected by Jarry and Ionesco (*cordoléance, trempler,* to take two examples from the latter) and to a lesser extent by Jacques Perret, is pitifully childish, the very quintessence of unfunniness, worthy of the "restaurant des maîtres-d'internat" in a provincial lycée. Dubuffet, the idol of the French lower-middle classes, is in much the same category ("Labonfam abeber kentele tankoler" = "la bonne femme à Bébert quand elle est en colère"); Boris Vian is not much better, though he is sometimes more inventive.

The range too of words that are physically descriptive is far less varied than in English, though *poitriner* (Barbey d'Aurevilly) is a pleasing discovery, especially when applied to an officer in his nineteenth-century uniform. It is perhaps interesting to note that the two authors who resort the most frequently either to archaisms or to the highly specialised language of the seas should have been of non-French origin, Huysmans and Looten (the same, of course, could be said of Apollinaire, but all his inventions are brilliant). Huysmans's words are like the neo-gothic

*Maurice Rheims, *Dictionnaire des mots sauvages,* Paris 1970.

crenellations, flying buttresses and rose windows of Viollet Le-Duc: "du faux moyen-âge", stained-glass painted "à la foire des croûtes", the syrupy language of late nineteenth century pseudo-troubadours (Huysmans would have written "trouvères", or even "trouveurs"); his use of language, like the "maison bourgeoise 1900" depicted by Darien in his celebrated pamphlet, *La Belle France*, might be described as "la gélatine, le nougat et le fromage mou": three ounces of Fourvière, half a pound of Notre-Dame-de-la Garde, three pounds of the Sacré-Coeur de Montmartre, one pound of the Basilique de Lisieux, with a sprinkling of pseudo-Chartres *pour relever*.

Audiberti too almost ruptures himself in his efforts to be clever, to turn verbal somersaults; his borrowings from Provençal are as unconvincing and as irritating as the language so preciously affected by Jean Giono— "les paysans du Cantal, en costume régional, munis de vielles", received by Le Maréchal, after his siesta, in the gardens of the Hôtel du Parc ("Pâturage et labourage sont les deux mamelles de la France"). How lucky we have been to have avoided this sort of thing, at least since Stella Gibbons! The only interesting regional borrowings are those from Normandy (especially in Barbey d'Aurevilly), the Berri, the Nord (André Stil) and the Craonnais (Hervé Bazin). Huysmans, it is true, is something of a period-piece—the worst of many; he had his counterparts in England at the turn of the century.

Finally, and there is no parallel in English, there is the pseudo-regionalism, the forced masculinity, the querulous scatology and the grindingly unconvincing *fausse bonhomie* of some of the fascist writers, especially Léon Degrelle (in his *Journal de marche*) ("Des Russes venaient le soir tâter le terrain à la gribouillette", "une aube alabandinée", "des femmes qui enveillotaient les foins"). If Huysmans represents nineteenth-century Gothic at its most indigestible, Degrelle is 90 per cent "Vieille Belgique", guaranteed false; his joviality inspires no joy and his constant harping back to Walloon bucolic slang is unconvincing and indecent, especially when used to describe his experiences as an officer of the SS on the Eastern Front. Nor is Degrelle the only fascist writer who aims at some sort of literary acceptance and respectability by thus dressing up in an assumed regional outfit. Jacques Perret is equally rumbustious, even more salacious, and even more insistent in displaying—see the hands, see the feet, see the dirty bottom—his impeccably *bressan* origins. The *Dictionnaire* is yet another useful reminder of the connection between regionalism—generally of the *appellation non-contrôlée* variety—and various forms of authoritarianism. Barrès, represented in M. Rheims's book, was much given to borrowings from Lorraine dialects; while Péguy, once he had discovered the spire of Chartres Cathedral and his pseudo-peasant origins, showed an equal taste for *beauceron* "rustic" gleanings.

But there is a wealth of real enjoyment in *Dictionnaire des mots sauvages*. Not surprisingly, the richest sections can be categorised under the headings military, religious, feminine, sexual, collective, gastronomic (including liquids), proper names, place names, criminal, political, period-pieces, and sonorous. There are various possible subsections (regional, pejorative, pronunciatory) and Raymond Queneau and Céline must be considered in categories of their own.

The French military vocabulary has always been rich, *vert*, alert and affectionate with a sort of concealed tenderness (General de Gaulle has drawn on it frequently, especially in conversation). The Army is represented here primarily by Apollinaire : *artiflot* (he was one), *bobosse, fanta bosse* and *fiflot*. Anti-militarism comes up with *papatrie* (Henri Michaux) and with Rimbaud's admirable double-entendre *le patrouillisme* ("trouille" being slang for "fear") inspired by the experience of the Franco-Prussian War in the Ardennes. Degrelle contributes the ancient expression, *grippe-jésus* ("gendarme").

Religion too is well represented, though with less verve and originality than in Jean Follain (*TLS*, 19 May 1966), which was the language of the clergy about themselves, whereas M. Rheims's is that of the outside world about the clergy. Among the verbs, one can single out : *ascensionner, assomptionner, bullifier, extrême-onctionner* (the clergy's and Brittany's *extrémiser* is more elegant and final), *génuflecter* and *itamissaester* (a typical Queneau).

Women are described through the eyes of men; that is, generally bitchily. There can be no objection to a woman ("une demoiselle de la haute noce") living off "une banquière belge" (Jean Lorrain : *le Tréteau*). There have been *banquières* even in France, and there is no law against living off them if you are a woman; the profession (*banquière*) exists, if the word does not. A bow for "la haute bicherie" (A. Daudet, better at this game than his son) in the same category as *la banquière* and her friend, but in the collective. *La blanchecaille* is a very ancient *argot* expression for *la blanchisseuse*. *La bombeuse*, for a woman who enjoys the good things of life, is a happy, if obvious, discovery; so is the adjective *fragonarde* for one of delicate beauty. *Les dégrafées*—

> C'était dans le temps et c'était dans les moeurs qui faisait que les noceurs, ou, comme on disait, les soireux, les cercleux, les péripatéticiennes et les dégrafées qui hantaient Maxim's . . . [Fargue]

—is superb. *Radeuse* is a long-established Paris word for prostitute ("mettre une fille sur le rade", from *rade = trottoir*). Boris Vian, for once, has come up with something good when he describes a *voyante* as a *reniflante*. But the best is from Rabiniaux's *L'Honneur de Pédonzigue : uniprix* ("belle fille standardisée")—"Les messieurs du jury saluent. Les belles uniprix marchent vers le vampire dans le matin surpris". Michaux has: "Elle refuse le chatouillis, le compromis, la veulerie, la sentimentalité niaise et uniprix des capitales."

Fargue is the most fertile inventor for Sex, as well as for Women. He even provides a hero both *gondolinant, matamorant* and *don-juanant*— he must have been quite an all-round athlete, even in the preliminary stages—whose name is Sexavant Rinçouette. The théâtre du Palais-Royal type of comedy is appropriately described as *caliçonnades* (Paul Guth)— lover with trousers off takes refuge under the bed or in the wardrobe, enter husband ... Those who wish to know the meaning of *la fellation* should turn to their Latin dictionary. Pichette's *la godemichienne* can be identified as a regular and no doubt satisfied practitioner of the *godemichet*. *Le pigeonnage*, we are told, is one of the more innocent pleasures of Jesuit colleges; but, as Roger Peyrefitte reminds us, it may go too far. Clébert's verb *tapeculer*, in the hay, has a rural ring, though it might be possible to do it in the Bois, if not in the Luxembourg.

French has always favoured *l'agglomérat*; there is something about that last syllable. So collectivities are well represented with M. Rheims; apart from "la haute bicherie" and such like, we have *le concubinat*, *l'indicatorat* (Queneau) and *la gradaille*, a group, like so many others, intensely hated by Céline. For collectivities in terms of place Vian offers *députodrome*, but one misses in a dictionary of this kind the expressive and ever-popular *baisodrome*. The Goncourt brothers produce *le souffroir*.

Predictably, the dictionary is rich in words expressing sheer capacity, in food and drink. Just as the inhabitants of a small town in Upper Normandy proudly describe themselves as "les maqueux de Neufchâtel", so we have *les gobichonneurs* (les Goncourt), and *les goinfraniers* (Rabiniaux), people similarly disposed. *Relicheur* is a very old word for drinker; *reginglet*, used by Céline, is a Paris expression dating back at least to the Revolution, for a bitter-tasting wine such as would now be described as "le vin de Bercy" or, more simply, *le pikrak*.

A large number of words, witnessing both to the French sense of irreverence (at least when it is merely verbal) and to historical memory, as well as to an ironical humour particular to big cities, are composites of proper names, the original owners of which would hardly have felt honoured by an unexpected fame that was not always posthumous. Fargue uses *bornioliser* ("enterrer"), a testimony to the nineteenth- and early twentieth-century fame of "la maison Borniol", Audiberti proposes *breguetteur*, from Breguet, for "airman" (Queneau offers *autoplaniste*). A *collignon* was originally the Paris slang for a cab-driver; a man of that name, after having had a dispute with a family over an excessive fare and having been denounced by the father to the police, went to their apartment the next day and slaughtered the lot; it was the most famous crime of 1855. After Collignon had been guillotined, the word was extended to the whole profession and was used subsequently by Céline as a more general form of insult. It has since disappeared, never having been applied to taxi-drivers.

Crébillon is the principal, most fashionable street in any town; it is of western origin, the rue Crébillon being the principal shopping centre of Nantes; Valéry Larbaud refers to "le crébillon de Bourges", meaning "the centre of Bourges". Revel, in his truculent pamphlet, *En France*, mentions what he calls "le frégolisme du Général de Gaulle"; that is, his ability to undertake a series of almost miraculously rapid changes of political clothing—not to mention ordinary clothing—from Général de Brigade to civilian-style President—his capacity too to be in many places in quick succession, and to be many things to many men (from Fregoli, a nineteenth-century Italian actor, credited with being capable of taking as many as twenty successive parts, with a minimum of interruption, in the same play). In the same pamphlet, he speaks of *le style gaulien, les gaulöides* and *les gaullophiles.*

We move from these heights to *gisquette,* a Paris word for prostitute, the origin of which is sometimes attributed to the name of Gisquet, Prefect of Police from 1831 to 1836, who introduced *la mise-en-carte* (a derivation which, if accurate, recalls that of *poubelle,* from the name of another Prefect, Eugène Poubelle—see also quai Poubelle, on the Seine). The Goncourt brothers use both *homaiserie* and *hugolâtrie* (the latter an endemic malady of the French Left). Proust, in the context of the Dreyfus Affair, uses *japhétique.* "Le professor Petdeloup", synonymous with an academic bore, is an invention of Nadar. *Rambuteau* has the same sense as *vespasienne,* though it is less deserved. Céline uses *tafaresque,* in reference to the Emperor of Ethiopia ("Tafari") to describe, unfavourably, the anti-fascists of the late 1930s. *Thierroriste* is self-explanatory. A number of late nineteenth-century writers, not without envy, have used the adjective *zoliste* to describe a novel that enjoys an exceptionally high rate of circulation; "sans compter les sommes fabuleuses et zolistes qui me viendront de ces romans si beaux que j'aurais enfin le temps d'écrire."

Place-names are less in demand. *Enversailler* is a particularly happy invention of the Goncourt brothers, as anyone who has seen the long straight avenues at sundown would agree; it means, of course, "to sadden", "to depress", *Verduniser* (Audiberti) means "to decimate": it also applies to the purification of water (*eau verdunisée*). *Un laguiole* is a southern word for a penknife (from Laguiole, a small cutlery town in the Aveyron).

Crime pays its ancient homage to popular respect and popular humour. *Blousier* ("voyou"), *bracarpe* ("voleur"), *carroubler* ("voler"), *jasard* (adjective derived from "jaser", "to inform"), *rifodé* (a crook who claims to have been burnt out of house and home and who seeks alms, from *rifaud*—a fire) and *sabouleux* (a false *epileptic*, who uses soap to make himself foam at the mouth) are all well-established words of Paris argot. *Aumonnard* is an adjective proposed by Clébert, a master of Parisian popular speech and life (the dictionary owes much to his *Paris insolite* and his *La vie sauvage*).

There are a few concessions to the outside world. (We will return to Queneau's renderings of English.) *Marcaroniser* (Apollinaire) is to talk French like an Italian (or Italian like a Frenchman). De Montherlant proposes *nostalgérie* for the homesickness of the uprooted *pied-noir*; the word is not likely to survive now that the *pied-noir* has been completely integrated into metropolitan society. *Sabirer* (Étiemble) is a derivative of *sabir*. *Négritude* we owe to Aimé Césaire, who passed it on to Senghor.

Politics are under-represented. Céline has the excellent *drapeautique* (adjective); a character in Roger Nimier states "dans les années 30 j'étais du péhésef" (P.S.F., Doriot's fascist group). Baudelaire refers to *arriéristes*, Pichette to *barricadiers* (a breed, alas, still with us), the Goncourt brothers, in an anti-parliamentary mood, speak of *les médiocrates*.

A number of words have either not stood up to the test of time or have totally changed their meaning, Maupassant's *bockeur* is as dead and gone as Galtier-Boissière's *boulevardier*. *Tapin*, as used in the Year II and by Verlaine, no longer signifies a drummer-boy; "faire le tapin" is a peripatetic, rather than a musical, exercise. Mercier, in his *Dictionnaire des néologismes* (1802) refers to *lanterner*; before the Revolution it had the sense of "to dawdle", "to laze", in 1789, it took on a much more sinister meaning; but Péguy uses *lanternement* as "hanging about", "idling by the wayside". *Pacant* ("rustre") is a medieval word still favoured by Hébert but which disappeared in the nineteenth century.

French is no doubt less sonorous than English, but verbs like *empouacrer* ("souiller", but with a sense of wetness), *se glougloutir, susseyer* (Fargue), or an adjective like *picoléreux* are self-expressive. *Mèragosse* is one of Hervé Bazin's happier excursions into anti-feminism. One can appreciate the attachment of nineteenth-century novelists to the word *zinzolin* (reddish violet).

The *Dictionnaire* owes most to the sunny fantasies of Raymond Queneau, who has a very good ear for popular speech, both in le Havre and in Paris (not to mention Rueil), and to the volcanic rage of the incandescent Céline. Queneau specialises in the renderings of initials: *achélème* (HLM), *ératépiste* (employee of the RATP), as well as of English, a relic of his Havrais childhood: *mouvizes, godesavétequinge* (compare with Nimier's *bohiscoute*). We also have *haupouèl* ("au poil!" with a Norman pronunciation), and *avagivitévé* (agité, an example of *javanais*).

Céline is above all rich in Parisian and suburban argot: *banquiste, bignolerie* (gossip), *bignolon* (concierge), *cresson* (braggart), *goyot* (a very antique prostitute), *refile* (sick, "vomi"), *transat* (shoe, from "péniche", "bateau", "godille", etc.); *nuiteux* (night worker) is now used more specifically for taxi-drivers on the night beat (*une nuitée* is surprisingly not included). *Blancboula, botocudo* (from "botte-au-cul") and *pluricon* (adjective) are further examples of his incomparable use of slang and of his verbal inventiveness.

It is fitting that one should end this rich chronicle of popular wisdom and of verbal extravaganza, if not with *godesavétequinge* (rather out of date in any case, since it is now *godesavétecouine*), at least on the ultimate. Death, in the *Dictionnaire*, is treated, as is proper, allusively and with respect. *Troussegalant*, an old word used by Corbière, refers to those diseases which, like cholera and the plague, mowed down young men in their prime. But for discretion, it would be hard to beat *dépêchement*. "Des hommes d'un grand nom et d'un haut rang scientifique," writes Chateaubriand, on the subject of the assassination of the duc d'Enghien, "ne craignaient pas de louer le dépêchement du Prince." A polite word for a shameful action carried out by night and with indecent haste.

It is feared that, despite his *mots sauvages*, M. Rheims may be received in a place whither his wayward and wild words cannot follow him, in the polite company of "les Immortels". He could at least, one feels, put in some good work with that other dictionary, which, unlike his, no one reads and is never finished.

The new Harrap dictionary* is a useful guide to the sharp slang and irreverent language of the *Parigot,* to the extraordinary gift of visual observation of the Paris underworld, as well as to the rather cruel humour of the French schoolboy. It does not have the scope, the charm and the wealth of illustration of *Mots sauvages*; but it is very good as far as it goes and should be widely recommended. The puzzled Englishman will here penetrate the secret of the French popular passion for initials: BOF, DKV, GDB, J3, AJ (and *ajiste*), PBI, PD, PJ, PMU, PLV, SMIG (and *smigard*) are all included. There are also plenty of examples of rhyming slang (*ça colle, Anatole; tu parles, Charles!; A la tienne, Étienne*; etc.) and the *lycéen*'s Seven Ages of Man are partially represented: *amortis* (thirty to forty), *vestiges* (forty plus), *croulants* (fifty to sixty), *son-et-lumière* (sixty to seventy); but the authors have missed *archives nationales* (seventy to eighty) and *monument historique* (eighty plus). On first tackling the book, some readers no doubt *auront l'air de revenir de Pontoise*, though they may prefer to *aller à Niort* ("deny" it); it is to be hoped that, in the course of future stays in France, none will feel the need to *filer en Belgique*, the old stand-by, not only for would-be military dictators and OAS gunmen.

There are a few Mediterranean products, mostly from Marseille:

*Joseph Marks, *Harrap's French-English Dictionary of Slang and Colloquialisms*, revised and completed by Georgette A. Marks and Albert J. Farmer, London 1970.

fada and *fondu* ("mad"; the Marseillais call Le Corbusier's *la cité du soleil* rather more accurately—and they are careful not to live in it— *la maison fada*), *Martigue, Moco* ("a *Marseillais*"; cf. *Pépé le Moko*), while *baraka, fissa, moukala, moukère, mousmée,** *smala* and *toubib*, all included, illustrate the influence of military service in North Africa on the Parisian, though the authors do not in fact indicate their Arab origin.

The dictionary, however, sometimes stops short of a full explanation of the origins or meaning of a word. *Amazone* is not just "a high-class prostitute"; the important thing about her is that she plies her trade in a car, she is *motorisée*; nor is the proverbial *Marie-Chantal* just "an affected young lady"; she reads *Elle,* lives in the XVIe, attends the Institut Britannique, has a smattering of English and, of course, has at least one Maoist boy-friend (from the avenue Henri-Martin). It should be explained that *lampiste* originated as railway slang and that *limoger* has more connection with Limoges, at least in origin, than *aller à Niort* has to the chief-lieu of the Deux-Sèvres.

The compilers include *galéjer* ("to tell tall stories") but omit *galéjade*, the Marseille brand of tall story, from which the verb is derived. General de Gaulle could do better with *le chienlit* than merely offer "disorder", "bed-sitter"! *Chabanais* ("uproar") is no doubt derived from the celebrated establishment in the rue Chabanais. We have *fifille* but no *fifils* (yet boys are much more likely to be spoilt). A *carte* is indeed a "wet dream", but it is generally, and more accurately as regards contours, rendered as a *carte de France. Lanterner* does mean "to idle"; but, in the Revolution, it also meant "to lynch" (M. Rheims has both meanings). A *retour de flamme* is not quite "a late flare-up of love", it is rather the resumption of a love affair with a former girl friend.

The dictionary may be best enjoyed, under a tree, *boulevard des allongés* , far away from the *archers* and *Centrale*, perferably not in the company of *Alphonse*, at a safe distance from the *lazaro* and *la Borda* (uncomfortable places), and with one's imagination stimulated by *beaujolpif*. The Harrap volume is a useful collection; but it hardly replaces either Simonin or Rheims, in both of which *les apaisés* and *les allongés* lie more comfortably, former *Pantruchards* now resident in Pantin or Thiais, the end of the line.

---

* *Mousmée* is in fact a borrowing from the Japanese.

30

Tour de France

This* is much more than very good journalism; for the author is a journalist of international standard who has previously written primarily about China—he was himself born in Chungking—and the Far East. On returning, after many years of travel, following civil wars on obscure frontiers, colonial wars in Indo-China and Algeria, successful and unsuccessful coups in tepid, torrid capitals, with the smell of death constantly in his nostrils, with the killing sometimes audible, occasionally visible, never very far off from the airstrip at which he has just landed, the traveller, jaded but still extraordinarily energetic, returns to France, that of the Fifth Republic, the technocrats' *hexagone*. This is a report in depth on what might be described as the state of the patient, in the late 1960s, in the post-Gaullian era.

Les Plaisirs de l'hexagone is certainly a brilliant piece of reporting, both on a society and on individuals, both eminent and obscure, nearly always worthy of sympathy. But Lucien Bodard, whether he knows it or not, is also a social historian and a writer. He has the ability to depict the process of social change and to discover the hidden assumptions of the inhabitants of a city or a province. His first visit is to Ancenis, once a small market town on the Loire, dominated, during his childhood, by the local gentry, now just another new industrial area, run, like a computer, by young technocrats, and farmed by businessmen who fly in at weekends from Paris. Gone are the *belote* players and the cap-in-hand peasants. Even the *pharmacien* is anonymous, a mass product, with technocrat's glasses, selling, in white coat, the mass product of Rhône-Poulenc.

All individuality has gone, the town has lost its identity. The teenagers, rushing in droves to the pin-tables on their Vespas, are indistinguishable from those of la Courneuve or of Arcueil. Gone are the riding-breeches of the country squires, the blue smocks of the peasants, the black coats of the lawyers and the professional people. The whole population is clothed by Prisunic and fed by a *super-marché*. M. Bodard expresses no regrets, merely draws up the balance-sheet of change. This study of the death of a small country-town and the loss of a once stubborn

* Lucien Bodard, *Les Plaisirs de l'hexagone*, Paris 1972.

provincial culture is the most moving section of the book. For this is no homecoming for the traveller. All traces of home have vanished; even the old *mairie* has acquired Orly-type doors that open automatically, and the young *maire* speaks in statistics, in front of a map which dutifully responds to his fluent exposition by winking coloured lights. The radicals and the royalists seem to belong to an age that ended hundreds of years ago, but that in fact still existed in the 1930s.

Nor is this by any means his only contribution to contemporary urban history. M. Bodard returns, again and again, to Marseille, to the changing pattern of its criminality, to the cruelty and fickleness of its population, especially in terms of sport, with the same loving fascination and acuteness. The old Corsican villains, the *nervis, la pègre*, the dangerous little bars of the Quartier du Panier, all these are now as much the memories of an era as that which ended finally with the overthrow of the Guérini clan. Marseillais crime has become industrialised and anonymous, thriving primarily on heroin, with its invisible entrepreneurs and its chain of middle-men, its suburban laboratories along the coast, and its own fleet. Even prostitution has become depersonalised, at least as far as organisation is concerned, for the raw material remains much the same; the woman cannot be replaced, but the artisanal *souteneur* can. So the old gangs have been rendered redundant, along with the post-midnight stabbings and *revolvérisations* of the Tunisians, Corsicans, Niçois, Lebanese who have now moved into other trades. If one wishes to know what has become of the Marseille of Marcel Pagnol and of Cendrars, read M. Bodard. It has disappeared, almost without a trace. Mémé Guérini is now nearly as much a museum piece as the picturesque and abominable Carbone and Sprito, the killers of the 1930s and of the Occupation period. Marseille is now a much safer, and duller, place, save, of course, for the teenagers who have been sucked into the awful, closed communities of heroin addiction.

M. Bodard is equally good on the dark, dismal, cut-off, intensely proud town of Saint-Etienne. There is a passage about the empty, cobbled streets of that peculiar city on a Sunday that might figure in an anthology of urban literature. He is at his best when thus attempting to prise open a community intensely particularist and deeply suspicious of anyone not brought up in sight of the *crassiers*. The one way out, for so many young Stéphanois, is to be taken up by the Association Sportive; for this, the competition is savage, the training rigorous—the young footballers are brought up like seminarists. At the end of the road is the threat of retirement at thirty, the certainty of retirement at thirty-five.

Then there is M. Bodard the social, as well as the urban, historian. Particularly good is the section on the Théâtre du Palais-Royal : the plots and the clientèle are still much the same : "le cocuage", trouserless lover in the wardrobe; but the trappings are now those of a technocrat's "pseudo-gentilhommière", Domaine de Chilly-Mazarin ("son tennis, son parking, son équitation, sa piscine", and so on—see the advertisements in *Le Monde*, or anywhere else), the furniture of the converted mill in the Brie, as described in *Vie et campagne*. The cuckold is apparently still good for a few years—a decade perhaps—for the owner-manager is not very optimistic about the future. He gets grandfathers and grand-mothers; but already the forty-year-olds have lost interest; the bedroom scene will soon be confined to "la France de grand papa". *Le cocardier*, the red-faced gentleman who raises his hat to the regimental colours, attends the 14 July military procession, applauds the swift-stepped march of the Legion, has already been completely laid to rest. There is nothing military about Pompidou, upright, encased in black, like an undertaker, in his open car.

M. Bodard wanders from the Palais-Royal to the Casino de Paris and the Folies. Both have had their drains repaired, the old smell of sweat has gone. But Madame Février, of the Sentier, still supplies them with ostrich feathers; her family has held the monopoly of the industry since the great days of the Second Empire. But she too is the last of the line. He visits the great Madame Soleil, in her quiet study, facing on to a rustic courtyard, in the area of the old coaching inns, in the XVe. There is no decline in *her* clientèle; on the contrary. Has she not predicted the results of all the most recent referenda? She is a quiet, scholarly lady of good family, who knows about Quantification, keeps abreast with reviews —no doubt *Annales ES*, which devotes so much time to her sixteenth- and seventeenth-century predecessors. But she speaks with scorn of the great 1930s exponent, "le fakir Birman", who advertised in the Métro and wore a turban (although he came from Hasselt); he, apparently, was a fraud. Madame Soleil may yet enjoy a year as Visiting Fellow of Nuffield College.

Christs have always flourished on French soil, and they continue to do so. In the 1950s, there was near Avignon a healer and a postman who had a considerable female clientèle all down the Rhône Valley and even in Italy. M. Bodard visits the latest one, M. Hénaux, a plumber, father of ten, "le Christ de Compiègne"—a misnomer, in fact, for he lives in a suburb of the town, rue Demonchy, in a house, or rather half-a-house in red brick, within sound of the trains passing from Belgium to Lourdes and from Lourdes to Belgium. His vocation was not, however, revealed to him "en gare de Compiègne", but in his own kitchen, in 1933. For thirteen years, he steadfastly denied the evidence of his divine powers, but since then he has been officiating, on Sundays only, from a raised platform facing on to the street. The faithful can be counted in their hundreds and include Polish, Portuguese and Belgian immigrant labourers and a large following of women of all ages, both in Compiègne and in the surrounding *communes*. There have been a number of judicial inquiries, following the deaths of some of his worshippers, but, apparently, suburban healing is still going on, in rue Demonchy, within the sound of the frequent trains. M. Bodard describes "le Christ de Compiègne" as a fattish man, with watery blue eyes. He is served devotedly by some of his daughters; others, more sensibly, have cleared out of the saintly scene. M. Hénaux, a "Christ du dimanche", returns to plumbing during the week.

Interspersed between the respectable, well-spoken Madame Soleil and the alarming Hénaux, there is a fascinating section on the elaborate social hierarchy of the circus world. It is based on hereditary privilege and on inherited professional skills. It is not entirely, as might have been expected, the hierarchy of danger; for if gymnasts and trapeze artists come at the top, so do jugglers, with clowns—"les blancs et les noirs" (but the white-faced ones are slightly superior)—close behind. There is a teeming, despised, insecure proletariat of gypsies, stable-boys, children with bells, breathers of fire and professional strongmen, many of whom can expect only seasonal employment. Under the *ancien régime*, the expression *banquiste* was one of implied derision. Now, apparently, it represents the summit of the profession. What matters, in this strange, proud, closed community, is ancestry, several generations of "gens du voyage" behind one. But it is probably a hierarchy that is steadily declining.

Perhaps the most heart-rending part of this picaresque and compassionate chronicle is that concerning the old, magnificent Tour de France, the geography of which still closely corresponds to the map of French economic underdevelopment, the *coureurs* looping to avoid the Super-Regions and keeping clear of the dreadful network of *autoroutes*, to take in, on the contrary, a France forgotten by the Igames, and only nominally part of *l'hexagone*. In this respect, for these somewhat disinherited places, the Tour represents a brief, strident compensation, as the coloured riders flash by, a sort of royal progress that may give a kingfisher sense of importance to some out-of-the-way, dormant *commune*. It will be something to talk about for the rest of the year. If the place is lucky enough to be chosen as an *étape*—and for that purpose it will need a *stade*—there will be more material advantages, at least for the hotel keepers and the *restaurateurs-traiteurs*.

But what a sordid business it all is. M. Bodard looks into the rather seedy, one-star hotels in which the mass of riders—even the Emperors of the Road, Raymond Poulidor, the adored Poulidor (an old lady of eighty, all shrivelled up, tells M. Bodard: "Je suis grand-mère. J'ai envoyé ma photo et celle de ma petite-fille à M. Poulidor. Il a la bonté sur le visage. Dites-lui qu'il est aimé des grand-mères"), Luis Ocaña—snatch a few hours' sleep between massage, several to a room, the room cluttered with half-open suitcases, ointments and bottles of lemonade. The Tour has become a vast, relentless industry. Gone are the old heroes, the troubadors, the giants, the individualists, the eccentrics : Poulidor is the last of his kind. The new race of cyclists is typified by the terrifyingly effective Eddy Merckx, the Belgian, who has taken unpredictability out of what used to be a sport. Merckx is already a millionaire; he will retire at exactly the right moment. M. Bodard does not warm to Merckx.

And, never content merely to scrape at the surface of things—and nine-tenths of the Tour is just an immensely vulgar publicity stunt, to advertise an apéritif, a tyre, a brand of petrol; it is for this that the young men almost kill themselves on the relentless summer roads of a normally hidden France—he takes us momentarily away from the "ténors du macadam", to remind us of the pitiable plight of the young third and fourth-rate runners, the pacers, the hangers-on, those for whom the Tour represents a thin chance of breaking away from the clustered mass of some provincial club, those who pedal round this cunningly contrived route of Hell for nothing, for the remote chance of being noticed by one of the barons who run the show : those who, like two brothers, Flemish farmers' boys, will in all likelihood burst their lungs, or something else, on the Col de la Faucille, le Galibier, or on the dreadful Ventoux (that killed a young English rider), or smash their limbs on the way down, in attempting to make their escape from obscure provincial mediocrity, in order to reach the fabled world of sports shops, bicycle shops and chromium bars. M. Bodard, and only M. Bodard, has a thought for these *déchards*, the real victims of the exploitation by the hard-headed promoters.

The Tour which used to be the annual Te Deum of French popular culture, along with the Six Jours, and Paris-Roubaix ("l'enfer des pavés du Nord", the real killer, the one big chance for the Belgians and the *Chtimis*); the Tour which, even in the time of Bartali, could attract the interest of the Pope (Pius XII recommended to *il campionissimo* a cup of camomile tea every night as the surest method of obtaining a good night's sleep), was an international event that pushed rumours of war and revolution into the background, has now become a boring, pre-dictable, dusty, screaming, *klaxonnant* industry—a sudden flash of colour, followed by a motorcade of ambulances, vans, loudspeakers, open sports cars, jostling the bent-up riders. There is, as he says, from long experience, no joy any more in following it as a reporter. Or what little joy there is for him is an opportunity to rediscover those areas of a France that have been left out of the calculations of the planners and technocrats.

M. Chaban-Delmas and the new ruling class do not want to hear about the Tour, provided it does not interfere with their *bronzage*. It will never again be allowed anywhere near Saint-Tropez ("Saint-Tropez, c'est l'anti-révolution", comments M. Bodard) or Grasse; it must not disturb the peace of the holidays of those who think for France. So it is probably not very difficult for the authorities of Agen, or of Rodez, or of Saint-Etienne to lay a claim to an *étape*. Even thus disinherited, pushed out of sight of *les Grands,* it still takes its annual toll of young men; there is no friendship in it, though no doubt all the *coureurs* would be at one in hating Merckx.

After Merckx, after the sad evocation of the old heroes of the road, what a relief then to move on to the south-west, to "la France du rugby", to *le rugbyman* : those colossal, hairy—hair seems to sprout even from their immense flattened ears—hulking Basquais, Landais, Béarnais, Agenais, Toulousains, Rodéziens, Albigeois, Montalbanais, great, generous, warm-spoken, friendly, dark bison who when off the field, move slowly, lopingly, prudently, as if to conserve their energies and avoid denting people or objects. They—and their supporters—are surely the friendliest, most disinterested people in Europe. They are true knights of sport; and their enjoyment of food and drink is stupendous and immensely reassuring. M. Bodard on rugby is a timely reminder, in a chronicle of so much indifference, mediocrity and professionalism, of "la France de la gentillesse". All is not wrong with *l'hexagone.*

M. Bodard, then, is an incomparable social historian. But he is also a natural writer, not just a very able, experienced reporter. He knows how to write about men, about courage, danger, death and horror. But he is no Hemingway; battlefields give him no joy, no inspiration, merely pity for the cut-off lives of the young corpses. Unlike Hemingway, he is aware of the obscenity of death, whether revolutionary or counter-revolutionary. Nor is he a Jean Lartéguy; for him, *les paras* are professionals, not knights. He does not succumb to the literature of virility, like Jean Cau, who, as an intellectual, affects the terse literary style and the costume of a mercenary. In his warmth and compassion, in his ability to write about men in acute danger and sick with fear, he is in a class with Emmanuel Roblès and Jules Roy, both of whom have written much of war and of heroism and the lack of it, never with ostentation, but always with fraternity. M. Bodard has brought fraternity into journalism, and journalism into literature. He is a "voyageur sans classe" who, thanks to patience and a capacity to listen as well as to observe, can penetrate *any* class. He can talk to very old women as well as to *starlettes.* He has something of Georges Simenon's gift for describing places only briefly seen; for the one thing he is never offered is time.

Les Plaisirs de l'hexagone is a beautiful and very moving book which ranges through so many recesses of French society, in a clarity of style and with a patience, an understanding and an acuteness that make one thankful that M. Bodard, after so many sudden assignments, should at last have come home, home even to *l'hexagone,* which, in this endlessly inquiring book, still seems to have something to offer, both to M. Bodard and to his readers.

Index of places